LESSONS FOR TOMORROW

Bringing America's Schools Back from the Brink

Edward L. Davis

Orgone Press
Northport, Michigan

Published by Orgone Press
P.O. Box 833
Northport, MI 49670

Publisher's Cataloging-in-Publication Data
Davis, Edward L.

Lessons for tomorrow : bringing America's schools back from the brink / by Edward L. "Ned"
Davis.—Northport, MI : Orgone Press, 2006.

p. ; cm.
Includes bibliographical references and index.
ISBN: 0-9769661-0-7
ISBN13: 978-0-9769661-0-4

1. School improvement programs—United States. 2. Educational change—United States. 3.
Public schools—United States. I. Title.

LB2822.82 .D38 2006
371.2/00973—dc22   2005928635

Book production and coordination by Jenkins Group, Inc. • *www.bookpublishing.com*

Interior design by Michele DeFilippo
Cover design by Chris Rhoads

Printed in the United States of America
10 09 08 07 06 • 5 4 3 2 1

For Lindsey and Matthew
May you both discover the passion of learning
in your own way, in your own time.

Contents

Part III The Future

Appendix

Recommended Reading

Index

Acknowledgments

In the course of researching and writing this book, I had conversations with dozens of teachers who were generous in offering their perspectives on the flaws of public education, and the need for a complete redesign. Their enthusiasm for change often surprised me and buoyed me through difficult periods. I am especially grateful to Steve Wetherbee, sterling example of a "master teacher" right here in my own community, for the inspiration he has provided to so many kids including my own.

I deeply thank the master teachers in my own formal education, Mrs. Coston, Virginia Warner, Malcolm Mole and Red Thomas. I will never forget you. I wish there had been a few more.

Many friends and colleagues have been helpful in supporting, challenging and helping me to articulate the ideas and themes in this book: Susan Ager, Sandy Collins, Jay Cross, Rick Cross, Irv Fischer, Michael Foulkes, Dr. Patrick Greene, Cathy Harrington, Dr. Patricia Jones-Blessman, Richard Laermer, Greg Luther, Laura Minnegerode, Rob Molek, Brian Nunn, Dr. Julia Palacios, Peter Shaw, Helen Sica, John Smart, Jack Snedeker, Donna Tischer, and Dr. Eugene Yates. I am most grateful to all of you. To anyone I have left out, please accept my apologies.

Special thanks to those, who had editorial skills, and out of the goodness of their hearts, helped me with editing during various stages of the book: Barbara Ittner, Michelle Racich, Sharon Winberg, and Janet Capron. Your assistance was invaluable.

I am especially grateful to Dr. Steve Eskow, longtime colleague and fellow pioneer in the e-learning world. Steve, you kept me on task and on point when I most needed it. Your input was always thoughtful and challenging. Few had the courage to ask the most difficult questions and make blunt criticisms when they were needed.

This book would never have been undertaken if Sally Chasanoff had not encouraged me to write it and helped support me in the early stages of doing so. Thank you, Sally, for kick-starting a dream into reality.

Thanks to my publicist Michelle Sobota, who believes in the book and has come to know that it is a "mission from God." We both know that God has high expectations of us.

My mother and father, Mikki and Ned Davis were avid readers and learners. Their example has much to do with my own odyssey as an educator and writer. I love them with all of my heart, and thank them for encouraging me to learn without ever making it seem oppressive.

To my son, Matt, thanks for putting up with me, tucked away in my office all of those nights and weekends when I could have been hanging out with you. I hope this effort will come to mean something to you.

Writing is a solitary profession. It certainly requires commitment and forbearance. I couldn't manifest these qualities without much encouragement along the way. Thanks to all who supplied even a whit. Often it was a whit that kept me going.

Introduction

When I venture out into the little village where I live, I often run into a guy named Pat at the post office, the bank, or the market. Pat always offers the same wry greeting. *What do you know for sure?*

For Pat, it is kind of gentle nudge, a way to provoke a response other than the usual. For me, it is an exhortation. Pat gets what he wants, a pithy reply and a little conversation, but I am left to think about it. Some days, it takes a while to shake the words from my head. After all, I am writing a book about education.

What do I know for sure? Maybe I can finally exorcise the question by offering an honest answer. Now in my 50s, I am supposed to have made my mark, matured, accumulated a little wisdom, inspired my children to embrace life, and given something back to my community. To whatever extent I have done these things, I do know this: *There is so much left to learn, and time is growing short.*

We live in coevolution with what our brains produce. Our greatest potential lies in better learning how to learn. It is the mother of all issues, yet we have collectively failed to bring it to its rightful status.

Schools house our designs for the future. They represent our best efforts at cultivating knowledge and intelligence. We entrust our young to them roughly 196 days and 1,372 hours each year to animate our collective hopes and intentions. When I think about this, I am embarrassed.

Our formal institutions of learning are the beachheads from which new thinking and new civilization can germinate and take root. By the same token, they are the bastions of the status quo: economic, political, social, and intellectual. Homogenized education that does not take into account individual curiosities, motivations, aptitudes, learning pace, or style creates a kind of social and intellectual poverty in which learning is devalued.

As a nation, we have come to rely on a professional elite to ratify our convictions, to posit what we can imagine. Without the existence of an authentic present-day culture of learning to provide contrast, it is difficult for most of us to imagine what could be. But, you get to be 50. You look around. And then you begin to wonder.

In a society dedicated to learning, the true diversity is diversity of thought, of perspective, and of creativity. I suspect that we humans share many unconscious yearnings and that the freedom to follow our intellectual curiosities is one of the greatest. Yet there are forces in play that would render knowledge an a priori phenomenon—something transferred intact from one mind to another. These forces have less use for creativity and perspective than they do for the ability to perform prescribed tasks and ascertain what those licensed to profess knowledge want us to know and believe.

If we are not a society dedicated to learning, then what *are* we dedicated to, and where does learning fit in? "Educate" has three Latin roots: *educare*, to bring up, rear, or train a child; *educere*, out, bring out; and *ducere*, to lead, draw, or bring. Combining the roots, most scholars define "educate" as *to bring out*, as in *bring out the best* or *bring out knowledge*. This implies there is something within to cultivate, to bring out. Surely, we have strayed from the roots.

To put it simply, I believe we are failing to educate because we fail to bring out what is within. Knowledge has become an increasingly exterior phenomenon. What is within us is going to struggle to come out anyway. It is our prime directive. But, we humans would be so much more resourceful and powerful, our potentials and dreams unbound, if only education would cooperate.

The flaws of schooling are relatively blatant and well underscored by reams of research. The evidence accumulates, pointing to the need for a comprehensive new learning architecture. We have knowledge that can lead us to a collective place where learning flourishes, yet we systematically ignore it. The influencers in the environment surrounding education—instructional designers, publishers, legislators, researchers, unions, and administrators—are locked into place in a tightly wound, self-justifying bureaucracy.

Virtually every conversation we hear about better education is about more money, higher standards, and better teaching. With due respect to the many dedicated public servants in education and government and their advisors, these discussions are, to put it politely, off the mark. It's time to turn our attention to optimizing learning, not teaching.

To the learning professionals who read this book, I want to make it clear that what I have to say is not an indictment of people. There are many committed, well-intentioned, intelligent, and caring people associated with institutions of learning. All of these people, just like the rest of us, are generally unwitting parties to a paradigm that binds us to our present course. This book asks you to shed beliefs to which we are all a party. Read on at your own risk.

There is much talk of introducing competition into the system. The principle is sound. I believe the methods suggested are somewhat misguided. The best competition we can introduce is to offer students and parents the opportunity to compete with teachers and existing curriculum design by choosing from a range of learning resources within the system and anywhere else they can be found. Teachers need to compete with the effectiveness of other learning resources for the attention of learners.

The notion of universal education as the foundation of an authentic democracy was born in America. It was, and still is, the most radical idea to have come from our founding fathers. The great achievement of this experiment is that education is available to all.

But there is also a great failure in the largely unchecked growth of an overbureaucratized system that demands ever-greater funds for increasingly fewer results—a system that cannot respond to the needs and talents of individuals. On present course, it is not justifiable.

The other great failure is that schooling fosters learned dependence and a lack of participation in the search for truth and what is important. Formal learning is seen in terms of discipline rather than passion. The hardware of our "intelligence," our brains, is significantly enhanced by making learners archaeologists and architects of knowledge rather than receptacles for what educationists decide to fill with "official" knowledge.

The prevailing experience of school, for those old enough to have an independent opinion, is that it is boring. It does not engage. It fails to harness the natural enthusiasm, the drive to individuate that is inherent in all children.

Since public education became an American institution in the mid-nineteenth century, it has, despite many reforms, become increasingly unresponsive to a world that has radically changed. To understand what is dysfunctional about the present system is, in part, to confront our own intellectual limits. Fundamental changes call for new mindsets. Otherwise, we end up with old mindsets driving new ideas into predictable chaos—a pretty good description of the present.

Public education is a $700-billion juggernaut. Any insider who dares take on the power structure knows he or she will suffer political and economic consequences. Private schooling, higher education, corporate and military training, and e-learning have distinguishing characteristics but exhibit many of the same fundamental flaws.

I would put the creation of a twenty-first-century design for education as our first millennial priority. We certainly have the ability, but lack the social and political will. In 20 years, I fear the United States will be known as a declining civilization and a fast-declining world power if we haven't "retooled" our brains.

Just in business terms, we have much to gain by establishing global leadership in learning design. In a world where "time to competency" is becoming the most frequent barrier to competitive advantage and where learning can be exported anywhere, the market size is measured in trillions of dollars. There is an enormous and growing demand for interactive products that enable learners to eliminate the middlemen and take charge of a learning event.

Third world countries such as Indonesia and China, with less entrenched educational bureaucracies, cheaper labor, and a keener sense of the connection between learning and survival, are poised to leapfrog the United States in the next 20 years. The threat is real and imminent. Where we can't compete with cheap labor, we still have the option to provide better solutions with better-equipped brains. It is truly the leverage point for developed nations in a global marketplace.

The Industrial-to-Information-Age lag is most conspicuous in how effectively we learn. It is the primary barrier to our evolution as a culture and an economy. Some have already abandoned schools as the places where we prepare for the world, saying they can't, or won't adapt.

Futurist Alvin Toffler touched on a key enabling element of the future of learning when he suggested that "kids raised in a smart, responsive environment, which is complex and stimulating, may develop a different set of skills. If kids can call on the environment to do things for them, they become less dependent on parents (and teachers) at a younger age. They may gain a sense of mastery or competence. And they can afford to be inquisitive, exploratory, imaginative, and to adopt a problem solving (learning by doing) approach to life. All of which may promote changes in the brain itself. ... A smarter environment will make smarter people."

At the individual level, learning occurs along the path untrodden. It is inherently nomadic, not homogenous. It relies on relevance and curiosity far more than memory. It is not instructed or meted out but sought relevant to unique inclinations and how each individual experiences the world. We must design learning environments based on these truths.

The "smart, responsive environment" Toffler referred to has to be built by humans with new thinking and new understanding. This new understanding will incorporate the social as well as the individual components of learning. A new learning architecture will not hinge on technology. Technology offers powerful new tools to augment learning, but the tools themselves are still subject to the boundaries of human awareness and ingenuity.

The New Mantra

It can't be fixed. It shouldn't be fixed. It's not broken. It's obsolete. The machinery and the factories of education are obsolete. No amount of retooling—higher standards, more money, smaller classrooms, or "back to the basics"—is going to alter the truth. We need to stop tinkering with what isn't broken and recognize its obsolescence.

It can't be fixed. It shouldn't be fixed. It's not broken. It's obsolete. Try these words, gently but firmly, in your next conversation with one of the members of the educational status quo. You'll find many of them in agreement but unable to act, not knowing where to start and not wanting to risk their careers. For the status quo and the fixers, the notion of a new design, a comprehensive new learning architecture, is just too complex, too risky, too far beyond the horizon.

It can't be fixed. It shouldn't be fixed. It's not broken. It's obsolete. To the "educrats," the politicians, and a large percentage of the biggest industry (more than three million K-12 public school teachers) in the U.S. this will be disruptive, disorienting, and threatening. Those invested in the status quo have much to protect. Those invested in learning have everything to gain from the implementation of a modernized, cognitive-based education system. The remedy lies in building strength through numbers—the strength that comes from having learned about learning.

Ignoring what we now know about teaching and learning, and failing to act, is surely our most costly national failure. It is invisible to us, in part, because the rest of the civilized world has copied our own approach. The differences from country to country, though worthy of note, are still trivial in the face of the possibilities.

This book will describe the characteristics and practices synonymous with the liberation of learning and will identify social dynamics, educational practices, and operating assumptions that keep outmoded thinking in place. It is an invitation for seminal thinkers to form the new field of learning architecture, to assemble a master blueprint for learning from cradle to grave. It is a call to the general public—all of us who are going to be affected by the future of learning—to join in the process of changing public policy.

The foundation for a new blueprint is in reversing the order of accountability in the old. At the top of the new order is the learner. How will we provide individual learners with the means to determine and meet their immediate and ongoing needs? Then, how do we hold teachers, providers of learning materials, and designers of learning environments accountable to fulfill these needs?

How do we insure that the customer has received quality service? How do administrators and managers of educational environments become accountable to teachers, facilitators, and counselors so that the input of the customer (the learner) is continually monitored to identify and address unserved needs, additional learning resources, and support for research processes to determine best practices? This can and should be a process that rewards teachers, counselors, and facilitators for meeting learner needs and exceeding standards for progress.

In the new order, instructional designers, content providers/publishers, and curriculum designers are responsible to a design process that allows individual learners to have a continuum of methods and pathways to realize a balance of societal and individual learning goals.

Learning design will be geared toward a variety of learning styles, interests, and rates of progress rather than a uniform grade level or knowledge or age standard by which learners are compared and judged. In such a context, remedial education, widespread failure, and wasted mental effort are profoundly diminished. The cost savings in this area alone would be enormous.

No one can yet claim expertise in the new architecture of learning. We need a renaissance where a variety of disciplines cross-pollinate and collude to create a new paradigm. We need an established profession of learning architecture where such collusion can take place and establish a platform of research and design that we look to and build on.

As a society, we must call on our institutions of learning not just to equip us to lead productive lives but also to encourage us to use our imaginations and our skills to improve the quality of everyday life. Learning is a process of individual growth, not a uniform end product. What isn't taught says more about us than what is. How effectively we learn mirrors our intelligence as well as our humanity.

Edward L. Davis III
Northport, MI
February 2005

Part I:
The Past

Chapter 1

DECONSTRUCTING SCHOOL

… Or "What we have learned from 2,500 years of teaching."

Education is central to civilization. The method, the style, the grace, and the philosophy we invoke in passing knowledge from generation to generation have more to say about societies than any other single endeavor.

Of course, most learning takes place on an informal basis. How much have you retained from classroom learning versus what the world taught you?

This book focuses on what has emerged from societies as a formal process of education and how the process has, in turn, informed history and culture.

This is not a book about history. So this chapter will be a romp, skipping over many events and seminal thinkers to provide an impressionistic view of how we got from there to here, what was lost in the process, and what is now newly possible.

Every historical era can be characterized by struggles for power and influence. As we proceed to the present day in this mini-history, I want to show the roots of the many struggles (i.e., classicism vs. modernism, behaviorism vs. cognitive science, authority vs. autonomy, religion vs. secularism, government control vs. local control, managed learning vs.

independent learning, etc.) that are alive in public classrooms, corporate classrooms, and everywhere else we participate in formal learning.

I will start with the Greeks, from whom education, as a formal practice, emerged. But first, it is important to note that formal education throughout most of human history came from priests or those connected with religious beliefs.

Before the growth of Western civilization and, in fact, throughout most of history, human concerns centered on agriculture, food preparation, family matters, war, music, and basic crafts and trades. The need for an education, in the formal sense, was minimal except in the service of religion.

Amid tribal strife, while coping with famine and disease, and the rigors of daily survival, the religious temple was a sanctuary and a place of superstitious awe. The mysteries of life were pondered and explained by religious leaders. Hopes of changing one's lifestyle and worldview were channeled to religion or conquest, or both.

This was true in virtually all of the ancient civilizations of India, China, Egypt, and the Middle East. Ascendancy to the priesthood or living a religious life was the circumstance that called for book learning or formal instruction. The priesthoods in ancient Egypt, medieval Europe, and elsewhere recorded ancient wisdom and contemporary events with great rigor and detail.

I will come back to the religious influence on education, but let us now move to the ancient Greeks, who sparked the genesis of institutional education.

Athens and Sparta Set the Stage for Education

There are those who believe that education, in the true sense of the word, was never more manifest than in Athens in the third and fourth centuries before Christ. The combined influence of Socrates, Plato, and Aristotle led to a cultural and political climate in which education became a national rather than a personal concern.

In Athens, school attendance was voluntary. Around the age of seven, parents sent their sons off to school. Almost all boys attended school until the age of 14.

Young men from wealthier families went to the equivalent of secondary school from 14 to 18. Men of means went on to higher education after two years of military service.

Socrates, the First Educator

History records Socrates as the first in Western civilization to develop an approach to education. The "Socratic Method" left us an enduring legacy, though rapidly dying out as an approach to teaching as will become apparent throughout this book.

By understanding the core values of the Socratic approach, we get a glimpse into the heart of what's missing today.

The way Socrates taught is consistent with what research on cognition tells us about learning. As he saw it, we begin to learn by first uncovering our presuppositions of knowing and our habits of understanding.

As a teacher, Socrates was constantly dealing with the question, How do we learn in the face of an already constructed world that has been placed, through much reinforcement, beyond question?

The beginning of this approach is always to pose a question. The listener is then enjoined to participate. At its core, it is "teaching by asking rather than teaching by telling." The fulcrum of learning rests on the ability to inquire.

The Socratic approach is designed to penetrate the world of appearances and repeatedly reveal what is beyond the obvious. The student is compelled to take a more critical stance, to ask the questions "What is it I'm not seeing here?" and "What lies beyond my assumptions, the way I usually see it?"

Even before beginning to question assumptions, Socrates exhorted all students to ask the primary question "How should I live?" meaning that everything learned was intimately connected to an identity, a place in the world. Behind this fundamental question are questions such as "What kind of knowledge do I need to get along in this world?" "What kind of knowledge do I need to become part of the world that is possible?" "How have I put the world together, and what have I accepted that prevents me from knowing how best to live?"

Clearly, Socrates understood that learning occurs in a social context. He knew that language has social and historical variables that skew understanding. Most of all, he knew that an examined life was the cornerstone of learning. *These were the fundamental tenets of an education almost 2,500 years ago.*

The importance of developing students' critical faculties, their curiosity, and their ability to formulate key questions, to express themselves clearly, and to frame an effective debate was essential to a Socratic education. What kind of a society would these values encourage? How would such a society differ from ours?

In a class of 20 or 30 students, nothing is more important than monitoring student understanding by asking questions designed to elicit assumptions. This provides the opportunity to make adjustments by asking another question designed to clarify a student's comprehension. Socratic pedagogy began with learning what to teach from gauging the level and background of each student's understanding.

How does this square with accepting and memorizing what a textbook says? How do you know that the content of a lecture is going to be applicable in a learner's life? When students dutifully complete worksheets and prepare for tests, what are they actually learning?

If what is learned is not going to be used, of what importance is it? Should it be part of your curriculum? These were key questions in the world of the ancient Greeks. Are they now?

The world has changed. We now provide education for every child. We live in a world of diversity. Not every teacher can be Socrates. Education has to prepare us for success in the world. Adults want practical education, not philosophy.

I do not take issue with these aims. But those who use them to explain why we don't incorporate the Socratic Method when third graders take math or when immigrants take English or when 300 college freshmen take Biology 101 are simply missing the point.

Plato, Socrates' student, continued to develop a theory of education based on the Socratic Method and founded the Academy in 387 B.C. Historians record the Academy as the first formal institution of higher education in the Western world.

Today the term "academy" is used to refer to the institution of higher education itself. Plato's Academy lasted nine centuries, closed down by the Roman emperor Justinian in 529 A.D. With a tenure of that duration, something was done right!

So, it was the Greeks who developed a "classic education"—not to be confused with an education in the classics. The core curriculum of classic education was language, segmented into three components (the "trivium"): grammar, dialectic, and rhetoric. In those times, "grammar" meant learning to talk; "dialectic" meant how to talk sense, to argue, to prove, and to disprove; and "rhetoric" meant structure and style, the way you framed your debate or inquiry to give it impact.[1]

The key components of "classic" were equipping students with the skills to learn, to express themselves honestly and courageously, and to develop according to their own insights about themselves and the world. It was understood that language was the medium in which these skills occurred.

Twenty-three centuries later, "educrats" have become fearful of imbuing students with these qualities. To comprehend what's wrong with modern education, it is important to understand the source of this fear.

Above all, Socrates knew that the basic value of education came from what was brought forth from the students' minds, not the teacher's. His primary commitment was to give students the ability to search for what is worth knowing and believing.

Socratic teaching exemplifies a combination of honesty, intellectual rigor, and humility. Interventions in the classroom always convey that what we all know and believe (even the experts) is subject to question and never off limits. Remember your own experience in the educational process. When were these qualities evident in one of your teachers?

Long before Athens reached its pinnacle, in another part of Greece, another form of state education was thriving. Sparta was a military city-state, at war with other states during most of its existence.

The laws and standards of Sparta were very much in contrast to those of Athens. The machinery of state was directed to the creation of skilled soldiers. The citizen existed for the state, not vice versa, and the notion of individualism was rigidly suppressed.

Education in Sparta was compulsory. At age seven, boys left their homes to enter the public educational system. They lived communally, under very strict conditions. Discipline was the hallmark of their education, and the curriculum was extremely demanding, physically and mentally. The goal was to produce a physically fit and mentally disciplined specimen that would be loyal to the state.

In the Spartan curriculum, literacy and the arts were of little importance. Virtue and a desire for glory were values stressed in Spartan society and reinforced in the educational process. The Spartan male's education continued until the age of 30 and grew increasingly demanding and strict as it progressed.

In the world of Socrates and Plato, knowledge was vital and open ended and could survive only where inquiry and critical faculties were encouraged. Independent thinking, oratory skills, and the ability to penetrate deeper truths were the hallmarks of an excellent education.

In Sparta, knowledge served a different purpose. It was for the survival of the state. Spartan citizens, men and women alike, were judged on how disciplined and unquestioning they were. Competitions were fierce, even brutal, with much glory going to the victor. The Spartan mind greatly valued brevity and simplicity and rejected all that was foreign to it. The options were command or obey.

Athenian culture was about self-development, while Spartan culture hinged on self-sacrifice. Though they were very different, both systems of education were extremely effective in producing citizens imbued with their stated goals. Much of their mutual success was predicated on single-mindedness of purpose. Today's schooling, with its many goals and socio-political underpinnings, shows a stark contrast to the ancient Greeks.

As we take a look at the purposes of education today, it will become apparent that they are multiple, not clearly defined at the user level, and can even contradict one another. The Athenian and Spartan traditions still exemplify what is best about schooling that works. They also can be seen as metaphors for contrasting ideals within our own culture and the partisan education wars that have been going on in the United States since public education came into existence.

Athenian and Spartan ideals were combined in the Roman Empire and spread throughout Europe.

It was Augustine, a classically educated Roman, who converted to Christianity in 386 A.D. and created the most influential adaptation of the Greek classical tradition with Christian ideals in the Latin-Christian world.

As a Christian teacher, Augustine pointed out that every individual was a citizen of the city of God. The prime purpose of education was to bring man's soul into harmony with the divine order. "But Augustine did not abandon his trust in a solid classical education: though the ability to think clearly and critically cannot bring salvation, they remain essential allies of Good Will."[2]

The fusion of Greek classical tradition with Christian theology became the model for Western education and survived into modernity.

> The classical concept of the trivium in education survived as the sole educational model for two millennia because it worked—it consistently produced educated men, given to the pursuit of knowledge and the exercise of the mind in the cause of judgment. **From "Classical vs. Modern Education,"** *Christine Miller*

"In the Middle Ages, Christian scholastics consulted the Bible and the writings of the early church fathers for answers to all questions. Investigation of the physical world and consultation of secular sources was forbidden."[3]

During the Middle Ages (until the thirteenth century), monasteries and convents were the recorders and preservationists of knowledge. Several became centers of intellect and culture. The education of children was exclusively the province of the church.

During the Protestant Reformation in the sixteenth century, Martin Luther broke from Christian tradition in placing the responsibility for education with civil rather than religious authorities.

The next big influence on education came through the thought and influence of those who gave birth to the scientific revolution. Although René Descartes (1596–1650) did not write about education, he had a profound influence on it. A devout Catholic educated in Jesuit schools, he nevertheless broke from religious authority and classic Greek ideals to develop an analytic method as the basis and model for inquiry.

Only that which could be observed and then separated from the inexactitude of the senses and ideation by mathematic measurement and calculation could be depended upon as truth. Descartes' work lauded the mathematical scientist as the new authority.

> Although he takes scientific truth to provide the new moral authority, Descartes nevertheless adheres to a provisional morality: he will obey the laws of his country and follow the guidance of the church, presumably in the unexpressed hope that scientific advances would eventually improve those institutions and their laws. **Rorty, "The Ruling History of Education,"** *Journal of the Encyclopedia of Philosophy of Education*

The new moral authority of science gradually took over as the prevailing belief now referred to as modernism. Modernism stressed observation, experimentation, and technical advancement. Theoretical and imagined realities have far less importance to the modern mind than they did prior to modernism. In fact, the notion of rejecting what we think or intuit in favor of what we observe is fundamental to modern thought.

What we now view as realistic or as common sense rests on believing that which can be observed. "Realism is the philosophy of science. It leads us toward an inductive view of truth and a skeptical view of anything we cannot directly perceive."[4]

An inductive orientation to learning depends on what has already been proven or asserted as truth. In the classical approach to learning, one was taught to be skeptical, to question the truth of observation, and to assume that ultimate truths were not available to us.

The distinction between these two approaches is profound and fundamental to the emphasis of schooling today. It is a quick leap, in the inductive approach, from accepting what is written on the page of a textbook or asserted by an instructor as truth to a passive acceptance of what the "experts" say must be learned.

John Locke (1632–1704) further distanced education from religious control with his concept of the *tabula rasa*, the blank slate of the young mind upon which the five senses write evidence of the external world. The implication of Locke's writings on education was that childhood was a state to be overcome by elders who molded a child's thought into maturity.

Locke's detailed descriptions of the workings of the human mind were extremely influential on other thinkers for the next 150 years. He was the first major figure to create a thorough and mechanistic model of human thought.

Locke's notion gave rise to the paradigm through which virtually all of us today have been schooled.

Locke, Descartes, and Isaac Newton ushered in the age of scientific determinism. We are now so imbued with the precepts of science that it is the "water we swim in." Any of us put into a classroom with Socrates or Plato would exhibit the tendencies that four centuries of scientific rationalism have wrought. What do you think these tendencies might be?

The Siege of Behaviorism

By the twentieth century, empiricism had become the method by which advancements of knowledge take place. The empiricist would consider it implicit that learning and conditioning are governed by the law of cause and effect.

John Watson and Edward Thorndike, influenced by the thinking of John Locke, fused empiricism with psychology in their development of behavioral learning theory. In 1913, Watson published a paper declaring, "The time has come when psychology must discard all reference to consciousness. ... Its sole task is the prediction and control of behaviour [by "behaviour," Watson meant observable activities]; and introspection can form no part of its method."[5]

> Most contemporary educational practice is based upon the stimulus-response-reward model. It sees the student as a passive receptor of knowledge. The teacher, as the prime actor, determines objectives, selects materials, gives assignments, and evaluates student performance (all of this with the mediation of publishers, remote instructional designers, the U.S. Dept. of Education and Congress). The student follows directions, listens to and reads about the "right" answers or appropriate algorithms, rehearses those right answers, and provides the correct response on an objective or short-answer test.[6]

To knowingly or unknowingly accept the behavioral perspective is to be in favor of rewarding students for high performance and grading them by a uniform standard. The standard may be set by the teacher or by the state for an entire age group.

The behavioral notion of "programmed learning" says that subject matter is broken down into sequential, easily understood chunks, each followed by a question that has a correct answer. The object is to reinforce the learning process by stimulating an immediate response that comes with the reward of getting it right or the negative incentive of getting it wrong.

It is this approach to schooling that continues to dominate formal education, from top to bottom, today. It is also the primary approach to instructional design for corporate and military training.

In the behavioral approach, all learning is conditioned. Introspection forms no essential part of its methods. Learning becomes a process of conditioning reflexes (programmed responses) through the substitution of one stimulus for another.

In such a method, there is no context for learning, no built-in reason to learn a particular subject, simply an imposed doctrine of the right stuff to learn. "It says the learner should progress from step to step in a predictable sequence, interrupted by frequent testing and reinforcement, with each step getting progressively more challenging."[7]

As a corporate trainer working for a large training company, I was frequently told that I would be most effective by sticking to the basics, which were "Tell 'em, tell 'em what you told 'em, and then have 'em tell you what you told 'em." Think about your own schooling. How much of it was from this mold?

Even though behaviorism has been largely debunked as a basis for learning theory,[8] it continues to maintain a stranglehold on the practice of teaching.

Education for Everyone—the Great American Experiment

The notion of education as a strategy to build a nation of desirable citizens took root largely from the writings of Thomas Jefferson, John Adams, and Benjamin Rush, three of our founding fathers. These men felt that the American Revolution would be complete only when knowledge could be "diffused more generally through the mass of people," as Jefferson put it.

In fact, Jefferson declared that the real revolution would not be overthrowing the British but creating an educated populace.

During the nineteenth century, progressives from many countries would credit the growing proportion of educated Americans as the primary influence on cultural and technological evolution. On the other hand, as education became increasingly available to all, it was seen as a means to shape young minds as the elite saw fit.

In 1851, Massachusetts passed the first general compulsory education law and began the trend toward universal tax-supported education. At that time, most of the country was rural and agrarian.

Most children attended a one-room schoolhouse with four to eight different ages and an approximate class size of 60 to 80. How did kids manage to learn? They were self-reliant, and they taught one another. Teachers depended on independent and collaborative learning far more than their own instruction.

Our national character was very different 150 years ago. For example, we were a nation of readers long before public schooling existed. In 1818, Noah Webster estimated that more than five million copies of his *Spelling Book* had been sold. This was in a nation of fewer than 20 million. According to the American Library Association, only one in 11 Americans buys or checks out a book today.[9]

Common Sense, the book by Thomas Paine that helped foment the American Revolution, sold 600,000 copies within a population of 2.5 million—the equivalent of selling 65 million books today. A best-selling author, Walter Scott, sold five million copies of his novels in the United States in 1812 and 1815—the equivalent of selling 60 million copies today. In 1812, Pierre DuPont de Nemours published *Education in the United States*, a book that reported that fewer than four in every thousand people in the United States could not read and do numbers well.[10]

It is a great irony to look back at this, but it appears that at the time public schooling was instituted, Americans were educating themselves quite well.

At the beginning of the nineteenth century, most schooling took place first in the home and second through the church. In the mid-nineteenth century, when public schooling began, the school year was 12 to 14 weeks long, and most students left school at around age 13 to help support their families. By the beginning of the twentieth century, the balance between home and school had greatly shifted as we collectively turned over the care of young minds to public institutions and professional educators.

Parallel to the rise of public education was the shift from an agrarian to a wage-earning industrial economy. Immigrants were pouring in from other parts of Europe, and people were moving from the family farm to cities. The nuclear family was losing children to the larger world of factories and upward mobility. As we approached the twentieth century, the character of America was changing.

With growing ethnic diversity, the growth of densely populated cities, and the breaking up of families came a steady increase in social tension. Crime and poverty were on the rise. The American response was to inculcate its ideology (that of being a meritocracy) in the young through schooling—to build a homogenous society out of a diverse one.

In addition, the skills and habits of an industrial worker required "engineering." With industrialism came enormous economic growth and equivalent social decay. Americans were growing uneasy. Industrialists were growing very wealthy from the labor of the masses. The freedom associated with being an American was available to a shrinking percentage of a rapidly growing population.

During this difficult transition, much thought was put into the purposes of schooling. The primary driver among the nation's elite was anxiety about cultural diversity. Between 1821 and 1850, close to 2.5 million Europeans immigrated to the United States. More than a million were Catholics and represented a threat to the Protestant elite. Between

1865 and 1900, 14 million more immigrants arrived at our shores, most of them from the poorest socioeconomic groups in southern and eastern Europe—also mostly semiliterate and from diverse cultural backgrounds. This constituted an assimilation problem unparalleled in history.

"Although the personalities and behaviors of adult immigrants might prove intractable, the impending rot of Anglo-American civilization could be averted through the concerted effort to shape the still-pliable characters of their children into a native mold. This massive task of assimilation required weakening the connection between the immigrant child and its family, which in turn called for the capture of the child by an outpost of native culture. In short, fears about cultural heterogeneity propelled the establishment of systems of public education; from the beginning, public schools were agents of cultural standardization."[11]

The first Western nation to introduce forced schooling was Prussia in 1819. Several years later, a contingent of American leaders (including Horace Mann, the most influential educational thinker of the nineteenth century) visited Prussia and "fell in love with the order, obedience, and efficiency they saw there. (They) attributed the well-regulated machine-like society to its educational system, and campaigned relentlessly upon returning home to bring the Prussian vision to (our) shores."[12]

"The Prussian educational system was clearly designed to produce obedience, a subservient middle class, and citizens who thought alike about major issues. As a result of the lobbying of Horace Mann and other influential Americans, without any national debate or discussion, we adopted Prussian schooling or rather, most had it imposed upon them."[13]

Americans had a traditional disrespect for authority and needed to be adapted to a factory production-oriented social organization that was growing by leaps and bounds. The Prussian educational system seemed made to order for those who were pushing an educational design.

The Prussian model emphasized learning by memorization because its chief goal was to mold the thoughts of learners, not stimulate independent thinking. It was very much a continuation of John Locke's notion that children were to be programmed with the best thinking of the day rather than left to their own designs. How far we had migrated from the world of Socrates!

The notion of socialization grew in stature. Educators emphasized the need for schools to produce punctuality, obedience to authority, delayed gratification, orientation to the clock, repetition, and reward for best performance—the values of the Industrial Age, the routines of school.

In 1889, William Torrey Harris, the most influential U.S. Commissioner of Education we've ever had, told railroad magnate Collis P. Huntington that American schools had been "scientifically designed" to prevent "overeducation." In 1906, Harris published *The Philosophy of Education*, in which he declared that the purpose of schooling was "to alienate children from their families, their churches, their neighborhoods, and themselves."[14]

Harris was an important voice for the new status quo. Immigrants and potential industrial workers had to be given values and skills that the captains of industry needed to build a compliant working class. The lower classes could not be trusted to comply.

It was the American school that would separate children sufficiently from parental influence to produce the new citizen-worker. This was an overthrow of the "true American Revolution" that Jefferson and Adams had called for.

In the early twentieth century, the enormous growth of industrialization was creating greater and greater demands for efficiency. **Efficiency = profit = growth** became the mantra of a radically changing culture. The notion of efficiency and of mass production understandably, albeit tragically, became fused with the most ambitious educational task in history—to educate all of America's children to the practical needs of its society.

Controlling costs, producing a uniform output, and getting maximum productivity from human labor were great concerns as we entered the twentieth century. In 1910, Frederick W. Taylor began introducing "time and motion studies" and "scientific management" to the running of railroads and manufacturing plants.

It wasn't long before the same principles were applied to the training of educational administrators. The words "scientific" and "management" quickly sold the public, which was understandably impressed by the efficiencies of mass production. Unfortunately, under the mantle of "science," schools focused on producing uniform outputs and on lowering costs, with little to no focus on the quality of their product.

"They saw schools not as centers of learning but as enterprises which were functioning efficiently if the students went through without failing and received their diplomas on schedule and if the operation were handled economically."[15] Educational administrators did not have the skills or the inclination to conduct real scientific inquiry into the real efficiencies of learning. The social sciences did not then (and still do not) provide a reliable model to measure educational outcomes.

One of the most respected educational leaders, William C. Bagley, published a book in 1907 entitled *Classroom Management*. True to the times, Bagley characterized the issue of academic management as a business problem. He stressed the need for "unquestioned obedience" as the "first rule of efficient service" and described the circumstances as "entirely analogous to that in any other organization or system—the Army, the Navy, government or great business enterprises."

The influence of Bagley and Taylor was pervasive for decades. It still persists today, though now cloaked in egalitarian rhetoric.

By 1918, every state had a law for compulsory schooling. In the corridors of political and industrial power, schooling had become a means to produce a socially and economically cooperative populace. During this time, the influence of private money was very large in shaping public policy on education.

By founding charitable organizations, by endowing university departments and school administrations, and by literally spending more money than the government, the captains of American industry (the Carnegies, Rockefellers, Vanderbilts, Fords, and others) were able to build a system of public education to their values and sensibilities, not the general public's.

Because of the cooption of schooling for the purposes of nation building, American schooling, unlike its European counterparts, placed heavy emphasis on nonacademic curriculum. "The democratic aim of bringing the fruits of modern culture to the masses gave way in practice to a concern with education as a form of social control."[16]

The Influence of John Dewey (1859–1952)

A unique voice in American education, John Dewey is considered the most influential educational thinker of the past century. He was an ardent antibehaviorist when behaviorism was at its peak of influence on education.

Some of Dewey's best thinking related to his concern for "social intelligence." He said that effective schools must be "primarily a mode of associated living, a conjoint communicated experience." He often argued that the enterprise of education failed to the extent that it did not view and develop schools as a form of community life. Were they to succeed as such, Dewey asserted that students would develop "the capacity collectively to enlarge their own freedom and to create a more desirable form of social life."[17]

Nothing was more important, in Dewey's view, than communication, shared reflection, and the discovery of shared values in the classroom. He viewed the process of education as a concentrated growth process stimulating curiosity and developing a social consciousness. One of his famous aphorisms is "Education is not about life; it is life."

Like Thomas Jefferson, Dewey tied education to the creation of authentic democracy and became known as the premier champion of "democratic education." His writings linking the nature of an education to the genesis and perpetuation of true democracy are among his most eloquent.[18]

Were you to trace back many of the educational reforms of the mid-twentieth century to their roots, you would be led to John Dewey.

Maria Montessori (1870–1952)

No single person has influenced the development of alternatives to modern schooling more than Maria Montessori. She had so many of the basic tenets of learning "right" that it becomes difficult to separate the latest thinking from hers.

The core of the Montessori method is to give children freedom to explore, solve problems, and pursue learning exercises within a clearly understood set of limits—freedom within limits. Children work at their own pace, chose the materials (from an available selection) they wish, and work alone or with others when they prefer.

The child's innate drive to learn is honored, and the teacher plays an unobtrusive role. Much of the work in the classroom is creative, concrete in its objectives, hands on, and multisensory. A three-year age span is mixed together in the classroom.

Learning materials are carefully designed for developmental stages. Parents are considered partners in the educational process, which is aimed at developing the child's character and social skills as well as his or her intellect.

Montessori schools are prevalent today. There are even public schools that use the Montessori method, though the name is not legally protected, so the method and materials do vary. The *International Montessori Index* at *http://www.montessori.edu* provides an excellent overview of the method and detailed comparisons between schools.

Understanding Montessori is a good starting point for learning what needs to happen in education.

The Critics

Three major modern studies of our education system have identified obsolete forces still dominating today's schools:

In 1970, Charles Silberman published the widely read *Crisis in the Classroom*, resulting from the Carnegie Corporation's study of the education of teachers, which Silberman directed. *Crisis* was a severe indictment of American education and centered on the repressive nature of schooling as well as its total failure despite years of rhetoric to counteract social, racial, and economic inequalities.

One of Silberman's key observations about the dynamics of schools was that the nature of instruction and authoritarian control had created an environment where docility and conformity were the best strategies for survival.

Although Silberman's reasons for educational failure were flawed, his overall conclusions were sound. For example, he said that the problems in schools were reinforced and compounded by teacher training and instruction that ignored intellectual development and practical end results.

By the 1960s, the era of schooling as a sacred cow was over. Blistering attacks on the organization, design, and implementation of American education were common. During the '60s and '70s, there were some bestsellers analyzing the failure of public schooling. You may remember John Holt's books, *How Children Learn* and *Why Children Fail.*

Although we continue to complain about educational failure, general awareness and substantive debate have declined. We seem to have turned over the stewardship of public education to career politicians, CEOs with a cause, and the professional status quo.

One could reasonably make the argument that our education system has achieved its prime directive—a compliant and complacent populace.

Prior to the onset of our collective complacence about schooling was the increasing tendency of educators to find excuses, in the form of learning disabilities, to account for poor performance in school. Daniel Calhoun points out, in his 1973 book *The Intelligence of a People*, that eighteenth-century teachers assumed that a failure to learn was the fault of the teacher, as a result of poor methods or inadequate efforts. The modern trend to find fault with the student belies the confidence of our present educational system.

In 1983, the landmark government report by the National Commission on Excellence in Education, **A Nation at Risk: The Imperative of Education Reform**, was published. Never before had the government so publicly and scathingly attacked public schooling. By now, the consensus was overwhelming that schooling was failing us, but like Silberman's report, *Nation* failed to give substantive reasons or provide any real analysis for why.

A Nation at Risk accomplished its chief mission, to scare us about international competitiveness and our national security. Its most memorable line was "If an unfriendly foreign power had attempted to impose on America the mediocre educational performance that exists today, we might well have viewed it as an act of war."[19]

A Nation at Risk, with its focus on describing mediocrity and the need for a policy stressing excellence, was a public relations effort on the part of the government to set higher standards enforced by testing, a trend that is now in high vogue.

Consider an entirely different tact that the government's report might have taken: *A Nation at Risk or How Our Public Schools Are Failing to Provide Students with Crucial Cognitive Skills*. Were this the title of the report, we would be talking about how to provide young people with the ability to learn instead of force-feeding them more stuff to memorize, most of which they forget.

Instead, we have the "standards" movement, which, rather than developing learning skills, focuses on increased graduation requirements, tougher standards for teacher credentials, more rigorous standardized curriculum, and national tests to measure learning progress—**keeping the same methods and practices in place with more rigorous reinforcement**. More about the consequences of this focus as we progress.

In a 1989 conference of the nation's governors, the National Education Goals were created. The goals focused on teacher salaries, higher standards, graduation requirements, and state assessments to meet increased standards. Under President Clinton, the National Education Goals became Goals 2000.

The Tenth Amendment to the Constitution prohibits the federal government from telling states and local authorities what curriculum, operating methods, evaluation, and graduation requirements to use. However, through Goals 2000 legislation, the federal role in education was dramatically increased.[20]

Under Goals 2000, the feds have circumvented the Constitution by asking states to voluntarily submit their standards to the National Education and Standards Improvement Council (NESIC) for approval. If state standards don't line up with national standards on curriculum, operating methods, and graduation requirements, then guess what? No aid under various federal programs for school funding.[21]

If you look at federal policies closely, it is clear that they want education to be in service of the state, not the other way around. The federalization of educational policy assures that "We continue to subordinate education to its narrowest economic goals, a process reinforced and strengthened by uncertainty in the new economic context of globalism. And we continue to elevate corporate executives to the status of moral leaders on educational issues while educators are rapidly losing the moral and professional authority they once commanded."[22]

George W. Bush's education plan offers no significant departure from the ideology behind *A Nation at Risk* and Goals 2000. I have spoken to many concerned citizens and professional educators who feel strongly that current plans and policies do not get at the real problems, but when I ask them what the real problems are, the answers are usually fuzzy.

There will be no significant change in our learning capabilities without widespread understanding of the current flaws in the system. Without understanding, there will be no consensus. Without consensus, there will be no action.

The biggest enterprise in America, public education, is safe for now. It has lulled us into complacence. Our understanding about the process of learning and its implications for our future is at risk.

Summary

To visit a time when learning was widely undertaken for the sake of individual development, we have to go all the way back to Socrates. Even Plato, Socrates' successor, believed that children belonged to the state and should first serve its educational goals.

After Plato, we have a long period of time when learning was in service of God and parental designs. The primary goals of education were to train children to obey authority, become self-disciplined, and act morally.

The church was exclusively in charge of education in the Western world for almost 1,500 years. Its moralistic influence lives on, for better and for worse.

In the seventeenth century, science became the new God, and the notion of social engineering through schooling became firmly entrenched. The behaviorists developed a formal learning theory based on an empirical model that discounted inner experience and focused on observable behavior and programmed response. Contiguity, repetition, and reinforcement were the primary principles upon which teaching was based.

Under the influence of behaviorism, the balance of teaching and learning was upset in favor of teaching or "schooling." Despite the fact that behavioral methods have been widely discredited, they clearly persist in our emphasis on teaching over learning today.

Industrialization and the rise of a management class very much reinforced a factory model in which instruction was preprogrammed and rigidly controlled to the extent that students were assembled into isolated age groups, told exactly what to learn, how to learn it, in what depth, and in what time span.

Schooling for everyone is one of the most significant socioeconomic changes in modern history. It has provided the basis for economic growth and major changes in social organization.

Yet, as Christopher Lasch so eloquently puts it, in *The Culture of Narcissism*, "The democratization of education has done little to justify (its) faith. It has neither improved popular understanding of modern society, raised the quality of popular culture, nor reduced the gap between wealth and poverty, which remains as wide as ever. On the other hand, it has contributed to the decline of critical thought, and the erosion of intellectual standards, forcing us to consider the possibility that mass education, as conservatives have argued all along, is intrinsically incompatible with the maintenance of educational quality."

It can be fairly said that fear has long fueled our educational policies: fear of unruly and possibly disloyal immigrants; fear of the tensions between diverse cultures, races, and religions; fear of social impediments to a wage-earning, controlled production-oriented worker class; fear of loss of dominance in the world economy; and more. Can we introduce educational policies based not on competition and the survival instinct but rather on the development of personal wisdom, individual conscience, and innovative thinking?

Another enormous influence on learning has been television. It introduces children to a bigger world yet isolates them from family and community. It entertains us and, at the same time, lulls us into passivity. It substitutes serial pseudoacquaintances for real-life encounters. It passes the time.

It passes the time so much that combined with the increasingly longer school day, children are effectively isolated from their families for all but a few hours each week.

Television reflects choices to kids: which channel to watch, which world to enter, and when to turn it off or on. School is just the opposite, telling kids what to think, how to think, how long to think about it. Television becomes the outlet for the linear, lockstep, and authoritative world of school. Both remove us from our unique imaginations, our own creativity.

When you look at public education closely, its design was intended to separate children from unpredictable and less controllable parents. It has increasingly become the means by which we civilize each generation and convert it into human capital.

To the immigrants who came here at great risk, America represented a place to find economic security and express individual freedom. As the powers of government grew, and as the pattern of social life moved from farms and villages to factories and cities, schooling became the obvious vehicle to mold subsequent generations as the ruling elite (in government and business) saw fit.

And as Americans increasingly became tied to jobs that required longer hours and greater distances to get to, school became the nanny that most of us couldn't afford, even to the extent of taking increasing responsibility for our moral education.

Benjamin Rush wrote in 1786, "Let our pupil be taught that he does not belong to himself, but that he is public property." In a 1914 bulletin, the U.S. Bureau of Education declared, "The public schools exist primarily for the benefit of the State rather than for the benefit of the individual."[23] This policy was shared by most of our early influential educators and politicians and still thrives today through our complicity with public schooling.

Learning has become, more and more, a commodity as we have reinforced the need to decide and orchestrate what people learn. The commodification of learning has upset the balance of learning in favor of teaching.

We have learned less and less in accordance with our instincts, tastes, and immediate needs. The enormous consequence of schooling is that it has molded us from a distinctively self-reliant people to a people inclined to learn about the world instead of learning from it. We grow up thinking that knowledge is in the hands of sanctified institutions and that our ability to find our place in the world depends on these institutions, their grades, and their diplomas.

As the social philosopher Ivan Illich put it, "Knowledge can be defined as a commodity only so long as it is viewed as the result of institutional enterprise or as the fulfillment of institutional objectives. When a man recovers the sense of personal responsibility for what he learns and teaches, this spell can be broken and the alienation of learning from living be overcome."[24]

The Prussians of the 1840s, the behaviorists of the 1930s, textbook publishers, management science from the Industrial Age, and your next education governor or president—these are the forces that continue to dominate how and what we learn through college and even beyond.

Until now, most of the criticism levied at schooling describes the shortcomings of schools, measures the shortfalls of their attainments, criticizes educational practitioners and their methods. The key flaw in this approach involves the focus on the terms "teaching" and "schooling."

If we shift our focus to "learning," interesting and profound questions arise. What is learning? How does it occur? What are the optimum conditions for it to occur? How would one differentiate a practitioner of teaching from a practitioner of learning? How do pedagogy (the art of teaching) and learning best coexist?

If learning is a natural process (and it surely is), what happens when we try to control its pace, its focus, and its outcomes? Can we strike a better balance between individual learning goals and what we collectively decide we must know? Can we better assist individuals to discover and pursue their unique abilities, interests, and aptitudes?

It is time to look closely at the conditions under which we learn. To what extent do they define what, how much, how thoroughly, and how rapidly we learn? Furthermore, it is vital in these times to incorporate within this examination the question of just what our intelligence is in service of. As Socrates put it, "What is worth knowing?" This is both an individual and a collective question.

What we have learned about learning returns us to Socrates, to the spirit of inquiry and dialogue. Minds stagnate when their contents become strictly a consumed product.

For learning to become an end rather than a means, we must put independent thought and whole participation first, before what is to be learned. We must emphasize learning over being taught.

Endnotes

1 Author unknown, Classical vs. Modern Education, *http://www.classicalhomeschooling.org*

2 Amelie Oksenberg Rorty, *The Ruling History of Education*, p. 4, *http://www.educacao.pro.br/ruling_history_of_education.htm*

3 Renee M. Newman, *A History of Formal Education*, 1998, p. 5, *http://www.shianet.org/~reneenew/HUM501.html*

4 *The Cognitive Paradigm*, p. 5, *http://wwweduc.drake.edu*

5 J. B. Watson, *Psychology Review*, 1913, pp. 158–167

6 Ibid.

7 Alfie Kohn, *The Schools Our Children Deserve*, p. 4

8 Alfie Kohn, *See the Learning Gap, The Schools Our Children Deserve*, 1999; M. Polanyi, *Personal Knowledge*, 1958; or Koestler, *The Ghost in the Machine*, 1967

9 Cathy Duffy, Foreword, *Government Nannies*, p. xi

10 Ibid.

11 Michael Katz, *Reconstructing American Education*, p. 18

12 Cathy Duffy, Foreword, *Government Nannies*, p. xvi

13 Ibid., p. xvii

14 John Taylor Gatto, Foreword, *Government Nannies,* and from an interview with Jerry Brown in *Dialogues*, 1998

15 Raymond E. Callahan, *Education and the Cult of Efficiency*, 1962, p. 247

16 Christopher Lasch, *Culture of Narcissism*, 1979, p.132

17 Carr and Hartnett (1996), taken from *Education from Democracy*, p. 9, see *Education for Democracy* in the *Encyclopedia of Informal Education, http://www.infed.org/biblio/b-dem.htm*

18 See John Dewey, *Democracy and Education*, 1916, MacMillan, N.Y.

19 National Commission on Excellence in Education, *A Nation at Risk*, p. 5, 1983

20 Cathy Duffy, *Government Nannies*, pp. 110–111

21 Ibid.

22 Dorothy Shipps, *Reconstructing the Common Good in Education*, p. 102

23 Cathy Duffy, *Government Nannies*, p. 115

24 Ivan Illich, *Toward a History of Needs*, p. 84, 1977

Part II:
The Present

- The Fatal Flaws
- Secondary Sins

Chapter 2

ARE WE DUMBER?

The *"dumbing down" of contemporary culture*—a phrase that has stealthily made its way into urbane conversation.

So, **are** we dumber?

The question is politically charged. Education pundits are known for pointing fingers and charging their political enemies with diluting cultural, literary, and academic standards for such purposes as playing to a lower common denominator, appeasing the need to sort through increasing volumes and decibels of information, bringing the largest numbers (through a homogenous set of inputs) to a state of cultural equilibrium, and preaching a political doctrine.

It seems to me that the question is important and that the subject is trivialized by political finger-pointing. Are we, in fact, dumber? If so, are we dumber by our own design, or is Mother Earth defending herself against us?

If it's dumber by our own design, then we can presumably do something about it—assuming we possess the will. Before you come to a conclusion, read through the following assortment of facts. What do they mean to you?

Literacy

- Roughly 60% of the adult population (in the United States) has never read a book, and only 6% reads as much as one book a year.[1]

- Only one high school junior in 50 (2%) can write well enough to meet national goals.[2]
- The U.S. Department of Education's reading "Report Card," released on April 6, 2001, stated that "two-thirds of U.S. fourth graders read below grade level and the weakest ones are falling farther behind."
- Also in April of 2001, the international Organization of Economic Cooperation and Development (OECD) reported that 60% of Americans aged 16–25 are "functionally illiterate" and that at such simple activities as filling out a form or reading a timetable, they scored "a the bottom of all industrial nations in testing."[3]
- The January 22, 1999, issue of *The Economist* (p. 55) reported that more than 40% of American 10-year-olds cannot pass a basic reading test and as many as 42 million adults in the United States are functionally illiterate. The January 29 *Economist* reported that more than 40,000 nine- to-ten-year-old Texans failed the state's standardized reading test, yet 90% were promoted anyway.
- In a 1999 newsletter to his constituents, State Representative Mark Ogles reported that "70% of Florida's tenth graders scored below the basic reading level."
- Every year, 40% to 60% of the students at the University of California find themselves required to enroll in remedial English.[4]
- In 1998, the Massachusetts Board of Education instituted a literacy test for teachers geared to the same level required for a High School Equivalency diploma. Of the 1,800 prospective teachers who took it, 59% failed.[5]
- The New York Times reported, Dec. 12, 2004 that the United States is 49th (out of 158 countries in the U.N.) in literacy.
- Something like 120 million American adults are illiterate or read at no better than a fifth-grade level.[6]
- In 1993, the first report from the federally funded National Adult Literacy Survey found that nearly half of all adult Americans scored in the lowest two levels of literacy, levels that the National Education Goals Panel has stated are well below what American workers need to be competitive in the global economy. Although the literacy survey findings made headlines, research shows that we are making relatively little progress in achieving a fully literate society.[7]

Numeracy

- A December 12, 2004 article reported that the United States ranked 28th out of 40 countries in 'mathematical literacy'.
- In 1992, the Educational Testing Service reported that 56% of American-born four-year-college graduates were consistently unable to calculate the change from $3.00 after buying a 30-cent soup and a $1.95 sandwich.
- The Third International Mathematics and Science Study (TIMSS), the most comprehensive and rigorous international comparison of schooling ever undertaken, was administered to a half-million students from 41 countries in 1995. Of the 21 countries participating in the twelfth grade general knowledge of math, the United States ranked nineteenth.[8]
- The second TIMMS study found that the "performance of the top 5% of U.S. students is matched by the top 50% of students in Japan."[9]
- A December 2000 report on U.S. eighth grader TIMSS scores indicated their performance on the last two exams (given four years apart) was behind 27 other nations.[10]
- A February 25, 1998, *New York Times* article reported that the 1995 TIMSS exam also ranked students who had taken or were taking precalculus, calculus, or advanced-placement calculus. The United States performed dead last.
- Mathematicians and scientists, including four Nobel Prize recipients and two winners of a prestigious math prize (the Fields Medal), deplored the U.S. Department of Education for math teaching methods they said were "horrifyingly short on basics."[11]
- In 1989, the National Council of Teachers of Mathematics (NCTM) called for a watering down or "decreased attention to" various aspects of the math curriculum from grade 4 through high school. Education research analyst Mel Gabler asserts that the "NCTM humors, conceals, and tests ignorance. They ask students to problem solve who have not first mastered necessary skills and concepts and hide crippled math skills through the use of calculators."[13]

Science

- In a survey of American adults conducted by the Natural Science Foundation in October 1995, 56% of those polled said that electrons were larger than atoms, 63% of the same group stated that the earliest human beings lived at the same time as the dinosaurs (a chronological error of more than 60 million years), 53% of the group said the earth revolves around the sun in either a day or a month (try 365 days!), and 91% of the group was unable to define the term "molecule."[13]
- A random telephone survey of more than 2,000 adults, conducted by Northern Illinois University, revealed that 21% believed that the sun revolved around the earth, with an additional 7% saying they didn't know which revolved around which.[14]
- In the March 9, 1998, *U.S. News & World Report*, education writer John Leo reported that half of the physical sciences teachers in U.S. secondary education did not major or even minor in physics in college.
- John Hubisz, a North Carolina State University science professor who led an exhaustive study of the quality and level of educational textbooks, was particularly horrified by science textbooks. For example, his researchers found that the 12 most popular science textbooks used in middle schools were riddled with errors, more than 500 pages of them. None of the 12 textbooks had an acceptable level of accuracy according to Hubisz, who estimated that 85% of U.S. school children use them. They "have a very large number of errors, many irrelevant photographs, complicated illustrations, experiments that could not possibly work, and drawings that represent impossible situations," he said. Errors such as misstating Newton's first law of physics and incorrectly depicting what happens to light when it passes through a prism are utterly unacceptable and have passed through screening by committees of teachers, administrators, parents, and so-called curriculum specialists![15]
- In the 1995 TIMSS test, U.S. physics students scored last out of 21 countries. The results would have been worse in both math and science had Asian countries participated in the international rankings.
- In a 1995 press release responding to the astonishingly bad international ranking of U.S. students in math and science, Dr. Neal Lane, director of the National Science Foundation, said, "This worries me.

It should worry us all." *A Splintered Vision,* a report issued by the NSF in response to TIMSS, asserted that eighth-grade U.S. curriculum, when compared with curriculums abroad, lacks focus and is packed with information, almost guaranteeing that no one topic can be taught in depth.

• In March of 2001, *Business Week* reported an annual rate of decline of U.S. citizen science graduates for several years.

History, Civics, and Geography

• A 1995 article in the *New York Times* reported the results of a survey indicating that 40% of American adults (upward of 70 million people) did not know that Germany was our enemy in World War II.[16]

• A U.S. Department of Education survey of 22,000 students in 1995 revealed that 50% were unaware of the Cold War; 60% of the same group had no idea of how the United States came into existence.[17]

• A 1998 survey by the National Constitution Center revealed that only 41% of American teenagers can name the three branches of government, 2% can name the chief justice of the Supreme Court, and 26% were unable to name the vice president.[18]

• Forty-seven percent of a sample of 17-year-olds, on the verge of becoming eligible voters, did not know the simple fact, according to a recent survey, that each state elects two U.S. senators. Half of the same group believed that the president appoints members of congress.[19]

• A Washington, D.C., grade-school teacher reports that many of the fifth and sixth graders in her geography class were unable to locate Washington, D.C., on a map of the United States. A survey by the Gallup Organization found that one in seven adults couldn't find the United States on a blank map of the world. In one college geography class, 25% of the students could not locate the Soviet Union on a world map, while on a map of the 48 contiguous states, only 22% could identify 40 or more states correctly.[20]

General

• A standardized test given to 26,000 Americans 16 and over "concluded that 80 million Americans are deficient in the basic reading and mathematical skills needed to perform rudimentary tasks in today's society."[21]

- A 1995 report by the international Organization for Economic Cooperation and Development reported "the effectiveness of the U.S. primary and secondary education system can be characterized as mediocre at best."
- A September 1997 report said that homeschoolers scored 70% higher than public school students on standardized national achievement tests regardless of race, economic status, or regulation levels. They scored 22.8 on the ACT Composite, which is higher than the highest state, at 22.7, and five points higher than Washington, D.C., at 17.8. The average SAT score for homeschoolers was 1,100, 80 points higher than public schools in 2000. A large study by the University of Maryland showed that the average homeschooler scored in the seventy-fifth percentile on the Iowa Test of Basic Skills, while the fiftieth percentile marked the national average.[22]

Adjusting the Standards

- The College Board, which administers the SAT exam to high school seniors applying to college, discovered that the average verbal score had dropped from 478 in 1963 to 424 in 1995 (this on a scale from 200 to 800), so it adjusted the scoring so that 424 became 500 and 730 became 800—a perfect score.
- In the previously reported situation in 1998, the Massachusetts Board of Education instituted a literacy test for teachers geared to the same level required for a High School Equivalency diploma. Of the 1,800 prospective teachers who took it, 59% failed. In response to this, the interim commissioner of education, one Frank Haydu III, announced that the passing grade would be lowered. The board finally reversed the decision, and the commissioner resigned. But the facts that 59% of a large group of potential teachers had severe problems with high school spelling and punctuation and that an educational administration would declare this no obstacle to the performance of their jobs are good indicators of the twilight phase of our nation.[23]
- Cornell University researchers Donald P. Hayes and Loreen T. Wolfer conducted an extensive research project on U.S. academic textbooks. One of their findings was that reading materials used in American schools were dramatically simplified several times between the late 1940s and the early 1960s.[24]

- Hayes and Wolfer set out to discover whether the long-term dumbing down of texts assigned to students has eroded their cumulative base of knowledge as well as their vocabulary and reading skills. Allowing for the phasing out of harder texts and when students using the easier texts would graduate, it was calculated that the low point for test scoring would be around 1977. Just so, reading scores began to fall in 1963 and continued to fall through the 1970s. Because educators have not increased the reading levels of the texts they use in classrooms, Hayes and Wolfer predicted that scores will continue to be low.[25]

- In a remark about the recent adjustment of educational standards, educator Gregory Cizek said, "In my home state (Ohio), as in many others, we've decided to raise standards so high for twelfth graders that we're going to make them pass a ninth grade test in order to get a diploma … over four years, (they) will get a dozen tries."[26]

- Within a few short months in 1997, Books & Co., one of the last great independent bookstores in New York, had to fold; Harper Collins canceled the contracts of more than 100 of its authors and sold basic books, its "intellectual" division; and the *New York Times* ran an article reporting that so-called midlist authors—those who didn't write best-sellers (probably more than 99% of American writers)—were now being heavily rejected by major publishing firms in favor of those few "stars" who could guarantee mass-market sales (John Grisham, Stephen King, Danielle Steele, etc.).[27]

- In 1959, a New York publisher made the decision to dumb down the famous Hardy Boys book series. The original versions were, given their audience, fairly complex in both intellectual and emotional terms. The rewrites, on the other hand, were stripped down to pure plot in a kind of cops-and-robbers formula, and words that might require looking up in a dictionary were eliminated. Any form of emotional nuance—any passage suggesting ambiguity, uncertainty, or awkwardness—was replaced by statements of bland avowal. The teenagers who were reading these books in the mid-1960s were no longer challenged by them; like so much else, the books had been reduced to mental chewing gum.[28]

What are we to make of this systematic "strip mining" of American culture? Are we anti-intellectual, anti-knowledge? Because of our material success, are we increasingly lapsing into complacency? Most of the European continent regards us as intellectual lightweights, yet it remains true that we lead the world in technical innovation and produce more Nobel Prize winners than any other country.

Comparing our students, including our intellectual elite, with other countries yields disturbing results, yet what is this information telling us? Educational experts have observed over the past century that educational systems have become extremely similar throughout the developing world.

Those of you reading these combined statistics for the first time are likely shocked—even in disbelief. Yet we are not shocked by the obvious fact that knowledge has become increasingly exterior. This is to say that, as a matter of course, neither teachers nor learners are given the opportunity to exercise their own judgment or ask key questions or explore ideas or implications of so-called fact. The acquisition of knowledge has been steadily disassociated from the training of minds.

What we call "knowledge" is an increasingly codified commodity. It has been distilled into bits of official text and stripped of nuance and context. It is then verified by testing that was designed to validate the efficacy of the teaching (not the learning) process. This is done in public and private schools, in universities, and in corporate training classes. Our subjective involvement in the process of learning, as well as what is to be learned, is on the wane.

This is what makes us "dumb," not scoring poorly on tests.

Curriculum design is created by remote educational "experts" who have no contact with students and little contact with teachers. Teachers have almost no say in what and how they teach. Textbooks are created by publishers through an iterative process that satisfies committees with divergent interests. They wind up being chiefly described as boring, excessive in breadth with almost no depth, full of nice pictures and multiple-choice quizzes. The United States is known for having the fattest textbooks in the world that offer the least depth of understanding on any given subject.

Whatever the cultural reasons for our intellectual decline, it is clear that our system of education is failing us. This has been clear for the past half-century, and yet the many attempts at "reform" have failed. The evidence of these statements is abundant despite the existence of defenders and apologists for the status quo.

Don't get me wrong. We should certainly be very concerned about the erosion of literacy and the decline of our performance in many areas of academic testing. But there is no comprehensive test for how effective our fundamental approaches to teaching and learning are. One could argue that Americans are more independent and freethinking and therefore more inclined to rebel against wholesale attempts to force-feed their brains.

It is fair to say that we are a pragmatic people and therefore may want to be assured of the relevance of information we are being asked to assimilate. Less steeped in tradition than other cultures, perhaps we have a greater need for context in order to see the need to learn.

Attempts to perceive the fundamental flaws in the system have mostly been made by insiders who are, with a few exceptions, least inclined to have the necessary perspective. For instance, if you are a teacher, it is not only heresy but also economic suicide to assert that the balance of teaching and learning is tipped to the extreme in favor of teaching.

Only a select few inside the system will speak openly about it, not because they are dishonest or uncaring but because (1) the extent to which they openly criticize will be met with a proportional lack of support from fearful peers and superiors, (2) they are largely unaware of the ideological directives that inform their work, and (3) no matter what their level in the hierarchy, they generally feel powerless to effect change through open criticism.

As awareness dawns that the real flaws of institutional learning are shielded from the scrutiny of insiders and exist as vague sentiments to the rest of us, it becomes clear that we must first openly recognize the pervasiveness and magnitude of our collective failure to learn. The recognition would certainly trigger a will to get at the truth.

As to the question "Are we dumber?" I would assert that there is no real evidence that our actual intelligence has diminished. Since 1900, IQ test scores, though subject to real question as comprehensive measures of intelligence, have climbed 9–20 points each generation in the United States and other Western nations.[29]

On the other hand, there is much evidence that we have become increasingly ignorant as a direct result of institutional schooling. And, to this point, I would add that our "dumbness" is in direct proportion to our ignorance of the process by which we learn.

Educators have developed an armamentarium of strategies to explain and mitigate failure—but whose failure? Eighteenth-century teachers had no such excuses. When a pupil did not learn, it was the teacher's fault, not

35

some failure or deficit on the part of the learner. Since the mid-nineteenth century, when enforced schooling began, we have steadily constructed an ever-more sophisticated constellation of "learning problems" defined as an individual inability to master what is taught.

In the early nineteenth century, when the prevailing American ethic was "do for yourself," literacy and numeracy were far higher than they are now. The line between teaching and learning was invisible. Teaching yourself was regarded as no more difficult than being taught.

As attempts to improve the existing system fail, we continue to dumb down the requirements. Education spending has increased astronomically. Each year, we graduate hundreds of thousands of students from high school who enter colleges and are promptly enrolled in remedial (high school-level) courses.

U.S. EDUCATION PRODUCTIVITY

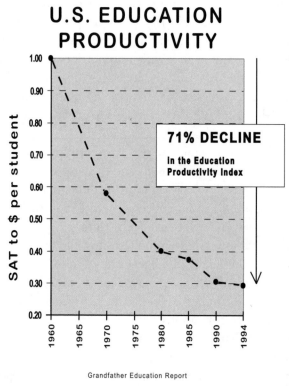

71% DECLINE

In the Education
Productivity Index

Grandfather Education Report

http://home.att.net/~mwhodges/education.htm

Adjusted for inflation, our per-student spending in public education between 1960 and 1994 tripled. Using the SAT scores as an index of productivity (starting in 1960 with a high of 100), the comparable score in 1994 was 29%. This relates SAT output to dollars of real spending per student. In this 34-year period, our educational productivity plunged 71%. In 1994, the SAT tests were revised downward to elevate future scores, so extending the curve beyond 1994 becomes problematical.[30]

We are dumber because we don't know why all of this is happening and don't have a comprehensive plan to remedy what is a bona fide national catastrophe.

Yes, we can do something about it, though the "we" is very important here. Real change, in this case, means radical systemic change—peaceful but not painless. It will come from outside pressure, not from the educators and trainers and those who make policy.

Obviously, we cannot blame all of our social ills on one institution. Drug addiction, consumerism, television, and divorce are all progressive conditions that have affected our society and are intermingled with schooling. However, it is reasonable to argue that we can maximize our impact on these social ills by focusing on a system of education that produces curious, resourceful, creative, industrious, responsible, self-reliant, and constantly evolving citizens.

Chances are that we are not biologically dumber, but the case can certainly be made that we are increasingly dumber for not tapping the enormous, unused capacity of our brains at a time when access to knowledge is vastly superior than it was a generation ago.

Some neuroscientists estimate that we actually use less than 10% of our neocortex (our "highest" or most recently evolved brain). True or not, there is strong evidence that "we seriously underdevelop our neocortex and hardly touch its potential, though we use all of it by default, simply because the brain functions as an integrated unit."[31]

As I look into the world with my history of longings, triumphs, hopes, and disappointments, I am most struck by the contrast between what is (and yes, it is awesome) and what could be. I have learned that there are different kinds of "dumb." There are people ruled by hatred with low IQs and low self-esteem who cannot seem to escape a preoccupation with their own survival. There are people who stumble from one relationship to the other, making the same mistakes and the same excuses, their unhappiness a contagion. There are people with brilliant minds who use their intelligence strictly to exploit others for power and financial gain.

I see that in our technological age, intellect and novelty seem to reign over emotion and conservation. Segments of our brains, out of balance and out of control, can wreak havoc in the world.

From all indications, it appears that where the brain is concerned, "structure remains in essential aspects malleable to such a degree that there are no narrow limits to the evolution of its functions (capacities). ... The iterative feedback between the inner and outer world may lead to the creative evolution of the mental structure. We can learn to see a situation 'with new eyes' and we become aware of it through a change in our emotional attitude. Depending on this attitude, we also influence the environment in different ways."[32]

The challenge of better learning how to learn, of enriching neural connections, is crucial and highly attainable. But, until we can demonstrate sustained progress in this direction, I fall on the side of dumber.

- Note—Although many of the statistics quoted in this chapter are several years old, you can be assured that none has changed dramatically.

Endnotes

1   Morris Berman, *The Twilight of American Culture*, W.W. Norton & Company, N.Y., 2000, p. 36

2   Charles J. Sykes, *Dumbing Down Our Kids*, St. Martins Griffin, N.Y., 1995, p. 20

3   *The Economist*, July 14, 2001, p. 84

4   Christopher Lasch, *The Culture of Narcissism*, W.W. Norton, N.Y., 1979, p. 128

5   Morris Berman, ibid., p. 36

6   Berman, ibid., p. 36

7   Daniel A. Wagner, from a 1996 issue of *Education Week*

8   Chester E. Finn Jr., "Why America Has the World's Dimmest Bright Kids," *WSJ*, Feb. 25, 1998, p. A22

9   Harold W. Stevenson and James W. Stigler, *The Learning Gap*, Summit Books, N.Y., 1992, p. 31

10 Michael W. Hodges, *The Grandfather Education Report*, *http://home.att.net/~mwhodges/education*

11 Hodges, ibid.

12 *Education Reporter*, "U.S. Math Scores Fail the Test," April 1998

13 Berman, ibid., p. 36

14 Berman, ibid., p. 36

15 M. W. Hodges, ibid.

16 Berman, ibid., p. 34

17 Ibid.

18 Ibid., p. 35

19 Christopher Lasch, ibid., p. 129

20 Charles J. Sykes, ibid., p. 21

21 Seymour Itzkoff, *The Decline of Intelligence in America*, 1994, p. 55

22 Michael W. Hodges, ibid.

23 Morris Berman, ibid., p. 37

24 Charles J. Sykes, ibid., p. 128

25 Ibid., p. 130

26 Gregory Cizek, "On the Disappearance of Standards," from *Education Week*, November 10, 1993

27 Berman, ibid., p. 47

28 Ibid., p. 47

29 Debra Viadero, "Nature x Nurture = Startling Jump in IQs," *Education Week*, January 23, 2002

30 Hodges, *The Grandfather Education Report*, *http://home.att.net/~mwhodges/education*

31 Joseph Chilton Pearce, *Evolution's End*, Harper Collins, 1992, p. 48

32 Erich Jantsch, *The Self-Organizing Universe*, Pergamon International Library, 1980, p. 171

Chapter 3

LEARNING AND THE BRAIN: SOME BASICS

It's not what you don't know that'll hurt you.
It's what you're sure is true.
—MARK TWAIN

Our brains develop from the knowledge of what we can see and touch to the awareness of our minds' own processes—from the concrete to the abstract—from direct experience to categories of experience. The potential to build on this process, through a better understanding of how it happens, is enormous.

At first, we see and touch, perpetually driven to explore. Then we begin to form impressions of what we have seen, touched, and acted upon. These early impressions are very intimately connected to and indexed by emotion. As intellectual growth begins, we project our impressions back into the world, thereby forming a gathering personal view of it. We do not separate ourselves from this "point of view." We lose ourselves to it and become increasingly subject to it. Ninety-five percent of what we learn occurs beneath our awareness.

To develop a higher mind, a self-evolving consciousness, we must enter consciously into the process of constructing and comprehending the world. We must continually seek out presuppositions that guide our perceptions and behavior inaccurately or inappropriately. All personal evolution, all creative thought, all new or deeper understanding is a product of this proclivity of mind. It is a skill that can be either stilled or fueled by our caregivers, teachers, and learning environments.

In the scope of this book, I will not take on the importance of infant-mother bonding and early nurturance on the development of the brain. Every teacher knows instinctively, if not intellectually, that developing brains have already been largely formed by the time children enter formal schooling.[1] Brains, however, have the capacity to continue to develop, and this is where our collective responsibility for learning comes to the fore.

We are born with brains that have been collectively evolving for millions of years. Above all, they are programmed to learn, to adapt, to relearn, and even to change the world we are learning about. It is in this ability that we are distinguished from other life. How well we use it portends our future.

Though it would be tangential to the focus of this book to cover theories of brain function and development in depth, there is good reason to touch on the basics. It is my contention that the functioning of our brains and the failure of our present approaches to teaching and learning are profoundly related.

The fundamental failures of learning design discussed in the next section of this book are in direct contradiction to the "triune brain" model developed by Paul D. MacLean, head of a laboratory for the study of brain evolution and behavior. Simply put, we aren't learning much because we aren't using our knowledge of how the brain works to design-learning processes.

For the purposes of simplicity, I will refer to the three components of the brain as the first brain (which could also be called the core, or reptilian brain), the second brain (limbic system, midbrain, or emotional brain), and the third brain (the neocortex, thinking brain, or higher brain).

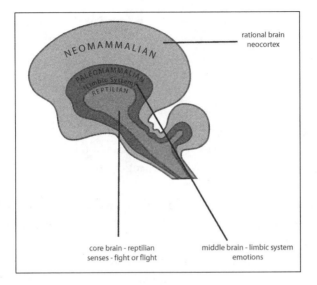

The first, or core, brain is the most primitive, having developed some 250 to 280 million years ago. It is primarily concerned with orienting and attuning us to the physical world. It is the part of the brain that includes our sensory motor system. It also stores what we "know" about the world into memory for immediate reactions to threat. Sometimes referred to as the "reptilian" brain (although far more sophisticated when it works in conjunction with higher brain functions), it is concerned with alertness to the environment, survival, basic physical functions, and the "fight or flight" mechanism that remains strong in our human makeup.

The midbrain, or limbic system, which evolved around 165 million years ago, forms impressions from the senses controlled by the core brain. It creates shades of meaning and preference between extremes. It is the source of novelty.

The limbic system governs our emotions and relatedness to all that is inside and outside of us. It does this by forming impressions and feeling tones in connection with what we encounter in the outside world. Many of these impressions are in the form of imagery, which enables the three brains to exchange information and integrate.

The limbic system is the source of creative thinking and translates abstract information to the higher brain. Because it is the feeling part of the brain as well as the part that mediates between the higher and lower brain, the feelings and emotions it experiences become guiding forces in learning and behavior.

The first two parts of the triune brain are reflexive. They mirror an outer reality they have already constructed in the inner world. Without the mediation of the highest-functioning part of the brain, the neocortex, thinking and behavior are without reflection and revision. They become hard wired.

The neocortex, or thinking part of the brain (which evolved roughly 50 million years ago), is five times the size of the rest of the brain and is responsible for reflection, intellect, creative thinking, and more sophisticated emotional responses such as empathy and compassion. It is this part of the brain that has the capacity for abstraction, which enables a kind of emancipation from the outer world—that which is agreed upon and seemingly obvious.

All three parts of the brain are capable of acting alone, strictly according to their own characteristics, or in collaboration with only one or with both other parts. The middle brain mediates between the lower (primitive) and the higher (thinking) brain and directs the attention of one part to the other.

In a situation that is (or is perceived to be) threatening, the lower brain will take over and direct the higher brain into a "How do I get out of this, escape or fight?" mode. The action of the middle or emotional brain as the mediator is to link the other parts to the outside world. It is connective by nature and governs relational patterns and emotional bonds, the caring for oneself and others.

A habituated brain, or one locked into automatic responses, is one that doesn't learn. The higher brain goes into neutral, and the lower brain tends to dominate. Learning is blunted and diminished. What is learned tends to be used for survival rather than one's personal evolution and the evolution of society.

If the emotional (limbic) system develops poorly because of the lack of social and intimate connections, it will diminish its capacity to utilize higher functions to make sense of the world. Instead, it will have difficulty making more complex connections and refer, more liberally, to the lower brain for marching orders. Venturing in new directions will be seen as risk, and the appetite to explore and make ever-increasing and more complex connections will be suppressed.

The brain's development is most dramatic from birth to roughly the age of nine. In the first four years of life, the interfunctioning of the brain's parts is about 80% developed. The same percentage can also be applied to the formation of our worldview. A six-year-old brain has five to seven times the neural connections it had at 18 months or will have as an adult.[2]

At the time children enter school, their brains are optimally configured for learning. The functions of their higher brains are starting to develop more rapidly. Mediating between classroom learning, individual experience, and real-world connections is the prime directive for brain functioning and building higher intelligence.

Of course, this mediation happens without the interference of teachers or curriculum. The great question affecting the future of learning is "What would happen if educators actually participated in this mediation?" In other words, what if they provided for us to learn in accordance with how our brains were designed to develop and function?

Jean Piaget identified the ability to retrace one's steps to see how a conclusion was reached as the gateway to higher thinking. "Reversibility thinking"[3] enables the process of thinking about one's own thinking, which, in turn, leads to more sophisticated layers of abstract and symbolic reasoning. Not everyone obtains a firm footing at this level of cognitive development.

What those who design learning exercises and environments need to know is how to intervene dynamically in the learning process (as it is going on) to develop reversibility and engage the higher structures of brain function.

By the time a child is seven or eight, instructors should be routinely developing the practice of reevaluating what has been understood from a lesson. Children must get in the habit of extending newfound principles and ideas to applications separate from the incidence in which an understanding or lesson occurred. Most formal learning environments from first grade to graduate school to corporate training do little of this. Hence, they are not training brains.

If we are unable to move from dawning familiarity back into unfamiliarity to create deeper levels of awareness, the brain encapsulates a category of experience without probing for new possibilities. This is the fundamental "muscle" of higher brain function.

The alternative is habituation to the known: drill and practice, learning to fulfill the expectations of a lesson plan (extracting meaning instead of constructing it), and becoming attuned to the expectations of a teacher. Habituation demands little of the brain except that it rely on its lower components for regulation. The controlled environment and practices of schooling rely on habituation.

Imagination is the ability of the brain to create images not present to the senses. It is the impressionistic and feeling middle brain that indexes these impressions. The higher brain deconstructs and reconstructs these impressions to create finer nuances of distinction and meaning. The ability to play gives resilience and scope to the imagination. To be able to play well is to be able to "play" with one's reality. Playing with one's reality is the cornerstone of learning to learn. This is why play is such a powerful learning catalyst. See "Learning as Play" in Part III, Chapter 15, of this book.

The optimal brain constructs from what it gathers, reconceives, poses new possibilities, integrates, and reinvents. It is these higher brain functions that we most need to develop.

As far as educating the brain is concerned, our ability to build connections between the middle brain and the higher brain is the key to building learning capacity. It is the key to being able to discover and construct meaning rather than simply extracting it (moving from the unknown to the known without question). It is also the key to balancing intellect with feeling and values.

"Intellect and its analytical enterprise, unimpaired by the positive-negative emotions incorporating it, may well be called upon to make our own justifiable violence thorough and efficient. Using intellect defensively we function in an anti-evolutionary mode. Our neocortical system serves our lowest and most primitive structures."[4]

The first intelligence is that of the heart, that which is formed by our alliances, our bonds, and feeling "a part of" whatever we participate in. If we strive to develop intellect without heeding the first intelligence and how it builds the links that integrate the brain, we produce disconnected minds that follow the dictates of mere curiosity and self-aggrandizement.

In order to engage and perpetually integrate all parts of the brain, we must:

- Ensure engagement of the senses and interest to involve the core brain
- Focus on "curriculum" as creativity, play, and conversation to involve the middle brain
- Always design learning experiences in context to engage the higher brain to integrate ideas, values, and place

When the three parts of the brain are functioning integrally, the higher-brain structures enable the processes of the lower and middle brain to bring new implications, meanings, and patterns of meaning into focus.

As we progress through Part II ("The Present"), I will argue that current teaching and learning practices run counter to brain function and even shut down the higher functions of the brain.

Endnotes

1 Recommended reading on early childhood development: Joseph Chilton Pearce, *Evolution's End*, Harper Collins, 1992; Alison Gopnick, Andrew Meltzoff, and Patricia Kuhl, *The Scientist in the Crib*, Perennial, 2001; and Jean Piaget, *The Origins of Intelligence in Children*, Norton, 1952

2 Joseph Chilton Pearce, *Evolution's End*, Harper Collins, 1992, p. 100

3 Reversibility thinking is the key cognitive skill to emerge from Piaget's concrete operational stage of intellectual development. Without this cognitive skill, children are less able to see other points of view. They remain stuck in egocentric patterns. See J. Piaget, *The Psychology of the Child*, Basic Books, New York, 1972

4 Joseph Chilton Pearce, *Evolution's End*, p. 107

Part II:
The Present

• The Fatal Flaws

Chapter 4

THE FOUNTAIN AND THE BOWL

Little learning is retained when it is learned on command.
—JEAN PIAGET

It is only because teachers (are obliged to)
*force students to learn that any unpleasantness
ever arises to mar their relationship.*
—WILLARD WALLER

The most fundamental flaw associated with the way we now learn is a prevailing lack of participation on the part of the learner. Schooling, as we traditionally know it, is *done to* us. We are generally not agents in the process of learning but objects of it.

The precursors of the "scientific" approach to teaching were the philosophers Locke and Hume. They both took the position that a mind develops on a cause-and-effect basis, which can be observed, validated, and measured in terms of behavior only. John Locke's ideas led the transition from Socratic thinking (where a learner must uncover and validate his or her own meaning and truth) to behavioral learning theory, which views young minds as a blank slate upon which it is the responsibility of educational experts to imprint the correct knowledge and behavior.

In the behavioral approach, innate abilities and proclivities are ignored in favor of what can be implanted. Of course, this has led to an approach to learning based on the centrality of a teacher and a textbook delivering a preformulated "instructional outcome." The notion of questioning the rationale of what is asserted to be so or of offering and exploring alternative perspectives is considered disruptive in this environment.

So the notions of inquiry and reflection have given way to deciding what should be taught, how it should be taught, and moving on in the shortest possible time. In the behavioral model, curriculum is strictly organized according to category and prescribed sequence. The learning environment is carefully constructed by the teacher to elicit and reinforce the correct behavior.

As learners adapt to this paradigm, they must become increasingly passive receptors of predigested information. Awaiting direction and providing the "right answer" are the prime directives of a behaviorally managed classroom. Accepting and remembering what is taught, without questing authority, are the prized outcomes.

These "behaviors" are then rewarded with a grade comparing each learner with the others undergoing the same set of inputs.

A common phrase that describes the current approach to learning is "the fountain and the bowl." It is a phrase that is familiar to educators. Imagine a stream of water (the teacher) pouring into a bowl (the student) and you have a pretty good image of what happens in today's classroom.

Add to this the two most important historical imperatives governing educational practice and you have the obvious reason for the condition of passivity:

1. The overwhelming influence of the scientific worldview: things must be observed and measured in a controlled environment in order to seek truth and accuracy. The classroom becomes a laboratory for "scientific" practice.
2. Behaviorism came into vogue from 1915 to the present. Its founder, John Watson, claimed, on the basis of animal studies, that he could make any child into anything he wanted, from a criminal to a judge, provided he was given absolute control of the child's experience soon enough.[1]

I suspect that most readers would describe such principles, as applied to learning, draconian, yet these are principles that have governed institutionalized learning.

How different a world this conjures than that of Socrates, where learners were set in search of what was worth knowing and believing. The teacher in Socrates' world was an intellectual midwife, bringing others' ideas and understandings to light. He understood that all learning revolves around who we think we are and who we see ourselves becoming or capable of becoming.

As Frank Smith, author of eight books on education, puts it, "The official theory of learning (roughly a hundred years old now) says that we have to learn something in order to understand it … this is totally contrary to fact. We have to understand something in order to learn it. We have to (first) make sense of it. And because individuals differ in what they know, in what they are interested in, and in the way they understand things, there is no way that the official theory can cope with approaching learning through understanding."[2]

Prominent education author and consultant Alfie Kohn describes his common experience of teaching:

> *The discussions teachers conduct are often fishing expeditions: they're not invitations to reflect deeply on complicated issues but attempts to illicit the right answer. Even in English or social studies classes, where the questions appear to be more open-ended, students inspect the teacher's face to see how nearly their responses approximate what's expected. I see this in classrooms all over the country. In a Chicago public school, a second grade teacher asks about the concept of tolerance. She pleasantly acknowledges a variety of answers until she hears the one she wants, at which point she nods vigorously, exclaims "Say that again!" and writes only that comment on the board. In a Seattle private school, the atmosphere is informal and the level is advanced, but the approach isn't all that different: the high school history teacher asks what makes a society "civilized" then gently tries to pull the right answers from students rather than inviting a real exchange of ideas.*[3]

Is this experience familiar to you? Haven't we all sat in a classroom where all the focus is on the teacher and what the teacher wants to hear? It is a form of mass production, a factory for filling minds. And when each mind is being stocked with standard information and is being scanned for correspondence with correct answers, what happens to our genuine curiosity about the subject? What happens to our enthusiasm and resourcefulness for seeking real understanding?

When your job as a student is to provide the correct answer, does this affect your desire to discuss a topic with other students, to explore alternative views or your own ideas?

Also characteristic of the "fountain and bowl" approach is the need to keep to schedules and to cover the prescribed topics at all costs. Some would call this "covering the basics." But, of course, the need to cover a wide array of topics, without deviating from schedules, to accommodate students' curiosity or need to understand is aimed at a predetermined result. "By Thanksgiving break, we will cover chapters one through eight, and the students will have memorized enough correct answers from each quiz to start preparing for the final in three weeks."

This whole experience is, of course, reinforced by bells that ring every 50 minutes, by textbooks with drills and quizzes that prepare one to move on to the next chapter, and by grades, which validate or impede forward progress. This same process continues right through high school, through college, and even, for the most part, in the world of adult learning.

In this race, the criteria for success are obedience and a good memory—certainly not creativity or reflection. Are the high achievers in this kind of race our most able? When these criteria become the primary preoccupation of students, they naturally become associated with learning. What impact does this have on our continuing motivation to learn? How does it affect our view of authority?

In a world where higher-order mental skills are increasingly called for to advance the interests of an individual or enterprise, do we want citizens and workers who are accustomed to being passive and obedient? If you own a chain of fast food restaurants, perhaps so, but as work becomes more complex, these characteristics become increasingly undesirable.

Schooling, with the support of television and other media, reinforces mindsets that undermine rather than empower our natural inclination to learn. The world is already explained. We need only wait for the answers at the end of every chapter.

How does knowledge come into being and advance itself in an environment that treats it as fixed and transmittable, something that is placed in our memory banks and then resides there until we find occasion to make use of it? Such an environment creates no vital practice of inquiry, no traditions of knowing through doing. It cannot develop the "muscle" of forming a new interpretation, of analyzing a new situation or locating evidence in support of new arguments or against anticipated counterarguments. These are skills that come from a participatory model of learning rather than a transmission model.

Transmission Model *Teacher-centric*	Participation Model *Learner-centric*
correct answers are primary	questions are primary
the object of teaching is designated content	the object of teaching is establishing interest
a wide range of focus (to cover the basics)	a narrow focus (to understand in depth)
recitation from memory	application of a concept or the implications of fact
assumes dependency and demands obedience	assumes and develops individual autonomy
break a lesson down into smaller easy-to-remember steps	look for patterns of connection to the interests and identity of the learner

What most characterizes "the fountain and the bowl" is the absence of dialogue in the classroom. Today's pedagogy has very little room for it. Of course, there are some notable exceptions, but the overwhelming approach to mastering academic material is what teachers often call "drill 'n' kill." It's not about depth of understanding but about memory and correct answers.

In a study of schools and teaching conducted in the '60s by renowned professor of education and educational researcher John Goodlad, he commented, "We were unable to discern much attention to pupil needs, attainments, or problems as a basis for individual opportunities to learn. … Teaching was predominantly telling and questioning (for recitation) by the teacher, with children responding one by one or occasionally in chorus. … Rarely did we find small groups intensely in pursuit of knowledge; rarely did we find individual pupils at work in self-sustaining inquiry."[4]

Fifteen years later, Goodlad published the results of another study, funded by more than a dozen foundations and the U.S. Office of Education. This research involved observation and data collection in more than 1,000 classrooms in seven regions of the United States.

In this study, Goodlad reemphasized teachers' reliance on rote learning and immediate responses. His observers almost never witnessed opportunities for give and take between a challenging teacher and engaged students. The student role was passive, and few teachers made any effort to adapt instruction to individual differences or nonintended questions.

The summary of chapter one of Goodlad's study began with these words: "American schools are in trouble. In fact, the problems of schooling are of such crippling proportions that many schools may not survive. It is possible that our entire public education system is nearing collapse."[5]

The Importance of Dialogue

The most important things in human lives happen between human beings; that which creates this "between" is dialogue or conversation. Dialogues are not necessarily face to face. Reading an essay is a form of dialogue with another mind. The frustration that many experience when trying to learn a foreign language is from the lack of conversation. An aspect of that lack may be the need to ask "Why do I need to learn this right now?"

A true dialogue presupposes that we are all agents in control of our own thoughts and actions, responsible for what we think and believe. It assumes that we are able to modify our thoughts and actions in accordance with discoveries prompted by entering, in good faith, into examinations of fact and belief, weather they be ours or others'.

What is most essential to our humanity, as well as to learning, is to ask questions, make assertions, conceive of possibilities, construct propositions, embellish existing ideas, heed the direction of others, respond, agree, and disagree. This all occurs in the midst of dialogue.

Without dialogue, we become the object of others' intentions; what is happening is done to us and not a dynamic or living process.

It cannot include what we suspect or desire to know or don't desire to know. It cannot include individual needs, perceptions, histories, proclivities, and aptitudes.

In conversation, it is implicit that participants are neither passive nor merely recipients of a ready-made message to be decoded, but rather participants in a conversation are simultaneously creating language in response to content, structure, style, and nuance. As water is to the fish, dialogue is to us.

Central to all dialogue is the implicit awareness that "I am different than you; I have different needs, perspectives, abilities, and sensibilities." Dialogue affirms our differences and at the same time builds connectedness.

What we call "mind" is characterized by curiosity, inquiry, doubt, proposing alternative views, and expressing awareness of other possibilities. If schooling involves more than preparing us for unknown challenges later in life, if it involves latent skills that must be used to be developed, if we are not just learning to recite from memory but also (and far more importantly) learning the art and skill of learning itself, it must include dialogue.

> *The aim of education is the acquisition of the art of the*
> *utilization of knowledge. A merely well-informed man is*
> *the most useless bore on earth.*
> —ALFRED NORTH WHITEHEAD

The experiences that we take away from school mostly have to do with being evaluated, being good performers and memorizers, and often having things we don't need to know explained to us—stuff we are supposed to take on faith as being important for later life. If this is the underlying experience of school, what does it really mean to us—beneath all the rationale for its existence?

If we are not coparticipants in the process of teaching and learning, with consistent opportunities to reveal our interests, our doubts, our problems, and the questions that arise from our own thinking, what of this process will reside—alive and well—in our consciousness? All retained learning emanates from who we take ourselves to be, what we see ourselves capable of, or who we are desirous of becoming.

The assembly line gave us affordable automobiles. Because we designed educational institutions with the same principles (time clocks, uniform inputs, breaking overall tasks into smaller and simpler steps, measured outputs, and strict controls), teachers and administrators became timekeepers, sorters, traffic managers, measurers, and disciplinarians, leaving no time for the unpredictability and unmanageability of real dialogue.

"Assembly line" schooling gave rise to affordable education. It sprang from our understanding of the efficiencies of teaching, not of learning. The price young learners have paid has been to become disengaged from the real affairs and necessary transactions of society—"real affairs" being those that our parents are engaged in, our community, our role models, the affairs that would bring our dreams and aspirations to life, the affairs that involve us in endeavors with practical and immediate rewards.

We are born into an undifferentiated state of being, necessitating the nurturance of parenting. We begin life with no awareness of an outside world, a reality separate from ourselves. It is only through conversation that we begin to have consciousness of the world, to differentiate its myriad components, subtleties, and possibilities. It is to the extent that this differentiation occurs that we become autonomous. And it is a process that continues as long as a life is lived.

If schooling is supposed to prepare us for this world, it cannot wholly succeed without the existence of authentic and vigorous dialogue to bring the complexities of the world into meaningful existence. If we are to uphold a tradition of quality and integrity or transform tradition into something new, it must involve relating to the words and deeds of others as well as comparing and integrating their understanding and deeds with our own. This doesn't happen without robust conversation. In the present environment of "school," we cannot expect to see genuine dialogue even though teachers may recognize its importance.

It is frightening for teachers and administrators to relinquish control of the process of learning. Efficiencies will be lost—the efficiencies of teaching, not of learning. When learning is generated through authentic conversation, classrooms are immediately transformed from platoons of good soldiers to communities of inquiry and resourcefulness.

Teachers then enter the subjective worlds of learners and break them into subgroups for problem solving. They break from scripted lesson plans and spontaneously compose lessons from understandings of common experiences, questions, and new ideas. The responsibility for learning is spread among all participants. It is a fluid process that generates collaboration instead of obedience.

All of us, in our compliance with passive schooling, are reinforcing a culture that sees what is true as obvious. Truth and knowledge are transmittable from one to another, and answers supersede questions. In such a world, we increasingly submit to external stimuli without question. In places of learning, we look for the cues that tell us what teachers want and provide accordingly. Why should we ask questions when we come to assume that answers await us at the end of each chapter in our textbooks or will be explained, in due time, by the teacher?

Then we leave schools to enter a society that was intended to be shaped by the practices we have submitted to. How do you see the results?

Endnotes

1   Frank Smith, *The Book of Learning and Forgetting*, Teachers College Press, Columbia University, N.Y., 1998, p. 58
2   Frank Smith, ibid., p. 35
3   Alfie Kohn, *The Schools Our Children Deserve*, Houghton Mifflin Company, N.Y., 1999, p. 56
4   John Goodlad, "The Schools vs. Education," *Saturday Review*, 1969
5   Goodlad, *A Place Called School*, 1984, p. 1

Chapter 5

WHY AM I LEARNING THIS?
Learning out of Context

*The right to ignore anything that doesn't make sense
is a crucial element of any child's learning—
and the first right children are likely to lose when they
get to the controlled learning environment of school.*
—FRANK SMITH

*The chief subject matter of school is school itself.
That is how most students experience it,
and it determines the meaning they make of it.*
—JEROME BRUNER

*The great end of education is to discipline rather
than furnish the mind; to train it to use its own powers
rather than fill it with the accumulation of others.*
—TRYON EDWARDS

Context is the background from which anything that comes to one's attention in the foreground makes sense. It is water to the fish. In our consciousness, it is the set of assumptions and beliefs that, usually unknown to us, governs our perceptions and actions. It is a participatory reality—one that we are always already part of.

School itself is a primary context for the young. It is the default imprimatur for the world we want our children to become familiar with. With few exceptions, we have all agreed, with little consideration for design, that this should be so. More important than the fact that school has a curriculum is that school *is* a curriculum. Everything about school has an effect.

Most every adult has a 12- to 16-year experience of being schooled—inculcated into the practices and often unexamined beliefs of this most ubiquitous social institution. It is a significant chunk of experience.

It is important for us all to consider just how we are products of schooling. What patterns of thought, identity, citizenship, child rearing, and basic association are conditioned from schooling?

Before any discussion of context can assume its true importance, we must first consider how education is not simply a preparation for later life but a significant and enduring aspect of life itself—particularly enduring in that it leaves us with a lasting orientation toward learning.

The most common of all dreams involves being unprepared for a test at school and knowing that you face the consequences. Untold millions of us, myself included, have awakened in the middle of the night in a cold sweat and have wondered why we should have such a dream.

It seems clear in principle, though absent in the consciousness of the architects and trustees of schooling, that the design of a learning experience is vitally important to any lasting impression its intent may confer upon us.

For more than a thousand years, schools have been preoccupied with order and control and with a representational (rather than experiential) approach to teaching and learning. These are crucial elements of the context of school.

Schools and educators have systematically ignored the crucial element of context in teaching and learning.

This is reflective of the view that schools must subordinate the individual to collective and institutional objectives. It also suggests an incapacity of schools, as presently construed, to imbue learners with the purposes of what they are to learn, to develop an aptitude for the relatedness of things, and to mediate between learning and life.

When I was in the eighth grade, I began the study of algebra. As I sat in class and tried to grasp some link between this strange new discipline and anything I would ever do with it, I became increasingly frustrated. It became difficult to memorize formulas for tests and increasingly difficult to understand what the teacher was asking of me. I felt myself falling further and further behind. I got my first and only "D" in algebra and developed a block against learning Algebra II and calculus.

Later on, as a freshman in college, I became very interested in the physical sciences but soon came to realize that I had no future in science with my "block" against higher math. This story is, of course, all too common. Millions of us have been turned off to one subject or another as educators systematically failed to establish its place in the world and its relevance to us as individuals.

"If students leave school thinking that 'school things'—such as reading, writing, mathematics, or history—are boring, difficult, and irrelevant to their lives and that they are 'dummies,' this is something they have learned both in school and outside. They *learn* to be nonreaders, or that they are nonspellers, or that they can't do mathematics."[1]

David Perkins, professor at Harvard and pioneer in the study of redirecting the emphasis in learning to reasoning, problem solving, and inventive thinking, advocates viewing knowledge as **design**. This necessitates inventing learning processes that require students to discover key facts, principles and patterns and then apply them to a new problem or issue to demonstrate comprehension.

Perkins says, "Treating knowledge as design treats it as active, to be used, rather than passive, to be stored."[2] "Knowledge as information purveys a passive view of knowledge, one that highlights knowledge in storage rather than knowledge as an implement of action."[3] This view goes beyond the merely instructive to the constructive. We will return to the notion of design as we discuss what it looks like to teach a subject in context.

If knowledge is to be memorized and stored, as it happens in school, it must be linked to some structure, some foundation of understanding that already exists in one's mind and relates to one's own needs or values. If it has not become part of your identity, like most of what we learn in school, it will be forgotten.

Many studies confirm that for something to be "learned," to pass from short-term memory (the kind we use to pass tests) to long-term memory, it must be linked to a complex web of related memories that can easily be recalled *because they are linked to who we are.* And yet millions of us have come to view ourselves as "learning challenged" in one way or another because these webs of memory were not woven into the design of our learning.

As renowned author and educational psychologist Jerome Bruner puts it, "Teaching specific topics on skills without making clear their context in the broader fundamental structure of a field of knowledge is uneconomical in several deep senses. In the first place, such teaching makes it exceedingly difficult for the student to generalize from what he has learned to what he will encounter later. In the second place, learning that has fallen short of a grasp of general principles has little reward in terms of intellectual excitement. The best way to create interest in a subject is to render it worth knowing, which means to make the knowledge gained useable in one's thinking beyond the situation in which the learning has occurred. Third, knowledge one has acquired without sufficient structure to tie it together is knowledge that is likely to be forgotten. An unconnected set of facts has a pitiably short half-life of memory."[4]

If we were to measure the proportion of schooling forgotten and never used in a practical or creative way, it would astound and shock us all. Its cost in dollars alone would be staggering.

Learning Is Social

Despite the early scientific view that little learning takes place without lecture, memorization, and recitation, research into early learning tells us otherwise.

Almost 2,500 years ago, Socrates, in one of his famous dialogues (the "Meno"), posited that the way we can understand an abstract concept such as *virtue* is not from our experience but because the abstraction already exists in our minds. As it turns out, Socrates was closer to the truth than the behavioral scientists who invented modern teaching.

For the past 2,500 years, "the dominant view was that children were essentially defective adults. They were defined by the things they didn't know and couldn't do. ... It was a picture of a sort of 'great chain of knowing' with babies at one end and philosophers at the other."[5]

We can still put Socrates, Niels Bohr, or Emmanuel Kant in front of a five-year-old in the chain of knowing, but what we've learned about children from close observation changes our understanding of their reasoning capacities and of learning itself.

In recent years, it has become important to study how brains develop by studying the evolving cognitive patterns of infants and young children. Through this research, we have vastly changed our general view of children's innate intelligence. "Twenty-five years ago, we still heard respected psychologists proclaim that newborn babies had no cortex, that they had only the simplest automatic responses, that they were, in fact, slightly animate vegetables—carrots that could cry."[6]

Now, after some 30 years of infant studies, young brains are seen as extremely complex and rapidly evolving bio-computers. Babies are capable of abstract thought that goes beyond the data of immediate sensation.

Psychologists have compared the way children progress and grow their brain capacity to the way scientists devise and revise theories. It has become apparent that human infants were designed by evolution to have unusually powerful and flexible learning abilities from the get-go.

Brain science now says that these capabilities are not just a program but that we actively participate in building our brains with enthusiastic inquiry. We are building axons and dendrites that allow cells to talk to one another and build cognitive capacity.

Sally Goes to School

At the age of six, Sally begins her first big adventure. She is carted off, Barbie lunch box in hand, to begin school. She was in day care for two years, and she went to kindergarten too, but these experiences were extensions of her playtime. She missed her mom and dad, but she got to play lots of games, hear fun stories, draw, paint, and, most important, make lots of new friends. She has similar expectations for the first grade. She is in for a rude awakening.

Sally's brain is now at peak performance, manufacturing neural connections and using energy at twice the rate of an adult brain. It has been this way since she was three, and it will continue to be as active until she is nine or 10.

Sally is a rabid learning machine, taking in information and impressions of the world at a rate that no computer can begin to match. She has done this primarily by expertly using adults in her familiar environment to help her with the particularities and the nuances of the world she can relate to juxtaposed with parts of the world she is still struggling to understand. And the adults who care for Sally are, quite unconsciously, adjusting their behavior to give her just the information she needs to "push the envelope" to make sense of what she is already struggling to express, undertake, and understand.

This is the way Sally's brain was designed over at least 300,000 years of evolution. It is exquisitely evolved to pattern itself from, into, and beyond its social and intellectual milieu.

When Sally sits down in a neatly organized classroom row, she intuitively knows that the boy sitting next to her has six years of individual history—a vast array of experiences, impressions, preferences, and proclivities that differ, sometimes profoundly, from her own. What Sally doesn't know is that her history and that of her peers, as well as thousands of millennia of evolutionary learning design, are going to be ignored in the classroom.

Through the highly evolved process of "natural learning" (how the brain was naturally designed to function), Sally was "taught" higher-order cognitive and linguistic skills. The activities in which Sally came to understand and to do something were not separated. They were part of her everyday existence, part of her existing and emerging identity.

Now, as she sits among her peers, about to receive a preplanned lesson, the way in which Sally has been learning will be regarded as peripheral, even obstructive to further learning. This is the single biggest mistake in the conceiving of "school."

Valued notions of curriculum and pedagogy are going to strip Sally's world of its context, ignore her sense of self, and fail to employ the higher functions of her already sophisticated brain. Though she may be only six and still naive, innocent, and ignorant of much of what society wants her to be aware, Sally is nevertheless far more adept at learning than the practices and routines school will provide.

"Babies start out with complex, abstract, coherent representations of the world and rules for manipulating them. They use those representations and rules to make sense of their experience. And they also use them to make predictions about what the world will be like … when there are discrepancies, they can modify their representations and rules."[7]

At six, Sally is probably most advanced, of the human arts, in language. She already has a vocabulary of some 10,000 words and a basic knowledge of grammar—although she couldn't explain its formal rules. She will continue to learn at a rapid rate of her own accord, but in the classroom, she will be taught 100 to 200 words per year. Many will be almost useless in practice, forgotten, or used improperly.[8]

The way Sally is learning language in school is very different from before. The teacher talks to 25 kids, not just to her. What she is told she will learn is not in response to her needs. She takes leave of her own world to become an accepted and performing member of the class.

In class, words and meanings, and the sentences that exemplify them, are self-contained "pieces" of knowledge, independent of real situations. Sally is asked to memorize and recite, to use words in sentences with no attention to nuance, metaphor, or what might be a better word. Sentences are used to highlight word usage with little to no regard for the sentence itself as a communicative act. The complex social negotiations in which Sally has been learning language have vanished in the classroom.

Researcher Dolores Durkin, in a classic study on reading, observed 300 hours of reading comprehension instruction and found that less than 1% of the time was spent dealing with units of meaning larger than a single word. Of all forms of instruction, one would think that conversation and the mastery of dialogue would dominate the learning of our native language.[9]

Language, of all things, must include coparticipation. It must involve the learner in improving self-expression in everyday dramas that occur at home, in school, and out in the world. Later, Sally will prepare for events in the future: writing to a newspaper, making a political argument, applying for a job, etc. Learning language must be immersed in real life, or it is out of context. The same applies to all learning.

To achieve teaching in context, educators must first understand that the classroom is itself a context. It is not the home, the workplace, an interaction with a stranger on the street, etc., but it is a place where activities and settings can be simulated to bring learners into such situations. Young learners are especially adept at role-playing. If orchestrated properly, it is not playacting but trying out real life.

In setting up real-life dramas that involve learners in negotiating their way to success or failure, teachers can become aware of learners' various comprehensions of a subject matter. Real-life scenarios draw in participation and draw out comprehension.

Suppose a lesson is on "how to get the best result out of an argument with your mom." It could involve vocabulary words as well as the opportunity for kids to play both mother and child. In the context of a role-play, they can focus on listening and negotiation skills, the role of emotion (tone of voice) in communication, alternative ways to handle conflict, the nuances between phrasing a response one way versus another, and more.

Another lesson for first graders might be listening to a story read by the teacher and then breaking into groups of four to discuss it. The discussion might include questions such as "What did you like about the story?" "What was important about the story?" "What could you say about the person writing the story?" The students could make up a different ending and then vote on whose ending was the most different, the most entertaining, or the most original. If there was a bad character in the story, why did the students think the character was bad? What made this character want to do bad things to others?

When listeners are involved deeply in stories, they begin to listen for elements of narrative, to struggle with their own sense of drama, and to prepare original responses to questions. By discussing the story with their peers, they relate their experience to others who can readily relate to them. They begin to learn about composition and the key elements of dramatic writing. By inventing new endings, they begin to explore their own creative skills with peers and to get feedback on elements of their creativity. They begin to distinguish concepts like "original" from "interesting."

Such a lesson involves all students because it is familiar, important to their lives, and a reason for practicing various elements of language. Yet what persists are lecture and recitation, memorization and quizzes, questions that relate to a single text, and uniformity of intended output.

Principals are required to recite instructions to teachers, superintendents to principals, school boards to superintendents. They all will be assessed by their ability to recall and follow instructions. The model is consistent from the top down.

The great paradox of school is that conversation is a horizontal plane, requiring a kind of equality and freedom to respond. Instruction implies authority and strict boundaries for performance. This gets at the need to swing the balance of teaching/learning to the middle—where the learner (the customer) is involved in consuming the services rather than simply becoming the object of uniform and depersonalized goals.

If Sally's language training was context driven, as she progressed, she would:

- Always know why she was beginning a unit of instruction and what relevance it has or will have to her life.
- Progressively learn the history of various aspects of language arts. Every subject has a history that puts elements of that subject's practice and its practitioners' orientation into perspective.
- Learn to practice reading and writing in more complex forms and in increasingly sophisticated settings such as analyzing a story, debating subjects with peers, journaling, writing an essay, writing and op-ed piece or letter to the editor, critiquing an editorial, conducting investigative journalism, working on performative language (e.g., how does a supervisor get better performance out of an employee), doing a job interview, writing a grant proposal, writing an advertisement, analyzing a scientific hypothesis, writing an executive summary, reading a legal brief, doing a storyboard for a movie, a play, or a video game, etc.
- Learn about the settings and learn to imitate the behavior and the unique jargon used by reporters, public relations people, lawyers, military personnel, media professionals, architects, and engineers by connecting with practitioners and communities of interest and practice.

These are the elements of learning language and any other subject in context. Everything Sally learns in context she will learn to put into practice as she will learn "know-how" just as she learns to "know what and why." Learning grammar and vocabulary will be incidental and integrated into lessons that put language to use in ever-more sophisticated settings.

As Sally progresses through mathematics, she will experience the worlds (and the orientation to math) of an accountant, a carpenter, a navigator, a physicist, a statistician, and a computer programmer. She will learn how these professionals use math creatively, not just to solve problems. She will learn the earliest uses of each branch of math, how algebra, geometry, and calculus were born, and the most advanced problems to which mathematics is now being applied.

As Sally progresses through these subjects, at some point, she will begin to be more in charge of their application in her life, first with the help of an academic counselor who sees that she is exposed to possibilities and careers that a subject will make available to her, and then Sally herself will begin taking charge of what she is learning and where it will take her.

But that is jumping ahead to a future where context is tacit in learning design. I have not yet adequately described the present. The adventure that Sally was expecting when she began the first grade is quickly transforming to the "tyranny of the lesson plan."

Learning, before a child enters school, is a rampant process fueled by insatiable curiosity, the desire to explore and make sense of what unfolds moment to moment. As Sally's brain is most intensively building the neural connections that will enable her cognitive, social, and biological growth, she is becoming literally disconnected from the stimuli that most efficiently and effectively develop her brain.

Learning shifts from being the result of ambient culture and family organization to that of explicit teaching. Cues that come from the supporting environment of friends, family, and creative play are ignored in favor of a more orderly approach.

In the classroom, Sally begins to wear the anticipative mask of someone waiting for direction. The social underpinnings of her makeup are being segregated from her "academic" regime.

Endnotes

1 Frank Smith, ibid., p. 10
2 David Perkins, *Knowledge as Design*, 1986, p. 18
3 Ibid., p. 5
4 Jerome Bruner, *The Process of Education*, 1977, p. 31
5 Alison Gopnik, Andrew N. Meltzoff, and Patricia K. Kuhl, *The Scientist in the Crib*, 1999, p. 12
6 Ibid., p. 143
7 Ibid., p. 150
8 See John Seely Brown, Allan Collins, and Paul Duguid, "Situated Cognition and the Culture of Learning," *Educational Researcher*, 1989
9 D. Durkin, "What Classroom Observations Reveal about Reading Comprehension Instruction," *Reading Research Quarterly*, 1979

Chapter 6

THE PRIMACY OF LITERACY

Literacy is not, as it is considered in our schools, a PORTION of education. It IS education. It is at once the ability AND the inclination of the mind to find knowledge, to pursue understanding, and out of knowledge and understanding, not out of received attitudes and values or emotional responses, however "worthy," to make judgments.
—RICHARD MITCHELL

The first curriculum and the first context we enter is that of language. Language is the clearest mirror of our evolution in its use and in the access to possibilities it creates.

The most endurable form in which to store experience, observation, and thought is in writing. The way it is retrieved, of course, is by reading. The magnitude of this uniquely human skill is difficult to fully grasp, and we should take the time to ensure that each learner does just that.

With written language, learning was released from the bonds of direct experience, imitation, and personal memory. Reading and writing greatly extend these capabilities in distance, in scope, in depth, and in time.

The centrality of reading and writing to human endeavor and to learning cannot be overestimated. Minds and ears attend to the words of a teacher with varying force, sometimes none at all. But, in the written word exists the perpetual opportunity to attend, reflect, assert, ponder, declare, and reinterpret.

To be a speaker, a reader, a writer, or a thinker is to infuse meaning (in all its depth, power, and nuance) to language. Every subject of human inquiry, every epiphany, and every message sent depends, for its influence, on this skill. It is acquired. It builds on itself. More than anything else, it distinguishes one as learned.

However, meaning does not effectively build on itself through the exercise of memorizing vocabulary lists and demonstrating that you can use them in a sentence. Such practices are boring. They attenuate rather than elaborate.

In the mid-1980s, researchers William Nagy, Patricia Herman, and Richard Anderson conducted an extensive study of language and how it was learned. They discovered that teenagers were still learning words at an average rate of 3,400 a year. At the higher extreme, they were learning well over 20 words a day and at the lower end around four. What accounted for the difference? They obviously looked to ethnic origin, socioeconomic status, parents' occupation and income, family size, and other dynamics for the answer. None of the usual suspects statistically held up. Guess what did?

The findings of this research team show how common sense is frequently abandoned in the so-called scientific world of modern instructional design. Nagy, Herman, and Anderson found that what makes one reader better than another was—what a concept!—reading.

They stressed the point that one didn't need a large vocabulary to begin with in order to read. All that was necessary to become a reader was the interest and the ability to relate to the subject matter. Readers who encounter words they don't know will learn them primarily through their use in context and the use of a dictionary.

Astoundingly, they discovered that people who read a lot become better readers: comprehension improves, writing and spelling skills improve, and—guess what?—readers become better students in general.

It's almost too simple, isn't it? You want to learn words, to spell them, to read, to succeed as a learner? Read—and read some more.

The next obvious question becomes, How do we turn nonreaders into readers? It certainly becomes more difficult once they've been turned off. I leave the question of converting the committed nonreader to experts in the area, but we can do much more to prevent the creation of nonreaders. It is, once more, an issue of context.

It stands to reason that reading and writing, conducted in context, would be as effortless as the mastery of speech. Remembering the analogy of neural connections, we know that reading, like no other activity, provides connections to the greatest minds, to the far corners of our world, and to ideas vividly and uniquely expressed by complementary and kindred spirits. Reading is the primary conduit to learning. It lets us learn selectively and unobtrusively and join the company of the greatest thinkers and achievers from around the world.

Learning to read and write in context might include some of the following:

- The anatomy of a newspaper—starting with the basics, some history of newspapers (how the printing press changed the world), a look at newspapers from different-sized towns, from different cultures and types of communities, etc. Then a breakdown of the typical daily newspaper, cover stories, editorials, letters to the editor, op-ed pieces, general interest stories, how newspapers are organized into sections including want ads and personal ads. Have the class break into groups and design and organize a newspaper according to what they think would be of interest to their peers. How would news stories be worded differently? What kind of news would they want to hear? What wouldn't they want to hear about and why? What new sections would appear in their newspaper? All of this will generate discussions, explorations of values, and practice in reading, writing, and design that uses their emerging skills.

- Have all students write down the three topics they are most interested in. Then have them pursue aspects of the question "How can I learn more about this?" Topics for discussion and action would include: using the library and using the Internet and search engines and discussion groups. Ask "How do you identify what you really want to know about your favorite topics?" Then ask "How do you organize yourself to find the best sources of information? How can you get to talk to someone who is an expert on your favorite topic? How can you become associated with others who share your interest?" Toward the end of the project, ask "Now that you know more, what do you want to do with this information? How will it help you in your life? How will you continue to develop your knowledge and your use of knowledge in these areas?"

- Have students read a story and discuss their responses with one another and then with the teacher and the whole class. Then have students listen to the same story on tape. Discuss the difference in experience between reading it and hearing it. For instance, ask "When you were reading the story, how did your own imagination make it different than when you heard the story?" Then have students view the story on video. Now ask the same type of question. "When you were watching the story on television, how was it different than when you read it or when it was read to you?" Acknowledge that reading involves the most effort but also gives your imagination the most freedom. Show links to famous people who read a lot and how their imaginations seemed to have developed more fully as a result.

- As television is such a key component of young learners' worlds, involve them in what it takes to produce a good TV show or a play. Break it into elements of writing, acting, and production. Show how a good drama begins with ideas expressed in written form, and have learners struggle with the production of a comedy, a mystery, and a documentary. What are the elements of each form that one must understand to get better at writing and producing each one?

In such major projects as those suggested above, context is enriched and extended when learners are presented the opportunity to find sources of help in achieving their assignments outside of the classroom *and* for bringing resources (including parents or community members) into the classroom that help to further each project.

Notice that all of the above projects include five elements. First, they encourage learners toward personal experiences and individual interests within the material covered. Second, they translate what is being learned into action. Third, literacy is attained through learners' involvement in conversations and individual as well as collaborative design. The motivation to learn vocabulary, composition, grammar, and other elements of literacy is built into their activities. They reach for such skills out of their own volition instead of being commanded to learn explicit and out-of-context words, sentence structure, etc. Fourth, each of the above activities tends to capture interests that peer groups have in common and put them to work toward collaborative learning. And finally, they reveal provocative connections between different disciplines and in so doing build lasting connections in the world and in the brain.

Elements of Context in Learning

1. Learning activities draw on the various individual experiences and interests of learners in a group.

2. Knowing what or why is integrated with action—knowing how.

3. Units of learning are designed to incorporate coparticipation (conversation and peer interaction) toward adapting what is being learned to one's own environment or familiar experience. The most valuable knowledge is recognized as being gained through insight, having engaged critical and creative thinking.

4. Learning design recognizes a critical element of context as making use of common experiences and shared perceptions within peer groups and communities of interest and/or practice. Learning is considered inseparable from identity.

5. Learning often crosses over subjects and disciplines and incorporates the fundamental axiom that what is worth knowing builds connections and interests in multiple directions.

Do we abandon recitation learning? Probably not (at first, anyway) but we can greatly diminish its emphasis in favor of seeking active involvement in learning both in and out of the classroom. We must also recognize the notion of immersion as key to effective (retained) learning.

Instead of covering a mile of breadth in an inch of depth, we (teachers and learners) must learn to cover a subject in sufficient depth that what we come to "know" is more implicit than explicit—a function of "heuristic" (exploratory problem solving and discovery) thinking rather than notes from lectures, memorization, and recitations.

> *"There are two modes of acquiring knowledge, namely by reasoning and experience. Reasoning draws a conclusion and makes us grant the conclusion, but does not make the conclusion certain, nor does it remove doubt so that the mind may rest on the intuition of truth, unless the mind discovers it by the path of experience."*
>
> —ROGER BACON

What has been truly learned has been "situated" in a manner, and that allows the learner to know that his or her own personal way of approaching the subject is valued—worth examining. Learning in context leads to intellectual autonomy. Learning out of context leads to the opposite.

The achievement of intellectual autonomy in learners, by definition, warrants that boundaries of inquiry and exploration are not rigidly set by teachers but are more likely to be "found" by learners. In the first curriculum, reading and writing, it is generally understood that composition is the pinnacle of demonstrating, reinforcing, and augmenting what has been learned.

Composition is "learning as design." It incorporates vocabulary, grammar, comprehension, creativity, and self-expression into a single activity. In composition, spelling is not its own subject but a by-product of learning language by expressing ideas. Yet composition is disappearing as the most advanced method of learning and being drawn into the language arts. "In 1914, nearly all universities required courses in English composition; by 1964 the figure was 86%; by 1996 it was only 36%."[1]

This statistic is a reflection of the fact that today we read and write, in school, primarily for the purpose of extracting rather than constructing meaning. The fountain fills the empty bowl. As writer and education critic Alfie Kohn puts it, "We are living in a time when such objectives as wanting students to learn how to write persuasively or solve problems effectively are dismissed as 'mushy.'"[2]

The future of learning will require a major shift in emphasis from knowledge as being "just there" to knowledge as constructed by human inquiry.[3] In the constructed view, the path of learning will include stumbling into provocative connections between different disciplines by extending insights from one event into commonalities, new applications, and new arguments that carry the learner away from discrete disciplines and fixed group lesson plans.

In the behaviorist view, knowledge is best broken down into discrete subjects—then further broken down into bits and pieces that can readily be memorized. What is remembered for an exam is the final product of the teaching process. Because knowledge is fragmented into bits and one subject is separated from another and because knowing is separated from doing, "knowing" principally happens without context.

Without a context to frame a learning experience, we cannot learn by doing. Memorizing math formulas, vocabulary words, or state capitals without a use that the individual can value and relate to avails no task that can anchor such "lessons" in long-term memory or in a hierarchy of value. It "assumes a separation between knowing and doing," with the result that students at best just "acquire algorithms, routines, and decontextualized definitions that they cannot use and that, therefore, lie inert."[4]

"Research shows that learners commonly acquire a store of knowledge they can retrieve in quiz situations, but which they do not bring to bear in situations calling for active problem solving. This is a serious problem in medical education, for example, where volumes of anatomy and physiology absorbed by medical students lie inert when they face actual problems of diagnosis and treatment."[5]

In a contextual learning environment, teachers and facilitators will know, above all, that the appetite to explore and understand must precede any content—that the motivation to learn must be intrinsic to be ultimately relevant. As the distinguished educator and writer Deborah Meier puts it, "A passion for learning ... isn't something you have to inspire (learners) with; it's something you have to keep from extinguishing."

The kind of thinking that assumes the motivation to learn is already there turns our present system inside out. With instructional design that desires uniform content, error-free assignments, and right answers with the ultimate outcome of a good grade, are we motivating students?

There is no authenticity to learning in a controlled and preprogrammed approach. We tend to create good and bad performers, and we perpetuate the notion that we can engineer learning with "efficiencies" that are, in fact, deficiencies: standardized curricula, standardized testing, rigid conformance to schedules and structured activity, emphasizing answers and deemphasizing questions generated by intellectual curiosity, etc.

Until now, I have addressed flaws that exist as a function of the way that "learning architecture" is practiced. The third fatal flaw addresses what present learning architecture cannot practice.

Endnotes

1   Phyllis Schlafly, *The Phyllis Schlafly Report*, 1996
2   Alfie Kohn, ibid., p. 47
3   David Perkins, ibid., p. 19
4   Brown, Collins, and Duguid, ibid., pp. 32–33
5   David Perkins, ibid., p. 19

Chapter 7

HERDING CATS
On Ignoring the Individual's Readiness to Learn

It is certainly incongruous in a society that highly values individuality that the individual is a threat to education. This is not because education professionals don't want individuals to learn according to their needs and talents. The current education model was designed in a time when values like cultural homogeneity, order and discipline, and the efficiencies of a manufacturing plant guided the thinking of educational leaders. With a little knowledge of history, it is easy to see how this thinking subjugated individual to collective needs.

Education, as we know it, is an enterprise that seeks to uniformly fill the human mind with content rather than train the mind to supply its own content as dictated by initiative and self-generated inquiry. In an age where knowledge has replaced labor, capital, and physical assets as our major source of value, this orientation is unacceptable.

Those of us at the higher end of the economic ladder (and those who aim to get there) get paid to think and learn. It is precisely these abilities that propel us up the ladder. The needs that we as individuals have to negotiate the ladder vary greatly depending on our ambition, talents, and energies.

If the education process is not incrementally teaching us what is important to us, how to use what we learn for personal and societal gain, and how to take charge of our own path to learning, we are not being prepared for the world in which we now live.

It is not realistic to expect that every person is going to be an optimum or even an enthusiastic learner. Many of us, for a variety of reasons and no matter how good learning design becomes, will opt for pursuits and preoccupations that do not challenge our higher-brain functions. This is to be expected. What we can expect basic education to produce in everyone is self-determination, compassion for others, and responsible citizenship.

An oriental proverb says, "When the student is ready, the teacher appears." Learning is a set of random opportunities that cannot be controlled or predicted. Furthermore, the process of learning is beset by mundane obstacles that are wholly ignored in our present teacher-centric approach.

The Bell Curves Not for Thee

What every teacher and every learner knows: Put 30 students in a classroom. Roughly 10 are keeping up and are engaged in the level and pace of instruction. Another 10 are struggling to keep pace and are falling behind, in need of, and usually not getting, extra attention. The last 10 are not challenged by the level and/or the pace of instruction and tend to be "going through the motions" to get the grade—to demonstrate their ability to perform, not to learn.

The material covered in our 30-person class may be highly relevant to some who can't keep up and irrelevant to several who are in sync with level and pace. If the class is a group of adult learners taking accounting, it might include a housewife, a small-business owner, a marketing manager in a large company who needs to better understand a balance sheet, a student who needs Accounting 101 to take statistics, etc. The teacher simply cannot accommodate the needs of each individual.

And it gets worse. Some learners have great difficulty comprehending an abstract lecture and need lots of sensory input, role-play, and/or actual practice in real situations to retain what is taught. Others can take in information more easily through analysis and reflection.

Active processors of information comprehend an experience by immediately applying it. Reflective processors think about it before they can act. Most teachers and curriculum designers are abstract perceivers and reflective processors. This means that instruction, testing, and even curriculum design tends to favor the same.

Though an individual learns in different ways, he or she will most likely have a dominant sense (e.g., visual—see it, auditory—hear it, kinesthetic—do it) that takes in information more readily. Personality also affects how each of us learns. For instance, extroverts succeed in different learning environments than introverts. There are people who need concrete details to make sense of new information and others who are intuitive and sense patterns of meaning.

There are numerous ways to categorize learning styles, though they generally fall into three categories:[1]

- Modes of perception—which of our senses tend to dominate the way we absorb data. This is physiological and hard wired.
- Information processing—designates the way we not only perceive but also organize and retain information. The way we process indicates how we think and solve problems.
- Personality types—describe tendencies of emotion, values, and the way we pay attention. Knowing a personality type can help one to predict how a learner will react to different situations.

One person responds to directions best with a drawn picture or a map, another with linear written directions, and still another with a retained image with a couple of landmarks to go by. These are all people who comprehend or remember things differently. Some types of auditory learners actually need to hear their own voice to process information. To a visual learner, seeing a picture or diagram can be far more useful than a succinct verbal explanation. A kinesthetic learner may have to get up and walk around or step away from a lecture for a moment in order to process information.

Research indicates that gender affects how we learn. For instance, boys tend to score significantly lower on the language arts sections of standardized tests. They also get disciplined more frequently, partly as a result of having to sit still for extended periods, which girls seem to tolerate better.[2]

Psychologist Howard Gardner defines intelligence as "the ability to solve problems, or to fashion products, that are valued in one or more community settings."[3]

To complicate the picture further, Gardner has a theory that there are multiple intelligences (at least eight and counting) that explain individual aptitude and enthusiasm for language (linguistic intelligence), logic and math (mathematical intelligence), the ability to perceive the visual world accurately (spatial intelligence), working collaboratively (interpersonal intelligence), solitude and reflection (intrapersonal intelligence), skill with one's body (kinesthetic intelligence), music (musical intelligence), and so on.

As the theory goes, we all share these forms of intelligence, though in different concentrations. They can all be developed, but we will be inclined toward some and not toward others.

Then there are the logistical elements of learning; we are predisposed to learn in accordance with individual rhythms and circumstances. For instance, I have noticed, over time, that I consistently do my best thinking and writing between 6:00 p.m. and midnight. We have different energy levels according to our metabolisms and circadian rhythms—the same for attention span.

Robert leaves the office after a particularly long day to drive to his management class at 6:00 p.m. (the only time the class is available during non-working hours). How much of him is going to be available for learning?

Robert knows that he doesn't really have the energy to pay attention in class tonight. But he also knows that if he doesn't go, he will fall behind and need even more time and energy to keep up.

Many of us in formal learning situations are on a lockstep treadmill. It is indifferent to our needs, to our circumstances, and to our preferences and what we have to contribute to others.

Because it is efficient to teach in groups, we are bunched by combinations of age, required (not desired) subjects, testing, time, and space allotments. All of these ways of grouping are likely to be unresponsive to our readiness (or the lack of it) to learn.

Learning does not proceed in a straight line. It cannot be organized and disseminated uniformly to groups. It is not a systematic stratification of facts and schemata to be regurgitated at appointed times.

One does not learn by surrendering to an established order but by discovering new orders in connection with individual experience. It happens in fits and starts. It is driven by questions generated by a learner's desire to know. It makes early leaps in one individual while stumping the next, only to be leapfrogged by the stumped one when he or she finally "gets it" on a whole new level.

Failures to comprehend are as important as epiphanies. Both are individual and move along paths that carry within them their own marching orders. To herd learning onto an appointed linear path and into a uniform conclusion is simply folly. This is common sense, yet we ignore it.

Philosophers Gilles Deleuze and Felix Guattari point out in their book *A Thousand Plateaus* that learning is "nomadic," a random function of "hunting and gathering" indexed to individual need. They describe formal learning as an assemblage, where all are putting connections together in the same way, for the same reasons, and because they are the same age or "slow" learners or "fast"— likening the process to rubbing a house pet's nose in its excrement after the fact in order to housebreak it.[4]

An unsavory picture but one that gets your attention. Recognizing the individual's readiness to learn will be a key organizing factor in the future of learning.

So if authentic and optimal learning cannot proceed at the same time, at the same pace, in the same place, or in the same way, what can we possibly do? It begins to suggest the unthinkable—throwing the baby out with the bathwater.

Yep!

This is when teachers, administrators, politicians, and pretty much all the rest of us begin to get nervous. There's a lot of infrastructure to learning: curriculum, books, blackboards, buildings, unions, laws, teachers, parental expectations, corporate expectations, schedules, and, mostly, that to which our minds have become habituated.

"Are you suggesting doing away with school?" you might ask. "If so, what happens to my kids after I leave for work? Or what do we do with the thousands of K-12 and college campuses, all designed to function in a particular way? Isn't it best to keep things pretty much the way they are and make gradual changes?" Good questions.

I introduce these questions now because they and others may be occurring to you at this point. The fundamental flaws are pretty fundamental. What does it take to reverse them?

It is important to recognize here that none of the continuing education reforms dictated by public policy and signed into law by "education" governors, senators, and presidents addresses the underlying faults of traditional and institutionalized learning as addressed here. Until they do, we are "rearranging deck chairs."

Even if we knew what to do, the larger problem would be how to get it done in the face of resistance to change: on what terms, in what increments, and to what audience? How do we influence the influencers?

Before getting to these questions, I believe it is necessary to cover a few more sins, including the big picture: public policy and the economics of learning. Then, we can begin to imagine a clean slate from which to build.

Endnotes

1   From *Learning Styles, http://www.learnativity.com/learningstyles.html*

2   Michelle Gallery, "Boys to Men," *Education Week,* January 2002

3   Howard Gardner, *Multiple Intelligences: The Theory in Practice,* Basic Books, New York, 1993, p. 7

4   From "The Teacher as Becoming-Student," *http://www.uta.edu/hypernews/get/delgua/24.html*

Part II:
The Present

- Secondary Sins

Chapter 8

TESTING AND THE PERFORMANCE CULTURE OF SCHOOL

Not everything that counts can be counted,
and not everything that can be counted counts.
—ALBERT EINSTEIN

Anyone can confirm how little the grading
that results from examinations corresponds
to the final useful work of people in life.
—JEAN PIAGET

It's testing for the TV generation—superficial and passive. ...
We don't ask if students can synthesize information, solve
problems, or think independently. We measure what
they can recognize. But this is very different from what
actually goes on in our information society.
No one goes to work and finds a checklist on their desk.
—LINDA DARLING-HAMMOND,
DIRECTOR OF EDUCATION FOR THE RAND CORPORATION

Children first enter school gleefully unattached to but highly engaged in learning. It is an unconscious process fueled by curiosity and the drive to explore an ever unfolding, complex, and alluring world: a world of the senses, a social world of peers, parents, and stories with heroes and villains. Then there is an unseen internal landscape that grows richer by identification and, by turns, differentiation.

The worldview of a child grows daily by leaps and bounds, fueled by imagining, questioning, experimenting, confirming, reaching, failing, mimicking, and musing—all toward comprehending what becomes immediately useful for purposes determined by the child's immediate needs.

Then children enter school. Something strange and unsettling occurs. The classroom removes them from their intimate and personal world, where the principal genesis of learning is discovery—simply being in the path of something that interests them. Now they are going to join a community that depends on doing the same things as their peers and then being compared to one another. Learning is going to increasingly become associated with competition.

The most significant thing that children learn as they enter this new world is that they are under constant evaluation and that they are going to be compared to their peers. They also learn that their own natural curiosity is a hindrance in class—they must now become attuned to what teachers want them to know. They must do this primarily by memorizing, not by the natural process by which they've been learning.

If judged by the criteria of their preschool learning experiences, the best indicators of a successful learning environment would be:

- Learners want to be there. They are aware of learning things they want and need to learn.
- They continue to be excited about learning.
- They are bringing what they learn in class into the world outside and vice versa—developing an increasing ability to describe and creatively solve open-ended problems that they will encounter as they become self-sufficient.
- Learning will directly be associated with growth—with understanding and mastering new worlds of their own choosing.

Clearly, for most learners, these are not outcomes of being in school. When they do happen, they are more likely the results of good parenting skills and the privileges of a higher economic status.

The experience of being compared to others (to determine whether you are satisfactorily progressing) does harm to us all. We can respond by becoming good, adequate, or poor performers. But, the operative word is "performer." Because performing is at the behest of others, it is at odds with learning. Knowing this, we might well ask:

- Do we want learners to be motivated by authority and fear or by curiosity and interest?
- Do we want learners to feel superior, inferior, or adequate, or do we want them to progressively feel competent and engaged?

These are not both/and questions. They are either/or questions, and they are crucial to how we want to design learning environments.

Central to the performance culture of school is testing. "Since 1910, 148 standardized achievement tests for elementary schoolchildren alone have been published in the United States, and only 34 of them have gone out of print."[1] In South Carolina, for instance, students take approximately 48 standardized tests between the third and the twelfth grade.[2] There was a recent push in Milwaukee to increase the total of tests during the same grades from 20 to 52. In some places, IQ tests are even given for admission to kindergarten.

After the 1983 report *A Nation at Risk*, there was a flurry of demands from politicians and corporate America to raise the standards of American education. Between 1982 and 1994, standardized tests grew faster than sales for school and college textbooks. By 1997, Americans were spending close to $200 million annually just on testing in public schools, almost double the outlays of 10 years earlier.[3] As I write this, the tally is up to $400 million. Now every state in the country except Iowa has some form of standardized test. Of course, this creates another problem because the standards vary from state to state.

Standards = Standardized Tests

The central principle now driving school reform is the raising of standards, an agreeable sentiment based on abstract reasoning with no proven method to back it up. We want schools and teachers to be accountable, and we want a reliable way of assessing how students are learning and progressing. Of course, we all want learners and educators to perform better in a climate where academic achievement and basic skills such as literacy and numeracy are declining.

The key phenomena that come with the standards movement are the quantification, standardization, and the measuring of minds. It would be so convenient if minds and learning progress were that easy to measure. As everyone who has been to school knows, they are not.

What this has translated into is testing—and more testing. Research does not back up the efficacy of testing for its intended purposes. The best research, though we need it to be more extensive, indicates a "statistical association between high scores on standardized tests and relatively shallow thinking. ... One such study classified elementary school students as 'actively' engaged in learning if they went back over things they didn't understand, asked questions of themselves as they read, and tried to connect what they were doing to what they had already learned. Students were classified as 'superficially' engaged if they just copied down answers, guessed a lot, and skipped the hard parts. It turned out that the superficial style was positively correlated with high scores on the Comprehensive Tests of Basic Skills (CTBS) and the Metropolitan Achievement Test (MAT). Similar findings have emerged from studies of middle school and high school students."[4]

Granted, this is not causal evidence but statistical correlation, underlining the need for advocates of testing to prove their case but more importantly to improve their methods of testing. There are several studies suggesting that the multiple-choice testing so frequently used in standardized tests results in a narrowing of the curriculum. They also add to the drill and practice work and rote memorization that is so endemic to schooling.

In October of 2001, five key national education associations (the National Education Association, the American Association of School Administrators, the National Association of Secondary School Principals, the National Association of Elementary School Principals, and the National Middle School Association) released a report highly critical of the increasing implementation of standardized tests. Individual states and school districts have also issued reports indicating that standardized tests, as means to better education, are poorly designed, overly simplistic, and even dangerous.

Two things we know for sure. One-size-fits-all exams are designed and built on the assumption that every child retains (or should retain) the same information, at the same time, and in the same way. The most consistent correlation that can be made to success on standardized tests is socioeconomic status. The higher the income level of a family, and, secondarily, the higher their level of education, the higher test scores will trend accordingly.

High-Stakes Testing

The growing assumption that accountability for standards lies in attaching higher consequences to standardized tests is wreaking the most havoc. "High-stakes tests" are used to make high-impact decisions about students, teachers, schools, and entire school districts. Often, a single test is used to determine whether a student will graduate, receive course credit, be promoted to the next grade, or get placed in "special" groups.

"Thirty-eight states, including districts in North Carolina, Texas, California, Colorado, and Kentucky, now award teachers merit pay, give administrators bonuses, and, in some cases, grant student scholarships to state universities based on performance on standardized tests."[5] Often, state funding is based on a school's performance on test scores. The better the test scores, the more money the school will receive. Imagine the mischief this kind of carrot can generate.

In most of the United States, high-stakes testing is a relatively new phenomenon. Test results were previously used as one gauge of many to measure a student's progress. In southeastern states such as Mississippi and Alabama, which have the worst-performing school districts in the nation, high-stakes testing has been going on longer with no measurable improvement.

What they have led to is a higher dropout rate. The National Board on Educational Testing and Public Policy, an independent organization that monitors testing in the United States, found (in 1986) that nine of the 10 states with the highest dropout rates used high-stakes testing, while none of the states with the lowest dropout rates did. The real victims of high-stakes tests are clearly minorities who perform poorly and leave school because of the use of a single test to determine their futures.

As the use of high-stakes testing grows, many organizations are coming out against it: the National Education Association, the National Council for the Teachers of English, the National Council for the Teachers of Mathematics, the National PTA, the American Federation of Teachers, the American Psychological Association, and the American Association of School Administrators. Against all of this opposition, the trend persists thanks to politicians looking for easy solutions to raising standards.

To force students to repeat a grade, or to withhold a diploma on the basis of a single exam, is simply absurd. About half of the 50 states are doing so or planning to. It is common knowledge that many of us, especially young people, have high anxiety and simply choke on high-pressure exams that focus on memorization. And clearly, the increasing preparation for standardized tests rewards memorization at the expense of deeper and more sustained reflection.

Even the American Educational Research Association, which represents the actual designers of tests, issued a statement saying, "Decisions that affect individual students' life chances or educational opportunities should not be made on the basis of test scores alone ... when there is credible evidence that a test score may not adequately reflect a student's true proficiency." The credible evidence is ubiquitous in every school where high-stakes testing occurs.

In January of 2001, Paul Houston, director of the American Association of School Administrators, made this statement: "Only on *Who Wants to Be a Millionaire?* can people rise to the top by rote memorization and answers to multiple-choice questions. The final answer to improving education is more than just memorizing facts for a multiple-choice test.

Children today need critical thinking skills, creativity, perseverance and integrity—qualities not measured on a standardized test."

It is difficult to comprehend the persistence of such policies in the face of so much vigorous and informed opposition. Has there ever been a better case of politicians hijacking an institution they know little about and "tweaking" it so they can claim far-reaching reforms?

George Bush's education plan calls for federally mandated testing of all schoolchildren in grades 3 through 8 in reading and math. If schools fail to improve, using the test as the sole criteria, the Bush plan reduces government aid. Urban school districts and poorer suburban and rural districts already receive thousands of dollars less per pupil than their affluent suburban counterparts. Is this any kind of solution to raising standards?

Let's Have a Look at Texas

The state where George W. Bush presided as governor for two terms is frequently held up by defenders of the standards movement as a sterling example of what raising standards can achieve. "In Texas we have found that when you raise the bar, people rise to the challenge," said Bush (*Time* magazine, May 31, 2001).

In his first presidential campaign, Bush claimed that the gains made by students in Texas were the "most fundamental in a generation." He further claimed that the number of students passing the Texas Assessment of Academic Skills test, or TAAS, increased by 51%, while the number of minority and economically disadvantaged students passing all parts of TAAS increased by 89%.

Sophomores in Texas must pass the TAAS exit test to move on to the 11th grade, regardless of their performance over the past 11 years in school. The real results of the TAAS test are nothing to brag about.

In the 20 years prior to the first TAAS exit tests, some 60% of black and Latino students made it from ninth grade to graduation without failing. Today that figure is halved. As many as 200,000 minority students have dropped out of the Texas school system between the ninth and twelfth grades. Driving students out of school is the more legitimate claim of tougher standards in Texas.

"Shake out the rotten apples, and we can show better test scores." Not a bad strategy to get results if you ignore the collateral damage. In Texas, 25% of minority high school freshmen are retained, and 98% of those retained drop out before their senior year.[6] Texas schools are heavily segregated by race and economic status. The casualties are mostly from underfunded schools with a high percentage of noncertified teachers. Texas has done very little to address this problem.

During Bush's governorship, Texas high school graduates lost ground in getting in to colleges. It ranked around forty-fifth overall and forty-sixth for getting its poor students into college. The performance of students on national standardized exams such as the SAT and the National Assessment of Educational Progress (NAEP) did not rise. What, then, does their state exam measure? Of what use is it?

The same phenomenon is happening in other states with high-stakes testing. Chicago uses the Iowa Test of Basic Skills to decide whether to pass students into the next grade. In 1997 as well as 1998, Chicago flunked some 10,000 students. In 1999, Chicago flunked almost 1,000 third graders for the second time. It is well known that grade retention is educationally damaging and harmful to self-esteem.

The collateral damage of high-stakes testing goes much further than dropouts and socioeconomic exclusion. "In a 1996 Who's Who among American High School Students survey, three of four students admitted to having cheated. 94% said they were never caught and five of six who were caught were never punished."[7] What's worse, in live interviews, students were unabashed in their justifications. "There's just too much competition to get ahead now, to get into a decent college. Everybody does it!"

Worse yet, as the consequences of poor test scores rise, the focus of teachers and students is narrowed. "Schools and classroom teachers, under intense pressure to boost test scores, have discovered the educationally dubious practice of teaching to tests. Subjects, ideas, and modes of inquiry not on the test and not easily formatted as a standardized test question are pushed out of test-driven schools. Teaching to tests also has had a 'dumbing' effect on teaching and learning as worksheets, drills, practice tests, and similar rote practices consume greater amounts of classroom time. The greater the consequences attached to the test, the more severe these distortions have become."[8]

Teaching to the test (organizing instruction around specific facts and subject matter known to be on standardized tests) and **teaching the test** (actually covering direct questions and answers known to be on standardized tests) used to be considered heresy by teachers. Now both are commonplace. In fact, teaching to the test is now referred to as "curriculum alignment" and is vigorously defended by it proponents.

In many states, standardized tests are tough, and preparation for them goes way beyond memorizing vocabulary words, historical dates, and specific concepts in alignment with state-specified standards. Kids are taught how to outsmart tests by recognizing trick multiple-choice questions. They are taught the specific expectations that go with test phrases such as "*compare and contrast.*" They are taught techniques for pacing themselves during tests such as "skip the harder questions and come back to them only if you have time." To sharpen these skills, students often take practice tests with questions that are very similar to their official state test.

- In Fairfield, Connecticut, district officials investigating the results of the Iowa Test of Basic Skills (ITBS) found that answers were erased and corrected five times more frequently at Stratfield School than at other schools in the district. Further investigation revealed that about 90% of the erasures had turned wrong answers into right ones. When students were retested under tight security, the school's scores plummeted from among the highest in the state to less than mediocre.

- In Maryland, state officials became suspicious when they saw sharply rising test scores at some schools in Baltimore. Upon investigation, it was found that a number of teachers were supplying answers to the Maryland School Performance Assessment Program (MSPAP). Although the state superintendent of education has the authority to fire or discipline teachers who abet cheating, no action has been taken against these teachers at this time.

- In Kentucky, the *Lexington Herald-Leader* reported that the state had received 151 complaints about cheating on the Kentucky Instructional Results Information Systems tests (KIRIS) since 1993. The paper said that the complaints should be investigated but that state investigators had followed up on only 11 of the complaints. This left the other 140 complaints in the hands of local superintendents, who have a professional stake in seeing the schools score well on the tests. Schools that perform well on the KIRIS tests are eligible for cash bonuses, while teachers and principals in schools that routinely score poorly can be fired.

- A 1995 *Reader's Digest* survey reported that "Eight out of ten high school students admitted to cheating; furthermore they say that their teachers often make it easy."

- Teachers and administrators at 32 schools in New York State were accused of providing kids with the questions to tests in advance and then marking the test forms for them.
- In Michigan, 71 schools were under investigation for cheating in 2001.

This list could be much longer, but you get the picture. What kind of culture are we creating in schools when pressure to conform to such standards results in this kind of behavior?

It is clear to most honest teachers, administrators, and others who make it their business to understand the testing phenomenon in schools that "large-scale testing programs are generally not useful in improving a student's immediate learning process, though clearly that is what most parents hope for from assessment." Furthermore, "they effect not only curriculum and instruction but also the culture of learning, student motivation, and the underlying conceptions of what learning is and how humans learn."[9]

It is fair to say that the very definition of "education" is being transformed by policy makers who have convinced the public that test scores, educational quality, and real learning are synonymous. Standardized tests have surely become the coin of the education policy-making realm. Many critics of education point out that this transformation took place a century ago and has now been resurrected on steroids.

Testing mania persists through high school and college and into the workplace. In suburban Detroit, dozens of middle school and elementary school students piled into seats at Brother Rice High School to take the SAT. For a $25 fee, parents could learn how their children were performing on the test used as a standard to admit high school graduates into college. Much of the material on the SAT isn't covered until high school, so younger children were destined to score poorly. In another Michigan high school, a mom pointed her video camera through a classroom window to capture images of her son taking his SAT.[10]

All of this hoopla is over a test geared only to predicting a student's performance in the first year of college. The real predictive validity of this test is about 16% for anticipating freshman grades.[11] Its ability to predict trends moves downward even further after the freshman year. Using high school grades and class ranking as predictors has proven to be considerably more accurate, as hundreds of colleges and universities will confirm.

At a May 1996 meeting of college leaders at Harvard University, it was suggested the SAT be eliminated from the admissions process. Despite general agreement that the test was not useful, several college presidents successfully argued that it would be unwise in the current political climate because it would foment a belief that colleges were going lax on standards.

The GRE, or Graduate Record Exam, which is used to admit students into graduate schools, has a predictive validity of under 10%, far worse than flipping a coin! Yet graduate schools steadfastly use it as means to predict a candidate's success in graduate school.

According to testing expert Peter Sacks, "Americans are taking as many as 600 million standardized tests each year in schools, colleges, universities, and the workplace." And at what cost? Calculating the true costs, Sacks says, would necessitate factoring in opportunity costs, such as what is "foregone when teachers spend inordinate amounts of time teaching to tests that might have a minimal connection to what students really need to learn. Research findings about the utility of test scores raise profound questions about the social and economic costs and benefits of a de facto national policy that has institutionalized the use of standardized tests for college and university admissions as well as the educational progress of individual children, schools, and states. Although the tests might be cheap to individual academic institutions, in many cases these institutions bear neither the direct costs of the tests nor the indirect social costs of testing."

In a 1993 study taking the above factors into consideration, Walter Haney, George Madaus, and Robert Lyons estimated that the U.S. taxpayers are spending as much as $20 billion annually in direct payments to testing companies and direct expenditures of time and resources devoted to taking tests and, most pointedly, teaching to tests.

If we were getting something of substance for this enormous outlay, it might be defensible. Let's review the following points about testing, and then you decide.

Standardized Tests

- Results tend to be highly correlated with socioeconor　　 ·°
- Result in a "dumbing down" of curriculum to enable ; and easy-to-answer questions
- Are disincentives to covering subjects in depth and　　 ꝑ ity and initiative in teaching and learning[12]　　 ꞈ

- Contribute to compromised ethics and poor morale in schools because the majority of teachers and students finds them superficial and unrelated to authentic learning
- Are used to make high-stakes decisions that affect the lives and careers of students, teachers, and administrators—the pressure to perform leads to frequent unethical practices to avoid negative consequences
- Are not useful as learning tools—helping students to understand their barriers to better learning
- Are used to compare school districts in newspapers without regard to issues such as school funding and socioeconomic status, which are known to be root causes of lower scores
- Expect students to develop in lockstep fashion—everyone needing to know the same stuff and at the same exact time
- Take an inordinate amount of time away from teaching for understanding and knowledge to administer and prepare for tests
- Are used to teacher-proof the curriculum—to take away any variance from specified standards
- Have not been shown to achieve their core purpose—to improve teaching and learning (according to a report by five major educational organizations)
- Are driving a wedge between teachers and administrators, who are forced to play the role of cops in tightly controlling teaching practices
- Are the principal cause of a high anxiety level, which is known to shut down the brain's higher functions
- Vary from state to state and are used by politicians (sometimes in the form of lowering benchmarks) to achieve high marks
- Fail to evaluate and compare students in a meaningful way (e.g., norm-referenced tests, which constitute the largest proportion of standardized tests, will always score 50% of the tested group below average)

And I saved the best for last. This deserves more than a bullet reference. Standardized tests don't measure things that really need to be measured. The vast majority of those round circles you blackened in with your pencil three or 23 years ago have no place in your memory now.

In West Bend, Wisconsin, 30 business leaders agreed to take a shortened version of the state's proposed graduation exam. They "had so much trouble with it that some wondered whether it truly will measure the quality of future employees," leading one bank executive to say, "I think it's good to challenge students, but not like this."[13]

As Bill Ayers (professor of education at the University of Illinois) puts it, "Standardized tests can't measure initiative, creativity, imagination, conceptual thinking, curiosity, effort, irony, judgment, commitment, nuance, good will, ethical reflection, or a host of other valuable dispositions and attributes. What they can measure and count are isolated skills, specific facts and function, the least interesting and least significant aspects of learning."

We are not teaching students how to learn in schools. We are teaching them what to learn. George Bernard Shaw said it succinctly. "We want to see the child in pursuit of knowledge and not knowledge in pursuit of the child." If you accept Shaw's statement, one must take pause. How did we get it backwards?

The Backlash

One of the few areas of good news in public education is that lots of people—teachers, parents, administrators, governors, senators, and students—are fighting back against the rising tide of high-stakes and standardized tests.

- In May of 1999, parents in Massachusetts made headlines by keeping their children home for two weeks while tests were administered. Parents in California, Michigan, Oregon, and Ohio did the same. Some districts in Michigan had up to 90% of their students waived from taking the test owing to parents saying "Not with my child you don't."
- In June of 1999, Wisconsin legislators voted down the hallmark of Governor Thompson's educational agenda, a new $10.1 million test to be required for graduation. Pressure from parents and education professionals killed the initiative.
- Lawsuits have been filed in Texas, Louisiana, Indiana, and Nevada to challenge the legality of high-stakes tests. In February 2004, Utah's House of Representatives passed a bill forbidding the state to spend any of its money meeting the requirements of No Child Left Behind.
- Petitions are being circulated in many states, legislators are being lobbied, and websites exist to support the effort to stop ineffective testing. At least 20 states are in direct revolt over No Child Left Behind.

- A number of high-profile members of state and local boards of education have resigned in protest of the unfair and punitive repercussions of standardized tests.
- In the county where my own children attended school, students from two high schools successfully boycotted (35% of one school sat out and 22% from another). Marin County School Board members supported the boycott, saying that standardized testing "warps the curriculum."
- Also in California, a child advocacy group joined with a protesting high school in Oakland to demand that Governor Gray Davis end high-stakes testing and redirect the $677 million allocated for testing to underfunded schools.
- The Massachusetts Teachers Association launched a $600,000 advertising campaign decrying the "one-size-fits-all, high-stakes, do-or-die MCAS test."
- A group of school superintendents in New York has set up an independent local school board to a more rational accountability system "based on multiple assessments and multiple forms of assessment." Representatives from business and higher education will participate in formulating the assessment criteria. The intention is that a county-sanctioned diploma will have more value and be issued on fairer terms than one sanctioned by the state.
- Even a few congress members have put their feet down. In Delaware, a Republican state legislator declared, "I cannot support, under any circumstances, a test that will be the be-all and end-all of a student's (getting a diploma). So why don't we just remove that?"
- Howard Dean, as the governor of Vermont, went on record as willing to forego his $25 million in federal funds to avoid the financial and social costs of the George W. Bush administration's testing policies. As a candidate for president, he referred to No Child Left Behind as "Every Child Left Behind."

These are the kinds of battles that will have an impact on education. Win one and we can begin another. For now, standardized testing is the battleground. To act, you need to be informed and in contact with sources that can help you stop the testing juggernaut. See *http://www.alfiekohn. org/teaching/fit.htm* for a document entitled "Fighting the Tests: A Practical Guide to Rescuing Our Schools." It even has a letter you can print out and just sign and address to your local school board, superintendent, or principal. There used to be standardized testing in Japan. It has been wiped out of existence by popular demand.

> *Making students accountable for test scores works well*
> *on a bumper sticker and it allows many politicians to look*
> *good by saying that they will not tolerate failure. But it*
> *represents a hollow promise. Far from improving education,*
> *high-stakes testing marks a major retreat from fairness,*
> *from accuracy, from quality and equity.*
> —PAUL WELLSTONE, SENIOR U.S. SENATOR FROM MINNESOTA,
> PH.D. IN POLITICAL SCIENCE AND COLLEGE PROFESSOR FOR 21 YEARS

Do We Need to Assess Learner Progress?

Of course. The "standards" movement is not wrong; it is simply misguided as to the methods that will achieve its goals. The solution is a bit complex and better contemplated in the context of the "future" segment of this book. For now, let it suffice to say that we need the participation of teachers, counselors, and the community (who know students well) and multiple ways of measuring progress to supplant the present system.

Quality assessment will give counselors and teachers information to guide students to improve their learning. It will take into consideration classroom work and independent projects that become part of a student portfolio. It will help uncover individual learning styles, problem-solving styles, and aptitudes leading to academic and career choices. Assessment will be used to broaden rather than constrain curriculum. Effective assessment will result in putting the child in pursuit of knowledge rather than the reverse.

Standardized testing has created the same problem in education that HMOs have generated in health care. Bureaucrats are making educational decisions. Jobs are on the line in the name of efficiency and performance, driving away talented teachers and administrators, and interventions that are viewed as expensive have been done away with in favor of the cheaper solution.

The culture of school is turning further away from what people can do and further toward how well they can take tests. Assigning academic merit to test scores, instead of retained, deeper learning and the ability to perform real-life tasks and solve real-life problems, is a very bad social policy. For one thing, it perpetuates an elite based on socioeconomic status and undermines the most precious of our democratic privileges, the opportunity for anyone to receive a quality education. It's a rigged game.

Standardized tests create standardized minds. They are too simple minded. Textbooks reflect this trend. For instance, the tests at the end of chapters are often created by the makers of standardized tests. Turning teachers and schools into assembly lines for testing and vehicles for implementing externally imposed standards is totally unresponsive to real needs.

The key question in response to this trend is "How can we create accountability without standardization?" After all is said and done, accountability simply cannot by indexed to a single source and to all learners uniformly.

The English philosopher John Stuart Mill (1806–1873), an admirer of democratic principle, put it this way, "It is not the minds of heretics that are deteriorated most, by the ban placed on all inquiry that does not end in the orthodox conclusions. The greatest harm is done to those who are not heretics, and whose whole mental development is cramped, and their reason cowed, by the fear of heresy." If Mill, a skilled essayist, were hired to evaluate how the American experiment in democratic education has turned out, what do you think he would say?

Endnotes

1 Peggy Van Leirsburg, "Standardized Reading Tests: Then and Now," from *Literacy: Celebration and Challenge*, Illinois Reading Council, 1993

2 John Goodlad, from an interview by John Merrow in the *Merrow Report*

3 Peter Sacks, from an excerpt of *Standardized Minds: The High Price of America's Testing Culture and What We Can Do about It*, Perseus Books, 2000

4 Alfie Kohn, from *Fighting the Tests: A Practical Guide to Rescuing Our Schools*, 2001

5 Meg Robbins, "The Failure of Testing," from Salon.com archives, May 2001

6 From "Just the Facts" at *http://www.nomoretests.com*

7 Educational Communications Inc., 1996

8 Peter Sacks, "Predictable Losers in Testing Schemes," *The School Administrator Web Edition*, December 2000

9 From "Testing Our Children: A Report Card on State Assessment Systems," see *http://www.fairtest.org*

10 Jeffrey Zaslow, "When Little Kids Take Big Tests," from *Time Magazine*, March 11, 2002

11 Peter Sacks, "Behind the Testing Juggernaut," *Rethinking Schools*, Spring 2000

12 A 1994 study by the journal *Education Policy* revealed that 77% of teachers polled "felt that tests are bad and not worth the time and money spent on them." The study also indicated that eight out of 10 teachers believe their colleagues teach to the test.

13 "Just the Facts" from *http://www.nomoretests.com*

Chapter 9

COUNTERACTING AND CO-OPTING MEDIA

If you decide to watch television, then there's no choice
but to watch the stream of electronic images as it comes. ...
Since there is no way to stop the images, one merely
gives over to them. ... Thinking only gets in the way.
—JERRY MANDER,
FROM *FOUR ARGUMENTS FOR THE ELIMINATION OF TELEVISION*

We have voted for a way of life with our time.
—TODD GITLIN, FROM *MEDIA UNLIMITED*

The electronic environment makes an information
level outside the classroom that is far higher
than the information level inside the classroom.
In the nineteenth century the knowledge inside the
schoolroom was higher than knowledge outside the
schoolroom. Today it is reversed. The child knows that
in going to school he is in a sense interrupting his education.
—H. MARSHALL MCLUHAN,
FROM *NBC EXPERIMENT IN TELEVISION, 1967*

efore a discussion of learning in the future can take place, it is
vital to recognize the enormous influence of electronic media on
contemporary society and on learning itself. The study of "media effects"
has rightly become its own branch of social science.

Language is our first form of literacy, our ultimate context. It is the
key link between self and society, between meaning and doing. It is the
stitching of our social fabric.

To think, question, brood, cast doubt, analyze, speculate, follow a
path of logic, conceptualize; to distinguish truth from falsehood; to elevate civilization from its entropic propensities; to connect others to a new
vision—events of this kind occur in language.

Language generates thought, insight, and, occasionally, wisdom. It
can be simultaneously literal and lyrical and can take new form through
its mastery. No other medium encapsulates and provides for posterity so
eloquently and completely.

Of course, what we utter can unstitch too. It may bore, offend, obfus-
cate, confuse, or enrage, or it can simply have no discernable meaning. It
is important for us to know this and develop a keen sense, the sense of an
artist, to know what our words (and those of others) have wrought. Some
have identified this as what most distinguishes the educated person.

In classic education, language arts (the trivium) was the first curriculum. Today, this is not so. As education critic Neil Postman puts it,
"Television is not only a curriculum but constitutes *the major educational
enterprise now being undertaken in the United States.* That is why I call it
the First Curriculum. School is the second."[1]

Images are primal and predate written language. They appeared
on cave walls to tell stories and express complex feelings before we
have any record of language. And over the ages, insightful and talented
artists have spoken to us at very deep levels with images. Images carry
power that words cannot possibly convey with the same economy. Many
who are gifted in the creation of images struggle to express themselves
in words.

As we live in a world of language, so do we live in a world of images
and sounds, all forms of communication. Most of us spend much of our
time in the grip of electronic images and sounds that literally overwhelm
us. With its economy and power, this tide is creating a new form of hu-
mankind worldwide—most blatantly right here where it was invented.

Electronic images are here to stay. They are often viewed all over the world simultaneously, communicating with enormous power. Imagine the impact of 9/11 without the images.

The importance of this discussion is to understand the impact of electronic culture in the form that we call mass media: television, advertising, music, and video games in particular. These media are literally altering the DNA, the brains of people in their formative years to an ever-greater extent.

We cannot make these things go away, nor do I think we should want to. But it is the task of this chapter to show that we must form a countervailing strategy to keep the electronic/visual tide from hypnotizing, homogenizing, and dumbing us.

Television creates isolation, false intimacy, and false community in school-age children. It penetrates their interior being and becomes yoked to their nervous systems. It tells them what to want and bombards them with far more adult information than they have the wisdom to apply. Furthermore, it does not provide any kind of commentary to mediate their experiences.

The way developing brains are used determines what their intelligence will be in service of and even alters developmental capacity. The more brains are "used" in a particular pattern of response, the less flexible they appear to become.

Television, visual advertising, music as mass media, video games, and even the Internet use brains by seducing them into repetitive, nonreflective, and subliminal attention. Brains being used by an exterior medium are selectively restricted to certain implicit messages—the messages of the medium and the messages of its owners and advertisers.

By the time your teenager graduates from high school, he or she will have spent 15,000 hours watching television, 3,000 more hours than those spent in the classroom. If we add video games, listening to music, and movie going, the time spent absorbed in mass media is virtually double the time spent in school. "Of children 8 to 18, 65% have a TV in their bedrooms."[2]

The average teenager spends more time in front of a television than any other activity besides sleeping. In one week, he or she will watch 25 hours of television, play computer or video games for seven hours, and spend four hours on the Internet.

In one year, your child will see 20,000 TV ads. Commercial messages have even made their way into educational television (i.e., Channel One) and into the hallways of schools and, of course, onto their clothes.

Children as young as three are influenced by pressure from ads.[3] Brand loyalty can begin to be established as early as age two. Research indicates that young children are not able to discern the difference between a commercial and regular programming.

Children now spend or influence $500 billion worth of purchasing in the United States and have turned marketing techniques upside down. Children, instead of parents, are the focal point of much advertising. It is recognized that children even influence the purchase of adult products such as cars.[4]

The main truth about the media is so obvious as to be forgotten: the shear saturation, the quantity of attention paid, and the repetition. "Media have effects on behaviors, not so much because any single exposure is powerful but because they repeat. And repeat. And repeat."[5]

> *The desire for pleasing windows on the world—and windows through which to escape the world—is nothing new, but only in modern society has it become possible for majorities to cultivate and live that desire, unwilling to accept anything less. Now, the desire for play, the desire for routine, the desire for diversion, the desire for orientation, the desire for representation, the desire to feel, the desire to flee from feeling—all these human desires in their complexity and contradiction are indulged in the vast circus maximus* (mass media), *our cultural jamboree of jamborees.*
> —TODD GITLIN, FROM *MEDIA UNLIMITED*

A massive study of media effects on the family published by the National Institute on Media and the Family in 1999 revealed some key predictors related to media saturation and school performance. Here are a few:

- Families that use electronic media less and read more have children who do better in school.
- Children who participate in more alternatives to electronic media with their parents' support perform better in school.

- Parents who report that their children play video or computer games less often have children who do better in school.
- Parents who report that their children more often watch television before bed have children who do more poorly in school.
- Parents who report that their children's behavior is less affected by media do better in school.

Such findings would suggest throwing your television and video or computer games out the window. We know this is unlikely, and for many, it is even unlikely that media exposure will be curtailed.

The Big Question

So how do we combat this overwhelming tide and its influence on developing minds?

More than any other factor, electronic media have destabilized the social control that schools and families previously exercised over developing minds. What is most clear from the facts, and from asking the question, is that school has a steadily diminishing knowledge monopoly, and whether it wants to acknowledge the truth or not, schooling is in competition with forms of mass media for the attentions and loyalties of its customers.

So far, the response to the big question has been understandable but one-sided at best—censorship and limited access. These are natural responses to an onslaught: to run away. But are they the most intelligent? With real awareness of the purposes, the utility, and the effects of electronic media, the effects need not be as bulleted above.

Let's break down the "big question" just a little bit, into how we can give young people the wherewithal to decide what is quality, what is trustworthy or what the effects of a violent movie or gangster rap recording are going to be on them. What's the difference between the unconscious impact and making conscious meaning of media ads, the artist's statement in a film, the values expressed in a TV series, etc.?

Looking at it this way, it becomes less instructive to simply dismiss media as superficial, insidious, or boring. Media are here to stay. They are constructed for specific purposes: to entertain; sell; dramatize; scare us; make us laugh, feel romantic, not sexy or beautiful enough, etc. Would it then not make sense to look at these various purposes and how they are achieved through various media? Do media reflect our own values, or do they influence or even define them?

When such questions about multiple forms of media are examined, deeper issues of method, quality, and standards naturally arise. Contemplating the use of different forms of media necessitates an understanding of context, subtext, and pretext that leads to greater literacy in any medium.

To deconstruct media is to learn how they are used and then learn how to use them. The ability to disengage, evaluate, experiment, and develop method (with still images, video, graphics, text, and hypertext) suggests a new kind of literacy and a way of making meaning that is more endemic to contemporary culture. Until there is a knowledge base from which to deconstruct and make use of these media, how can ethical issues and issues of value be authentically addressed?

Literacy cannot be separated from historical context. To pretend that the environment that we grow up in is the same as it was a generation ago and needs the same standards is just plain foolish. Now the young have their own culture with separate language, music, styles, and sensibilities. Today we have to draw from both ends of "culture" to engage the young and to provide them with a perspective that allows for such distinctions. What is enduring, classical? What is popular but temporary? What of each will endure, and what will fade away? To be educated in a culture that is undergoing change at today's pace is to anticipate where the collective is going and to learn where it has been.

The Constructive Approach

Today it would be unrealistic, given the skills needed to communicate and succeed in the workplace, not to provide young learners the skills to read, write, speak, debate, produce graphic statements to accompany text, produce video, create web pages, and mix media together to strengthen the impact of a narrative or message.

The constructive approach involves enabling learners to deconstruct and then have the skills to actually construct individual and mixed media. The end goal is to provide them with the ability to make discerning judgments based on their own experiences as contrasted with the analysis of peers, media professionals, and media analysts.

A comprehensive and contemporary literacy will also embrace various contexts. Conversations and forms of expression differ in the classroom, while "hanging with the homies," while gathering at the water cooler, at home, or in a community meeting. Part of literacy is being able to move fluidly from one context to the next. A contemporary definition of literacy needs to include this, and young learners need to be aware of it.

All of these cultures and forms of expression (media) can come together in the classroom such that they redefine literacy and use its various implements as a laboratory to develop new literacy skills. The chalkboard and textbook become part of a larger pool of teaching and learning media.

Some Tools for the New Literacy

Tool	Form of Literacy
video-camera	capturing full-motion images
animation software	creating simulated characters and action
Adobe Illustrator®	to create artwork for printed documents and the Web
Microsoft Power Point®	to create graphs, charts and slides to accompany essays and presentations
Digital Camera & Scanner	to integrate still images into text and websites
Web Browser	conduct research, compare points of view, search for pictures and graphics
MPG Software accompany	to create or capture sound to text and images
HTML - Hypertext software	to create websites with links to other text, websites and images

At present, media education has reached only about 5% of American classrooms.[6] It is clear that widespread acceptance of a new definition for twenty-first-century literacy is yet to come.

In Rowland Heights, California, Dave Master teaches 200 students media literacy every semester. "Today's students are citizens of the computer-video age and we have a responsibility to prepare young people for their electronic future. The creative citizen of the future must be an aware and active media viewer and a capable media doer. There is nothing inherently evil about modern technology any more than there is something inherently evil about a pencil. Creative, artistic, critical-thinking young people will help society realize the full potential of new technologies. It's up to them."

To those who would suggest that an expanded focus on new media to produce literacy would dilute the already atrophying level of reading and writing, I say it's purely a matter of design. Imagine an assignment to produce a docudrama of the life of a contemporary hero, someone sure to capture a place in history.

Your assignment, using multiple forms of media (see "tools" chart), is to create that place in history, complete with comparisons to others who went before.

The class breaks into three teams. Each chooses a worthy subject (e.g., Colin Powell, Hillary Clinton, Steven Spielberg, or Michael Jordan). The group then has to research a life and write a "treatment" that reflects the most meaningful aspects of the subject's life. Then comes a storyboard, which breaks the drama into its key components and story lines, followed by a narrative script that tells the story with accuracy and impact and combines images with words.

The team would then have to locate images and possibly video clips that could be incorporated into the story, followed by developing a shooting schedule that would accompany the script with visual dramatizations that give power to the script and help tell the story.

The story could focus on one famous incident in the subject's life, a critical or well-known period of his or her life, or a sketch that covers the scope of his or her character and accomplishments.

Research, reading, writing, rewriting for dramatic effect, piecing together a known person's life (or some aspect thereof) into a drama that will involve an audience, comparing and contrasting that person's achievements and personality with others in his or her field: there are more components to print literacy here than we are used to addressing in traditional classrooms plus the added dimension of combining visual media. Most important might be the practice of a literary craft or constructing a work of art rather than the usual reading, memorizing, and taking of tests.

It has struck me that my own children rarely volunteer any information about what they are doing in school. However, I always hear about it when they are doing a large project that involves independent research, some creative license, and other media besides their boring textbooks and workbooks. It is, in fact, the only time I have detected genuine excitement about their schoolwork.

The constructive approach is to design and build narratives using a combination of words and electronic media. It is also to involve learners in projects that give them awareness of different media and how they affect their perceptions, values, and attitudes.

For instance, have students pick three advertisements that have impact on them. One can be picked for its humor, but others must be picked for other reasons. Have them analyze what the advertisers wanted them to feel and how that relates to the product they are selling. Have them discuss their analysis with peers to see whether there are differences in perception.

Then have students estimate how many times they have seen each ad and what the effects of repetition are intended to be and what they actually are. Then give some facts about advertising and its generalized effects followed by an assignment to have students actually identify brands they are loyal to and why.

Another project would be to have students break into groups and choose from a group of simulation-style video games a single game and play it to mastery or until bored. Then have them discuss the following questions and answer them in a report: What did the game simulate well? What did it fail to simulate or not simulate well? What was real about it, and what was unreal? What did you learn from the game? What did the creator want you to learn? How could the game be used to teach other things? How did you learn differently than from a book, a video, a field trip, or actually doing the thing simulated?

The intention of such a constructive approach would be to build a kind of "deep" literacy resulting from the media that learners are immersed in yet unconscious of in terms of their techniques and effects. Such a curriculum, if designed appropriately, would underline, to a greater extent than can be done with text only, the primacy of language in communication. Every movie, TV program, video game, and advertisement has a storyboard that uses words to pair images together and a script to actually tell the story.

Conserving and Reviving

The counteracting part of a strategy to deal with the media is ecological. Ecology is about balance—in this case, the psyche in balance.

As Professor of Media Ecology Neil Postman put it, "Education tries to conserve tradition when the rest of the environment is innovative. Or it is innovative when the rest of society is tradition-bound."[7] Postman says that we are becoming accustomed to change but we have lost the arts of preservation. He further points out that "In a culture of high volatility and casual regard for its past, such a responsibility becomes the school's most essential service."

In the case of media, Postman's views are particularly apt. Without a countervailing view of electronic media, we risk losing perspective, diminishing our intellects, and losing access to the best thinking of those around us as well as those who came before us.

If television has any motive, it is to keep our attention. It has the advantage in that it is in our living rooms and our bedrooms, available 24/7. Its currency is emotion opposed to intellect.

In this sense, television knows something that educators do not. The key driver of attention is emotion. It drives the default system within our brains, the one that is concerned with survival—in particular with prospects of sustenance, threat, social status, and mating. Consumerism on television is a form of sustenance, and, of course, violence and sexuality abound.

Mass media show us how to consume, not how to produce, how to defend ourselves, not wage peace or cooperation, and how to treat sex casually, not seriously. We are made into voyeurs, and our appetites are constantly whetted. Because of this constant barrage of stimuli to the primitive part of our brains—the part that relies on automatic response, to act on impulse or fear or unrestricted appetites—we are increasingly out of balance.

The most primitive part of our brain, the size of a fingernail, controls such responses, and the media rely on our most primitive instincts for drama and commercial messages. The chronic activation of this part of our brain may account for all sorts of collateral social issues involving sex, violence, eating, and consumerism.

From my perspective, it is more realistic to give our young understanding of the media and a higher-quality exposure to the language arts than to insist on censorship and turning television and violent video games off. From this approach, we can assume that what developing minds bring to the media is more significant than the reverse.

The key countervailing element to mass media is the liberation of independent thought—something that schools are generally very incompetent at. Television does not ask you to consider or reflect upon an idea. Many books do. When kids read books in school, however, their independent thoughts are not encouraged or examined. Textbooks, in particular, are designed to prompt specific correct answers.

Interactivity and reflection are not possible in the TV curriculum. The TV curriculum also develops an expectation that a new focus or subject matter or change of scenery will occur every few minutes—a dynamic that surely contributes to the short attention spans and much of the "acting out" we see in schools today. These "biases" of the TV curriculum need to be consciously countered by the school curriculum.

Reading and writing skills have clearly declined in the past 30 years or so. The language arts of semantics, composition, and debate have been radically deemphasized. If we are to strike a balance between an image-centered world and a language-centered world, they need to be revived. Notions of complexity, ambiguity, big ideas, self-directed inquiry, and intellectual rigor (all antithetical to television) need to take center stage in a renewed approach to the language arts.

Digital game-based learning environments are becoming very legitimate media for designing learning experiences. It is time to recognize their validity and incorporate them into learning design. It is even more important to enable learners to experiment with different media as to their unique learning potentials. Books may be "slow" to a kid with an Xbox, but it is irrefutable that they represent the largest and richest repository of knowledge (and extraordinary thinking) by far. With more than 160,000 new titles coming out annually, it will be a long time before visual media can offer such quality in volume.

One of the themes central to the balance of media consumption is that of identity. Are children's identities going to be based on the images and messages of mass media (what Marshall McLuhan described as "Mass Man") or on the exploration of great ideas and learners' own interior space?

Schooling is not unlike television in that a bell rings every 40 or 50 minutes, suggesting that what is being learned does not require focus and depth of inquiry. Everyone is taught the same thing, at the same time, and by the same method. These are components of the media curriculum that need to be countered in order for school to send a different message than television. They call for a different design for school.

School and television are driven by a hidden ideology that does not encourage independent thought, free speech, rigorous dialogue, self-directed inquiry, and self-directed substantiation of truth. For school to stand for learning, it must redirect its focus in these directions and in conscious contrast to mass media.

Endnotes

1   Neil Postman, *Teaching as a Conserving Activity*, N.Y., 1979, p. 50

2   Tod Gitlin, *Media Unlimited*, N.Y., 2001, p. 18

3   Victor Strasburger, University of New Mexico, *USA Today*, December 17, 1997

4   Factsheet from the National Institute of Media and the Family, *http://www.mediaandthefamily.org*

5   Tod Gitlin, ibid., p. 8

6   Elizabeth Thoman, founder and president of the Center for Media Literacy

7   Neil Postman, *Teaching as a Conserving Activity*, N.Y., 1979, p. 19

Chapter 10

THE BIG PICTURE
Show Us the Money

The United States now spends about $740 billion on education, or nearly 10% of its gross domestic product.[1] This is more than we spend on defense and Social Security combined. We rank first among major industrialized nations in education spending yet rank last, or near last, by many international measures of student achievement.[2]

If one really takes a look at where the money goes in education, it becomes clear that one of the myths associated with ineffective education is lack of funds. The biggest excuse made by educators for falling short of our expectations is simply false.

Since 1960, public education spending has increased by 225%.[3] Test scores have fallen, and research has shown no increase in results correlated with increases in spending. In fact, the conservative National Review reported, in September 1998, that "Students in the top five states in per pupil expenditure performed far worse on the SAT than students in the bottom five spending states." Dr. Walter Williams, chairman of the department of economics at George Mason University, even asserts, "There is a strong case for a negative correlation between educational achievement and expenditures."

Using SAT scores as a correlate to spending for the purposes of measuring productivity shows that between 1960 and 1994, spending increased threefold while productivity plunged 71%.[4] Between 1960 and 1995, class sizes fell from an average of 25.8 to 17.3 with no overall improvement on achievement tests or any improvement measuring U.S. students against those in other countries.[5]

In Kansas City, which spent as much as $11,700 per pupil (more than any of the other 280 largest districts in the country on a cost-adjusted basis) and also had the highest-paid teachers and the lowest student-to-teacher ratio, test scores did not rise with increased spending.

At the state level, most tax dollars appropriated for education are skimmed off to pay administrative costs. In New York, for example, 51% of every dollar "is removed at the top for system-wide administrative costs. Local school districts remove another 5% for district administrative costs … the average school deducts another 12% more for administration and supervision bringing the total deducted from our dollar to 68 cents."[6]

Other nonteaching costs drop the actual amount for classroom instruction to 25 cents on the dollar in most schools. Out of a $7 billion school budget (in New York), there is a net loss to instruction, from all other uses of the money, of $5.5 billion.[7]

When lost interest is calculated, says two-time New York City teacher of the year John Gatto, "The cost for building a well-schooled child in the year 2000 is $200,000. That capital sum invested in the child's name over the past 12 years would have delivered a million dollars to each kid as a nest egg to compensate for having no school." Which would you rather have? It merits some thought.

The city of Milwaukee spent $6,951 per student in 2000. "Central administration there skimmed off $3,481 from the top, so $2,970 actually reached the school level. Of that $2,970, only $1,647 was spent on instruction—(again) just about 25 cents on the dollar!"[8]

The cost to taxpayers for homeschooling is nothing, yet homeschoolers outperform the average of any state's schools on the ACT Composite, the SAT, and the Iowa Test of Basic Skills. There are various estimates of the number of homeschoolers. Using a median estimate of 1.2 million times the average cost (2000–2001) of educating a student in the public elementary and secondary schools (rounded back to $7,000), that's $8.4 billion off the books.

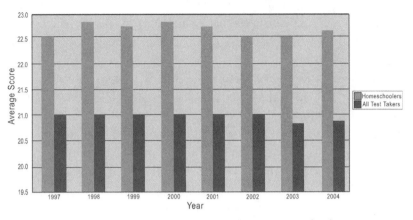

ACT Test Results for Homeschoolers vs All Test Takers

from *http://homeschooling.gomilpitas.com/index.htm*

What is wrong with this picture?

We have increased spending on primary and secondary education more than 325% in the past 40 years with no increase in return on our investment.

A 50-state analysis of the "Economic Impact of Government Spending" says that the growing percentage of administrative expenditures "tend to have negative effects on learning." Private schools, which have a much thinner bureaucratic structure, spend, on average, about 60% less per student.[9] Parochial schools, which cost two-thirds less per pupil and have an equivalent ethnic mix, consistently and dramatically outscore public schools on the SAT (and other) tests.

Spending has more than tripled. Teacher pay has gone up, and student-teacher ratios have gone down. Testing students has steadily gone up, and test scores have gone down. Colleges and corporations are putting their new students and new hires into remedial classes in the millions— another huge and uncalculated addition to the real cost of education.

Periodic education "reforms" have added a great deal of expense to public education. For instance, "outcomes-based education" (OBE), the brainchild of Dr. William Spady, is a reform method with some sound ideas behind it, but it makes the fatal error of assuming that every student in a classroom can be brought up to a single standard.

This assumption has generally resulted in lowering the common denominator to which all students are held, and it has added enormous cost to those states and districts that have adopted OBE. In Michigan, the state where I live, the OBE program has been widely declared a dismal and costly failure.

The State of Kentucky spent more than $1 billion converting to the OBE system with no evidence whatsoever of academic improvement. One strategic plan to implement OBE in a small school district of 18,000 students was to cost $18 million or an additional $2,250 per student. Other strategic plans revealed very similar costs.

The famous Littleton Colorado School District was held up as a model of OBE reform until, in 1993, a huge margin of disgusted taxpayers voted the entire school board out of office.

And then, there's the added layer of bureaucracy and befuddlement interposed by federal tax dollars. A congressional report issued in July of 1998 pointed out that the federal government has "more than 760 federal education programs." At least 39 federal agencies (each with its own bureaucracy) oversee these programs at "a cost of $100 billion a year to taxpayers."[10]

More than 20,000 pages of applications are filled out each year to receive federal education funds. After a "streamlining" of the Department of Education's discretionary grant process is complete, it will take an average of *only* 20 weeks and 216 steps to complete a review.[11]

Senator Bill Frist predicted that, in 1999, teachers and administrators would churn out 48.6 million hours of paperwork to pursue government money. "This is the equivalent of 25,000 teachers working 40 hours a week for an entire year," said Frist. The paperwork alone gobbles up 35 cents of every federal dollar spent on education.

All of this work to vie for funds that generally account for less than 10% of a state's education spending!

Money awarded at the federal level usually goes to school districts, still several layers of bureaucracy away from the classroom. We have created bureaucracies to administrate the doings of other bureaucracies and have thus added billions to the cost of education. According to the GAO, there is an equivalent of 13,400 federal employees funded to administer federal programs for state education agencies.

Many federal programs are redundant, and very few have demonstrated a return on investment. The largest education program, Aid to

Disadvantaged Children, "has spent over $100 billion since 1965 while producing hardly any evidence of positive lasting results."[12] It has not reduced the effect of poverty on student achievement.

States have created their own bloated bureaucracies to administer rules of conduct and to request and implement funds. Analysts from firms such as Coopers and Lybrand have tracked the increase of administrative overhead. From 1960 to 1990, the percentage went up around 15%. It has steadily risen in the past decade as well.

There is no benchmarking of standards for resource allocation in education. How is it that Utah gets along fine with one administrator for every 204.8 teachers, while nearby North Dakota requires one for every 17.7 teachers?[13]

I could go on and on, but it ought to become clear to anyone who takes a close look at public education spending that there is no accounting for and no relationship between spending and quality. Besides applying common sense to the scrutiny of education, following the money ought to convince anyone that we are pouring money into a bankrupt system.

Billions are added to education spending each year. It's like betting more money on a horse that never wins in hopes that increasing the bet increases the horse's chances. Who is going to stop the madness? It won't be politicians, educators, teachers unions, or economists. It will be only the collective, and it will happen only when enough of us wake up to what is really going on.

Let's reduce what could be an entire book on education spending to a few basic observations:

- University of Rochester economist Eric Hanushek, upon reviewing 377 studies conducted over two decades, said this: "Researchers have tried to identify inputs that are reliably associated with student achievement," but "they have not found any." These were decades when education spending was skyrocketing. As previous chapters have pointed out, such "inputs" have been culled out of the system.
- Per-pupil spending, adjusted for inflation, tripled between 1960 and 1994. This would be a two-thirds decline in ROI if the quality of education had remained constant, but as we now are keenly aware, output has gone down. Where is the accountability?

- Even without the radical systemic redesign that is needed every-where, charter schools and parochial schools outperform regular public schools with 35% to 60% of the funds.
- More than half of the money appropriated from our pockets never gets to the classroom. Much of the money goes to layers of fed-eral, state, and district bureaucracis that can and should be largely eliminated.
- Of course, a large slice of the educational pie goes to teachers' sala-ries. Recall the teachers who truly impacted your learning process. Most of us have clear recall of these special individuals and can count them on one hand. These teachers should be making significantly larger salaries. Mediocre and bad teachers can be replaced by more effective and less costly learning solutions.

Bottom line: We can cut education spending by 30% to 50% and dramatically increase learning outcomes with systemic redesign—a new architecture for learning. Study after study confirms that in the current system, we are throwing good money after bad.

When we get to the subject of a twenty-first-century architecture for learning, resource allocation becomes an important subject. Not only are we spending too much money, but also we are spending money on the wrong things. Let me make just a few suggestions for you to think about as we approach a discussion of the new architecture:

1. Eliminate layers of administration, and replace the simpler aspects of education bureaucracy with software that will be far more efficient and can be used to systematically increase efficiency in administra-tion. Train teachers to assume administrative duties. Bring in com-munity volunteers to assume administrative duties. We can cut the number of administrators by 75% at least, cut administrative costs by almost the same, and increase the efficiency and effectiveness of the bureaucracy by doing so.
2. Instead of hiring more teachers, reduce the amount of teachers in public education by at least half. One $30 million interactive com-puter history course can have several of the nation's best teachers on video. It can be supplemented with authentic and high-quality historical depictions on video and sophisticated computer games

that immerse learners in historical periods and mindsets. Finally, historical developments can be linked via game-centered activities in conjunction with other learners to reenact applying the thinking and behavior of a historical period to particular problems. Such an approach will allow learners to follow multiple pathways to mastering compulsory aspects of history curriculum while encouraging them to follow special interests in further depth and receive credit for independent projects. All of this at their own pace, in their own preferred learning styles, and with the ability to review and test for understanding at their own individual levels of readiness.

One high-quality course of this nature can replace thousands of mediocre and bad history, social studies, math, or science teachers. Furthermore, students with accelerated self-management skills can contract with schools to take courses by independent study by utilizing learning materials from private sources—thereby reducing costs further: homeschooling intertwined with classroom learning.

All students should have the experience of a few outstanding teachers who can stimulate their interest in a subject and augment their excitement about learning—undiluted by the legions of teachers who teach by the numbers and function as nannies. These master teachers should be accorded high status and high compensation, and their classes should not be restricted to assembly line routines and timelines.

3. There is much to be sorted out here. And, of course, the devil is in the details, but the billions saved by a new design for learning that incorporates steps 1 and 2 above can then be used to introduce new components to twenty-first-century learning—components that incur new costs. The overall effect will be to reduce education spending dramatically while leveraging the brain's capacities beyond our reckoning.

Endnotes

1   Michael Moe, education analyst at Merrill Lynch, January 2000

2   See *Organization for Economic Cooperation and Development*, "Education at a Glance: OECD Indicators," 1993 and 1995; and the National Center for Education Statistics, "The Condition of Education," 1995

3   Figure is adjusted for inflation

4   M. W. Hodges, *The Grandfather Education Report*, p. B, see *http://mwhodges.home.att.net/education-b.htm*

5 From a major report by Eric Hanushek, senior research fellow at the Hoover Institution

6 John Taylor Gatto, *A Different Kind of Teacher*, Berkeley, CA, 2001, p. 26

7 Gatto, ibid., p. 28

8 Gatto, ibid., p. 29

9 See the U.S. Department of Education Digest of Educational Statistics

10 "Education at a Crossroads," by the Subcommittee on Oversight and Investigations of the Committee on Education and the Workforce, House of Representatives, One Hundred Fifth Congress

11 Ibid.

12 Ibid.

13 Mike Antonucci, "Public Education Spending and Staffing," a Report of the Education Intelligence Agency, May 2001

Chapter 11

CENTRALIZATION VERSUS LOCAL CONTROL

> *Most people don't know who controls American*
> *education because little attention has been given*
> *to the question by either educators or the public. Also*
> *because the question is not easily or neatly answered.*
> —James D. Koerner, "Who Controls American Education?"

W ho sets educational policy and who governs have been increasingly contentious issues in the past few decades. Since the federal government began funding programs in schools back in the 1950s, states and the feds have been creating special interventions, reforms, mandates, standards, books of regulations, and layers of bureaucracy.

All of this has been going on while the quality of education has been declining. Before the escalation of remote controls and bureaucracies, the highest authority was the local school board, and teachers had far more discretion concerning what to teach and how. A little more than half a century ago, there were more than 100,000 local school boards. At that time, elected citizens (in the form of school boards) made decisions based on their wisdom, common sense, and most of all, intimate knowledge of their own communities.

In 1930, one citizen in 63 sat on a local school board. Today, it's one in 5,000. Citizens and parents have been displaced by the wisdom of so-called scientific educational principles applied uniformly to all learners. Since the beginning of the twentieth century, the authority of teachers has steadily eroded along with their status in the educational hierarchy. Today's curriculum is purposefully designed to be "teacher proof."

Control of education is now diffused among parents, local school boards, municipal and county governments, state legislatures, state departments, state boards, state superintendents of education, independent educational agencies, institutions of higher education, judicial bodies, administrative agencies, state employment relations boards, and federal statutes and judicial decisions. Then there are researchers, testing organizations, textbook publishers, teachers unions, activists for industry, private educational foundations, and think tanks.

Talk about "too many cooks"! The result is that creative input, breadth of perspective, oversight, and input at the level of implementation have virtually disappeared.

What we have is a system where the buck is endlessly passed, which serves to protect the millions who make their living in it and to justify the need for more resources to make the system work. Public education is a case study of the failure of accountability in a socialized system. The cries for competition present the ultimate threat to the system. They come in many forms. Competition is now inevitable, and the form it takes will be critical.

In the current environment, local administrators carry out centralized state and federal policies and standards. The State of California has more than 7,000 pages of educational code with which teachers and schools must comply. Failure to comply with rules and meet standards is likely to mean further loss of control at the local level.

Teachers increasingly prepare students to meet very specific one-size-fits-all standards for advancement. They and parents have very little input into what students are learning and how. Teachers, like learners, have largely become cogs in the bureaucratic machinery.

The centralization of control is a reaction to poor performance in schools, yet it has accelerated the downward trend and is clearly not the solution. When we measure productivity by dividing particular measures of student achievement against per-pupil spending in inflation-adjusted dollars, we see that productivity in public education has fallen virtually 50% in the past 30 years.

126

Federal mandates to "raise the standards" continue despite overwhelming failure. The first President Bush's America 2000 education plan and Goals 2000, signed into law by President Clinton, failed to achieve *any* of their goals.

Reams of research about how the brain works and how we learn have revealed highly effective new approaches to education, yet they are ignored by politicians in favor of the rhetoric of "higher standards," "more money," and "smaller classes." While all of these political solutions have proven ineffective, they remain at the core of public policy.

The latest presidential education reform, the No Child Left Behind Act of 2001, which the U.S. Department of Education lauds as "the most sweeping reform of the Elementary and Secondary Education Act since ESEA was enacted" (in 1965), is frankly more of the same: more money (an additional $6.5 billion), smaller classes (we know what the research says about that), and even tougher standards of accountability (even though previous standards remain unenforceable).

The basis of the new architecture for learning is that learning is an inherently individualized activity. It requires interaction with others and with the world at large, but it depends for its effectiveness on individual inquiry, resourcefulness, and discovery. Therefore, all central planning and bureaucratization of the learning process not only creates layers of unnecessary bureaucracy but also stultifies learning by turning it into a mass-produced and uniform process.

In the name of efficiency, we have progressively created millions of "educrats" who now outnumber teachers. This bureaucracy cannot focus on the individual learner, but rather its energy is consumed, devising its own governance and self-perpetuation. It does not know whether its customers are parents, students, the local community, the broader needs of corporate America, local universities, or the regional economy. The truth is that all are customers, but there must be a hierarchy of priorities and organization around the needs of the different constituents.

The need to organize education and its priorities around the marketplace is clear. Centralization and bureaucratization have failed. But who is the market? If there are multiple markets, can we satisfy them all? How can we decentralize, deregulate, decontrol, depoliticize, and debureaucratize? How can we satisfy the needs of individual students without sacrificing the needs of society? These are the truly big questions that accompany the need for a new learning design.

The common sense of the marketplace says that competition will tend to drive costs down and drive quality up. But competition will have trade-offs—expensive trade-offs if not engineered properly. There are many forms of competition.

Charter schools are a form of competition that keeps competition in the public arena. Most of the funding (from all sources) to charter schools cuts out the administrative skimming and goes directly to the school. They are free from most government regulations, and they can teach whatever (and however) they want as long as they can demonstrate adequate academic progress.

Charter schools generally have fewer than 100 students. They can require uniforms. They can focus on vocational training or the arts. They have been founded by Christian fundamentalists and disenfranchised minorities. In short, they can serve diverse sociopolitical groups and learning styles. Kids who are unhappy underachievers in traditional high schools often find relevance and a supportive environment in charter schools.

In California, which has the most charter schools, they have outperformed public schools on 60% of per-student funding. Some see charter schools as the most important development in modern education. They are decentralized, they have a large degree of autonomy, and the prime directive is simple. Perform or you get shut down.

From an interview of Los Angeles charter school Principal Joe Lucente:

The handcuffs have been taken off, yes, but we are in a fishbowl too. Everyone watches what we do and how we do it, and we do it very well because we have local control. We set policy at the local level and we have control over where the money goes and how it is spent.

Interviewer: *The superintendent doesn't have any say over you? Who is your boss?*

Mr. Lucente: *160 staff members, the community, 1,300 parents ...*

This sounds very reasonable, but in the context of modern schooling, it is radical!

Charter schools are public schools that operate under complete autonomy in exchange for higher scrutiny and accountability: accountability to parents, to students, and to the local community in addition to state standards.

Another form of competition and decentralization is the concept of schools within schools. Large schools are broken down into specific learning cultures with their own approaches to optimum learning design, student activities, and parental involvement. Under such a model, a particular group or "house" (as described in the British system à la Harry Potter) builds an intimate learning culture around shared interests, ambitions, and aptitudes.

Smaller, theme-based "houses" are likely to produce a sense of identity and belonging absent among many students in large schools. Discipline problems would be inclined to diminish. Students would participate in their own governance and in defining their own measures of excellence.

Key to this model is the close relationship of each student to a faculty mentor. This functional role is a combination tutor, coach, and counselor. It is most effective when it endures for the entire school experience and beyond. The notion of having a confidante, confessor, tutor, mentor, and coach throughout one's scholastic career is paramount to decentralization.

The Department of Education and private entities such as the Annenberg Foundation, the Pew Charitable Trust, and the Bill and Melinda Gates Foundation have already committed millions to downsizing schools and making learning environments more intimate.

The new architecture will emphasize radical decentralization of control over education toward the ultimate goal of self-determination in the learning process. The effects of decentralization will create a new kind of need for centralized organization. This is brought about by the need for a national information infrastructure for administration, individualized curriculum, and a standard (including a software platform) for learning management.

Telecommunications and computer technology create new domains of efficiency and unprecedented access to information and individuals linked to specific areas of knowledge and interest. The combination of access and efficiency will change how we learn in yet unimagined ways.

Because we are just beginning to invent how technology will transform the distribution, the organization, the management, and the very act of learning, the critics of technology have the most to point to. Applied learning technology still emulates the mass-production model from which we have yet to extract ourselves.

Any kid who uses computers knows there is something inherently wrong when walking into a computer lab with rows of PCs lined up on desks. If he or she were carrying his or her own laptop with e-mail capability and shareware (such as Lotus Notes), tied in to local area network

(LAN) that would allow access to homework assignments, collaborative simulations, and game-based learning projects, special communications from teachers and staff, software for note taking and turning in assignments, etc., he or she would be in the real world of computers in which the device itself disappears and simply becomes a powerful tool to learn, distribute, and access information as well as work in collaboration with others.

In order to usher in learner-centric environments supported by technology, centralized efforts will be needed on the federal as well as the local level. Here are some suggested roles for the federal government under the new architecture:

1. Disband the Office of Education and appoint a nonpartisan commission of experts in learning design to record an evolving blueprint for the new architecture and to apportion federal funds for research to validate evolving aspects of design and administration.
   Education is not a domain that should employ sticks and carrots to effect change. Furthermore, partisan politics has no place in education at the federal level.

2. Pass legislation that insures the end of education reform based on political agendas at the federal level. The main venue for proposing new educational imperatives, based on the nation's interests, would be the Commission for a National Learning Architecture (CNLA). The federal government thereby legislates itself out of the business of educational administration and resource allocation.

3. Create an information technology (IT) infrastructure that houses an evolving research agenda. It would issue to states and localities descriptions and results of all ongoing and completed research. It would issue the criteria by which to record, receive funds for, and publish the results of research. Priority is given to "action research" or research that actually puts new operating principles and learning design into practice. The need for research to continually build and refine the new architecture is key.

4. Create a secondary federal budget to assist educational institutions in adopting proven learning design and acquiring the resources (expertise, equipment, software, training, etc.) for implementation. Funds of this nature will be apportioned on the basis of a demonstrated readiness to adopt and implement proven innovations. The federal

role, here, would be strictly to confirm that the readiness is in place to apportion funds and to record the implementation and effectiveness of sanctioned and proven programs. They will avoid creating bureaucracies and rules to manage the process of implementation locally. Once it has begun, the federal role will be to verify implementation and verify recorded information as required. This will require a higher degree of trust between the feds and local school districts as well as serious consequences for fraud in recording required information.

5. A third segment of the federal budget will be for the CNLA to approve curriculum design that can be administered on an individualized basis in any school nationwide. More will be said about this in *The Future* segment of the book. Some curricula would be funded by the federal government, and some would be approved to be offered for academic credit by private vendors. Some may be the product of a public-private partnership among the federal government, a state, a large school district, and one or more private enterprises. A scholarship program based strictly on economic need could be attached to this segment of the budget to help underserved students with remedial and privately offered curricula.

6. Finally, a crucial component of the new architecture will be a web-based information infrastructure that would house learning management software, administrative "groupware" for teachers, learning facilitators and administrators, record-keeping software for administration, research templates and archives, online courses, and databases of approved "learning objects."

Needless to say, getting from where we are to a radically decentralized (and newly centralized) structure as defined above presents an enormous challenge. I believe it is safe to say that the payoffs will be well worth it.

The upfront costs to switch over to a new system as described above will be, at first, very high. The business model of this approach should look very much like that of a software company: lots of upfront investment in research, design, and infrastructure build out with enormous cost reduction in the ongoing implementation.

Eighty percent of the cost of our current educational system is paychecks. This amount could be halved in the long run. The money spent on bricks, mortar, concrete, and buses, etc., could also be substantially reduced. Yes, there would be new costs, and yes, all of this is debatable, but the economies of scale enabled by technology combined with the efficacies of new learning design cannot be ignored.

It is important to know that other countries, unencumbered by entrenched bureaucracies, unions, and the politicization of educational policy, are making great strides toward a twenty-first-century architecture for education.

For example, the Malaysian "Smart Schools" initiative, begun in 1996, is a complete reworking of learning/teaching design in keeping with many of the principles discussed in this book. Its purpose is to prepare Malaysian students for globalization and the social and technological changes in the nature of work and learning. This initiative, which is proceeding briskly, has significantly leapfrogged our traditional approach to learning design.

It is difficult to make predictions, but the stakes are too high not to take a stab at it. I think that we have a 20-year window to redesign and implement a twenty-first-century learning architecture. If we fail to stake a claim to leadership in this area, it will most certainly be claimed by others.

> *For over a generation, the public secondary school system*
> *has produced graduates who are less qualified than those*
> *of our major competitors. If this deterioration continues,*
> *the nation runs the risk of losing its lead in productivity*
> *and innovation (the two factors that most account for*
> *economic leadership in today's global economy).*
> —SAM LEIKEN,
> DIRECTOR OF PUBLIC POLICY AND GOVERNMENT RELATIONS

> *Our high schools were designed...to meet the needs of*
> *another age. Until we design them to meet the needs of*
> *the 21st century, we will keep limiting-even*
> *ruining-the lives of millions of Americans every year.*
> —BILL GATES, CHAIRMAN & CEO, MICROSOFT

The fallout, in a time when learning itself is the currency of economic leadership, definitely puts us at risk of becoming a second-class power. It has happened every time a civilization takes its wealth and its assets for granted. It happens when centralized control suppresses innovation and becomes self-perpetuating. Certainly, these phenomena, in themselves, are synonymous with the decline of learning.

Chapter 12

TEN CONVERSATIONS FOR THE ACTIVIST TO HAVE WITH FRIENDS, FAMILY AND EDUCATORS

Changing education is going to require the strength of numbers. Most of us are vaguely irritated about the state of education. Now it's time to convert your irritation to clarity and clarity into fuel—fuel for mobilization.

I'm reminded of the bumper sticker "If you're not outraged, you're not paying attention!" I can't think of a more apropos context for this sentiment than the society of schooling in which we now propagate with our assent and tax dollars. To move toward an authentic learning society, we might well be fueled by some good old high-octane righteous indignation. Most of all, we have to start paying attention—knowing that change isn't going to come from within the system. Try a few of these conversations out, and then let us know what you have wrought at *http://www. lessonsfortomorrow.com*

1. School is not responsive to my daughter's (or my son's) real needs.

Two millennia ago, Plato warned those who read books that a totalitarian juggernaut would eventuate, resulting from the urge to homogenize societies and teaching. When our founding fathers defined education for all as the foundation of a true democracy and the final stage of the American Revolution, Benjamin Rush called for an overriding allegiance to the common good. "Let our pupil be taught that he does not belong to himself, but that he is public property. Let him be taught to love his family, but let him be taught at the same time that he must forsake and even forget them when the welfare of the country requires it." This call was for each individual to "perform (his part) properly in the great machine of the government of the state."[1]

The "welfare of the country" so far as education has been concerned has gone through many phases, but since the beginning of the twentieth century, the primary welfare has been to make better workers and better spenders of us. In a 1907 speech, Henry Pritchett, the first president of the Carnegie Foundation for the Advancement of Teaching, declared that it was "more and more necessary that every human being should become an effective economic unit." Furthermore, he argued that the educational system "must seek to produce economically useful knowledge and to sort people efficiently into the various positions that need to be filled in the stratified occupational structure."[2]

The 1983 *Nation at Risk* report was rather blatantly designed to scare us into producing higher-skilled workers to compete in the new global economy. It worked in that it created much alarm and gave rise to the "standards" movement now in vogue.

It failed miserably in that it has produced no significant rise in student performance.[3] In fact, in most categories used to compare our students with others around the world, there has been further decline since 1983.

But this isn't the worst of it. The *Nation at Risk* report did not identify the skills needed for this new economy, nor did it indicate new methods for educating learners in a postindustrial economy. It didn't even identify the principal causes of our failure to educate—neither has any federally commissioned report since.

So, we are left with the one-size-fits-all method of education and recalcitrant policy makers who are largely ignorant of the new skills needed to compete in the global marketplace and ignorant of methods (based on cognitive science) that would greatly increase the efficiency as well as the effectiveness of teaching and learning.

Even if your child is diverted into a special education or gifted program designed to deal with conditions beyond the norm, he or she will not be educated according to individual talents, interests, ambitions, or learning styles. If this is not the kind of school system you want, you need to get personally involved.

Only the will of an informed majority will generate change. To move toward a system that educates individuals (while also serving economic mandates), we need to want what's best not just for our children but also the children of our neighbors and those across the economic spectrum.

2. "Big Brother" doesn't want us to be smart.

Most of us have heard the rhetoric: businesses have to innovate to stay ahead of the curve; companies can no longer afford the "mindless" worker who simply records and files information or performs repetitive tasks without thinking about them. Knowledge workers are the vanguard of our economy. They get paid for their knowledge and their ability to learn and innovate.

Certainly this is true for the vanguard. But how big is the vanguard, really? And what about the rest of us? Is having thinking employees in the interest of America's largest private-sector employer, Wal-Mart?

I went to the Bureau of Labor Statistics to conduct a little research of my own. Here are the 10 largest lower-wage employment sectors with a bit of commentary to specify what they mostly do:

The Ten Largest Lower Wage Occupations (In Round Numbers)

1. *Office & Administrative Support* - mostly clerical — 23 million

2. *Sales & Related* - mostly cashiers and retail sales — 13.5 million

3. *Production* - mostly assembly line workers and fabricators — 12.5 million

4. *Food Preparation and Serving* - waitresses, fast food workers counter attendants, etc. — 10 million

5. *Transportation and Material Moving* - mostly people who transport others or deliver goods — 9.6 million

6. *Construction and Extraction* - workers with highly specialized and repetitive technical jobs — 6.2 million

7. *Installation, Maintenance and Repair* - again, technical jobs that, once mastered, become highly repetitive - focus and precision are more important than thought — 5.3 million

8. *Building and Grounds Maintenance and Cleaning* — 4.3 million

9. *Healthcare Support* - home health aides, nurses aides, orderlies, attendants, veterinary assistants, massage technicians — 3 million

10. *Protective Services* - mostly security guards, correctional officers, parking enforcement workers, bailiffs — 3 million

Granted, a proportion of these workers are either in management or have job functions that require complex or creative thought. I think it is fair to say, however, that if you interviewed a representative sample of each category, most of them would describe their jobs as relatively mindless.

Add to this other large employment categories with low-end jobs (e.g., management, personal care and service, business and financial operations) and surely you could add several million more workers who would say that their jobs consist of following strict policies and routines with relatively little thought or innovation.

At the present time, how many of us can truly be described as knowledge workers? Corporate leaders and consultants are inclined to exaggerate such numbers, while employees, who would rather play it safe than stick their necks out, downplay opportunities to use their knowledge for advancement.

I certainly think it would be fair to say, being very conservative, that less than a third of us are actually retained to use our brains to advance the goals of an occupation or enterprise. The rest of us would innovate or suggest real change at our peril.

Pointing this out raises some very important questions. What are the implications of having a populace that is self-actualizing? What happens if we shift from a culture that is being taught what to think to one that is taught how to think and how to learn? What happens in a culture that is widely drawn to learning for its own sake?

The dark side of the American character is that our wealth and dominance depend on a compliant and complicit underclass that has the illusion of attainment or at least the lack of knowledge of alternatives. It is on the backs of these lower- and middle-class workers that the economic elite amass great fortunes.

Twenty-five percent of U.S. families own more than 80% of private assets. Well over half of those assets are in the hands of the top 5% of that group, or the top 1% of all families.[4] Former Secretary of Labor Robert Reich pointed out that between 1973 and 1993, the top 20% of our population gained $275 billion per year directly from the middle class. In 1998, Bill Gates's net worth ($46 billion) was larger than the combined net worth of the bottom 40% of American households.

The disparity of wealth in the United States is the worst among developed nations.

Note only have these developments eroded the economic base from which schools are supported, but also the consequences, when added up, have created a growing sense of deterioration of culture and opportunity in our young. Young learners sense the fault lines in American culture even more keenly than the rest of us.

Do the captains of industry want us to think, to become entrepreneurs like they were? I noticed that in the late 1980s when corporate "re-engineering" was in its heyday, business really was being reinvented from top to bottom. The notion of an "intrepreneur" sprang up: a corporate employee who would think like an entrepreneur within an organization and streamline work processes.

Many of these "intrepreneurs" were replaced or rendered less essential by the very processes they invented. Much of their work was replaced by information technology. They and others became the entrepreneurs (dot-commers) of the '90s and often, despite many failures, cannot bring themselves to return to the "risk-averse" cultures of large corporations.

The lesson implicit in recent corporate history: *don't innovate or you may be downsized or devalued.* The divide between those who are clearly designated as knowledge workers and the rest of us has grown. As impressed as we were with the boy billionaires of Silicon Valley, we now view following in their footsteps in a different light.

It is true that more new wealth is created in our society by entrepreneurs than by any other group. But the learning environments we provide for children are not inclined to produce entrepreneurs. Even at the highest levels of achievement, we are more likely to produce professionals who follow already-trodden paths.

Researchers for the Board of Governors of the U.S. Federal Reserve System identified the following trend regarding human capital development in 1997: "By identifying alternative means of accumulating human capital, we are able to show that an economy in the early stages of development may have too little education, but in the later stages of development may have too much education. … When entrepreneurial human capital is more important than professional human capital in determining the level of technology, the steady state will have too many professionals and too few entrepreneurs."[5]

The inevitable conclusion: we are not educating our young for the real opportunities that are proliferating in the economy, **and** we are over-dependent on formal schooling to be the vehicle for such new learning. This conclusion leads into directions such as vocational education and alliances with organizations outside of school to increase entrepreneurial thinking and activity.

Such an observation may seem contradictory in an economy where multiple careers and lifelong learning have become a reality, but it really isn't. The contradiction is in the fact that learning is not tied to individual needs, interests, and learning styles. A shift in the balance from teaching to individualized learning combined with the early acquisition of practical skills will certainly generate more entrepreneurs.

The present system has isolated learners (and learning) from the real world of work and achievement. If we expose young learners to this real world, they are likely to develop earlier independence and a greater sense of control over their lives.

When the United States made the leap to take responsibility for educating its populace, the pressures on young people to develop themselves were greatly reduced. Getting ready for the real world became defined by the state, not according to what individuals chose for their own purposes. We need to acknowledge the deep dynamics of this policy and define a new one.

But policy makers and big corporations do not favor such directions. They are the guardians of the status quo, of big money, and of predictable outcomes. Too many smart people represent a threat to the status quo—a growing segment of the population with creative initiative and a lack of tolerance for those mindless jobs.

Today, around 90% of high school seniors expect to attend college and be prepared for the higher-paying jobs that come with an advanced education. We do a very poor job of preparing them for the realities they face. Many of these students face severe disillusionment when their dreams and ideals collide with the real world. About 37%, overall, of those who enter two- and four-year colleges drop out in their freshman year. Only about 58% of those who pursue a four-year degree actually complete it.[6]

3. Politicians will never provide the solutions.

One of the core problems with schools is that they have become ideological battlegrounds. Principals experience this every day between the dictum of assigned curricula and what teachers believe, between parents who object to rules, discipline, or the lack of it and what their kids are or aren't learning.

The policies and regulations that govern educational personnel and students are now staggering. Teachers no longer design a class, and principals have very little opportunity to lead. Everyone is governed by remote control—policies that are a product of political ideology at the state and federal levels.

In the 1960s, we saw the pinnacle of liberal idealism in education. The political left had taken the higher ground. Education was their issue. Some of the ideals that informed their policies coll'''' better society through the benevolent intervention ment. Layers of bureaucracy were created. They a centered education and couldn't figure out how to the other.

As a result of liberal policies, more roles were given to teachers and administrators. They needed to build self-esteem, adapt to the cultural differences of their students, deliver sex and drug abuse education, and resolve incidents between students according to strictly prescribed sequences. Separate and often overlapping programs were developed to deal with social ills. Critics began to point out that schools were diluting their purpose by overdiversifying and trying to become social welfare agencies in addition to educators.

Government benevolence supplanted parental concern. Parental involvement diminished. An extreme form of liberal educational ideology was that in a multicultural society, cultural literacy was impossible and that many of the standards of the past should just be relaxed or abandoned. Manners, discipline, and communication became complicated by cultural diversity; better to back off than enforce our WASP traditions and language on African Americans, Asians, and Hispanics!

Of course, much of this ideology was in direct contrast and direct reaction to the prior era of schooling, that of building homogeneity and preparing for industrial expansion. The sentiments of progressive policy were mostly good, but the execution was often disastrous. The many attempts to improve or fix teaching were undertaken by politicians and other leaders who did not understand learning. The social agenda of liberal education was never integrated with learning science.

Then we had the next political swing of the pendulum. Conservatives took the higher ground. The rise of conservative ideology in the Reagan era brought with it the "back to basics" movement. Conservatives rightly pointed out the lack of standards in education but were unable to define authentic standards and engineer a method to realize them.

What was to be learned became more strictly defined as content, and how it was to be learned was memorization. The parameters of learning were narrowed to increase focus on the basics. How basics were to be more effectively taught was never really addressed. Accountability and measurability became the new mantras. They sounded good as a reaction to the excesses and chaos of the '60s, but they didn't use sound cognitive theory to provide a substantive solution.

The sentiments of both sides of the political divide are often well placed, but the progression from sentiment to logic to practice simply doesn't take place in an ideological context. George W. Bush wants "no child left behind." I believe him, but his solutions have already been proven inadequate, even counterproductive.

It is time we recognize that ideology can be represented in different approaches to schooling without universally controlling it. We can have military schools that emphasize discipline, schools that emphasize vocational rather than intellectual development, and schools that emphasize "emotional intelligence" and self-directed learning all in the same community.

When Jerry Brown, mayor of Oakland, California, suggested the idea of having military schools in underprivileged areas of Oakland, he provoked a vigorous outcry from the liberal community. Having been to a military school (and hated it), I still thought he had a good idea. Students who thrive in military schools find the discipline helpful and learn to have pride in themselves.

If the suggestion had come from within the community with some research to back up its benefits, along with information about the military being an equal-opportunity employer, perhaps it would have found a receptive audience. If we can segregate educational policy from the political arena, we will be taking a giant step forward.

The political right won't come right out and say that public education is an expensive nuisance—that it should be done away with altogether—though many of them feel that way. Politicians on the left won't tell you that they are fearful of alienating a voting block of three million voters, mostly democrats, who reliably vote.

A politician running for office should have little more to say about managing or reforming education than about managing or reforming the post office. He or she wants to buy your vote with high-minded rhetoric but doesn't have the time or the expertise to back it up with real solutions. The cost of this folly to you will be billions more spent on nonsolutions. We can effectively remove politicians from the process by telling them to separate the innovation process from political deliberation and leave it up to people with real depth of knowledge.

Then, politicians (especially local ones) can be congratulatory toward schools that adopt and effectively execute workable learning design. They can work toward a system that does not deny equal opportunity to districts that lack a tax base to put them on par with wealthier school districts. Finally, they can work toward partnerships among the private sector, communities, and public schooling to create new kinds of learning opportunities invented outside of the official channels. These are goals that belong in the political arena.

4. Teachers unions are not on our side.

We tend to think of unions in a couple of ways. Those with a sense of history tend to have deep appreciation for the role unions have played in giving a voice to worker grievances and to improving their working conditions, salaries, and benefits. Others view unions as creating needless self-sustaining adversarial bureaucracies in organizations where employees already have adequate leverage.

Public education is a special case where it is very hard to argue for the traditional view. In the first place, the unionization of taxpayer-supported public services is viewed askance by many. As a government monopoly, public education does not have competitive forces to respond to. This invites teachers unions to pay no attention to cost-benefit issues.

And isn't the welfare of our children adequate motivation for legislative bodies to ensure the rights and benefits of teachers? Is it not in the interest of school boards to provide for teachers' welfare? Imagine the U.S. Armed Forces with unions.

This is not to say that a union has never stepped in to protect a teacher from a vengeful principal or superintendent. However, the truth is that state governments and even the Supreme Court have intervened to create guarantees (of free speech and due process) that protect teachers from school boards and administrators who exhibit biased judgment.

The NEA (National Educational Association) and AFT have more than three million members. They not only represent a huge and influential voting block through political action committees (PACs) but also have an enormous influence on public policy. At the 1996 Democratic National Convention, 405 of the delegates were NEA members.

As the lobbying body for the largest employer in America (public education), teacher unions are not going to favor any kind of innovation that threatens their influence or the expansion of their labor markets. Consequently, they are opposed to vouchers (or any other form of privatization), charter schools, homeschooling, tuition tax credits, most forms of online or electronic learning, and large-scale innovations or experiments.

Teacher unions are an excellent example of producer groups that seek government protection of their interests without the benefit of demonstrable gains for their efforts. They spend huge sums of money influencing politicians. In 2000, the California Teachers Association contributed just shy of a million dollars to Governor Gray Davis and just over $400,000 to the State Superintendent of Public Instruction Delaine Eastin. Among other things, this money bought them one of the best tenure deals in public education—two years of teaching and you're in for life.

Just look at the record of productivity in public education. Coincidentally, or maybe not, it started to decline most sharply after unions reached their peak influence in the 1970s. During the same period, in today's dollars, teacher salaries actually declined.

Teachers pay substantial dues to their unions, and many union employees make in excess of $100,000 in salary and benefits. What do teachers get for this? What does the tax-paying public get for it?

It can be argued that the extended conflict within school districts, propagated by unions, has reduced the status of teachers. For a teachers union to get the public's attention, it must characterize the school board and/or the administration as inept. In response, school boards and administrators are obliged to point out that the teachers are relatively well paid (especially when pay is correlated to the number of days they work) and sometimes air their own dirty laundry by pointing out the lack of improvement in performance by teachers.

Clearly, this industrial-style, combative approach undermines public confidence. What then happens when voters go to the polls to vote for school bonds? Presumably, the real power of a union is to go on strike. Strikes further erode public confidence, put students at peril, and fly in the face of our laws.

In the new architecture of learning, unions may well disappear or else transform themselves into professional associations instead of collective bargaining entities. With a more proactive approach to representing teachers, they might think in terms of creating professional certifications and professional tiers for teachers that result in elevating their status and economic value. Professional dues could be used for training and monetary awards for exceptional performance instead of lobbying and lining the pockets of union bosses.

5. Schools do not develop initiative, creativity, or independent thought.

The natural cycle of maturation (and learning) is to move from tight controls and the supervision by elders to becoming self-managing and self-determined. Yet the practice of modern pedagogy is to control groups so that they may reflexively respond to universal inputs.

Were educators to declare that individuals have different needs, aptitudes, sensibilities, and values, it would lead to the inevitable conclusion that at the core of a free society is an imperative for individuals to make judgments about what is best for their own development.

In such a climate, schools would emphasize the development of self-management skills over external discipline. Their prime directive would be to bring young learners to a point where they are directed (with guidance from the community and counseling professionals) by their own judgment and where much of their learning is independently initiated and managed. The impulse to take charge of our own lives, to exercise our own judgment, is most crucial to encourage and develop us in making our own way in the world.

Yet, at the very time this impulse is generating the potent energy of adolescence, at every turn our schools are sending this message: "First know yourself? Forget about it. You aren't ready. You can't be trusted. This is when you need maximum controls over what you are doing and learning."

The very act of controlling thinking and behavior at this crucial time, I would assert, contributes greatly to the violence we see in secondary and middle schools. It is one of the prime directives of adolescence to challenge conventional wisdom and to overturn tradition.

When we respond with tight controls or with carrots and sticks, we rob adolescents of the dynamics that would encourage initiative, self-discipline, and the sense that they are free (in fact, welcomed) to develop into adulthood with its attendant freedoms and responsibilities.

There are potentially far more effective ways that the rebelliousness and experimentation of adolescence could be used proactively to develop young minds in positive and self-actualizing directions. This will be a cornerstone of the new architecture.

Ivan Illich's landmark treatise, *Deschooling Society*, was based on the assertion that the business of education is primarily to convince us that we have needs that can be satisfied only by the institution of schooling. As a society, we have to disabuse ourselves of this notion. Kids, by the millions, are doing so without knowing it by throwing the baby (learning) out with the bathwater (school).

It is a national tragedy that many of the same children who reject intellectual curiosity and mental discipline along with their rejection of school are highly intelligent and industrious people. They just don't want to "waste" their time in the stultifying atmosphere of school. They want to get out into the "real" world.

We now have the highest high school dropout rate of any industrialized nation when only a generation ago we had the highest graduation rate. To add insult to injury, we provide a second-chance credential to high school dropouts called a GED. Many think the first two letters stand for "graduate equivalency."

In fact, GED stands for "general education development" and consists of an eighth-grade-level reading test with some math thrown in. Its authentic purpose is to prepare the 860,000 plus who take it annually for the lowest-level jobs on our employment pyramid. But colleges are happy to take them in, even knowing that up to 75% will not make it through the first year. They want the tax money and the tuition.

The sad truth is that a significant proportion of our most independent, creative, and self-directed young people have nowhere to turn within the educational system and must reject it to validate these very qualities. This is a tragedy that must be corrected, or we will pay a steadily higher price.

6. Schools cannot accomplish the educative tasks of modern civilization on their own.

The most compelling classroom will always be the world at large. One of the major blunders of modern schooling is to separate and insulate children from the larger world.

You can be exposed to the abstractions and the formulas of geometry in a classroom. Some will have the discipline of a good student to memorize formulas for a test. But when you have to build a wall at a 75° angle and then install flooring and a roof to match, you don't have an option. The discipline developed by Euclid over 2,000 years ago is no longer a curiosity or an arcane discipline but an indispensable tool.

Consider how much kids would learn—the kind of learning that sticks—if they were to spend one month of their high school career building houses for Habitat for Humanity, Jimmy and Rosalynn Carter's charitable organization for building low-cost housing. Consider the skills integrated into a single experience (e.g., various aspects of carpentry, practical use of mathematics, learning about the underserved population of a particular community, working in teams, taking instruction effectively, training others to duplicate a task, the economics of designing and building low-cost housing, etc.).

In the scope of another book, one could describe experiences where schools collaborate with charities, social agencies, families, industry, professional associations, and civic agencies to contract or broker educational opportunities that pair intellectual underpinnings with real-world experiences. One of the major themes of such a book would be the integration of social and emotional competence with technical and intellectual knowledge.

There is much talk these days about emotional IQ and self-esteem but next to nothing in the way of a design to build these components into a secondary school curriculum. I believe this is because such qualities can be cultivated only in the real world, where learning becomes immediately invested in doing.

There are multiple (and sometimes overlapping) opportunities for volunteers to help fulfill a task in the educational community as it is presently conceived. These opportunities are not well publicized or promoted because there is a countervailing force in the hidden curriculum of schooling that says "leave it up to the professionals." A quasi volunteer organization modeled after the Peace Corps would be immune to "professional" resistance if, like the Peace Corps, its prime directive was to provide people with "real-world" skills that encouraged autonomy and self-reliance.

We are currently squandering an enormous resource by not finding ways for "boomers" to impart their skills (e.g., vocational trades, business, management, law enforcement, agriculture, engineering, etc.) to children and young adults. There is no better context in which to resurrect John F. Kennedy's maxim "Ask not what your country can do for you ...." Back to our chapter on where the money goes, I think an analog of the Peace Corps devoted to creating educational experiences in the real world (à la Habitat for Humanity) would allow for significant reductions in educational costs.

Back to the importance of harnessing the quest for freedom and identity, what schools often see only as adolescent rebellion, I would underscore the importance of directing young people into learning self-reliance-building tasks and skills no later than age 14. Up until the twentieth century, most 14-year-olds were already in the workforce.

There is more than a principle at work here. There is the need to change a paradigm. Earlier in this book, I brought up the philosophy of behaviorism and the thinking of early empiricists such as Locke (the mind is a blank slate) and Descartes. For purposes of identifying the paradigm, it might be useful to use Descartes' famous maxim "I think therefore I am" as indicative of the predominant mode of "academic" thought.

"Because I think, I am" begs the question "Am what?" The very word "academic" is associated both with "higher learning" and with "having no practical or useful significance."[7] The meaning we make from "thinking" is made not from thinking alone but comes from an interpersonal context that defines us through engaging with other humans in projects that are not solely limited to the solitary activities of our brains.

We don't think of a paradigm or about it. It thinks us. It is a built-in lens of perception. How many times have you heard an instructor say something like "Let's think together about what the terrorists really want"? There are no conventions in schooling for identifying the cumulative, meaningful relations that occur in patterns of mutual activity. Yet this is a profound and ubiquitous method of learning in the "real" world. It is the social basis for meaning and understanding that we are asked to dismiss in formal schooling.

In a new architecture, we must expand the definition and understanding of learning very explicitly beyond the realm of what an individual mind does by itself into the realm where we are what we share in thought, language, and deed with others through mutual commitments. In this realm, performance is evaluated by a socially negotiated standard that may issue from the community at large or a narrower community of practice.

As educational researcher Lauren Resnick puts it, school learning is individual and involves generalized theoretical principles and pure thought, and nonschool learning is shared and involves tool manipulation, contextualized learning, and situation-specific competencies.[8] It is absolutely imperative that we integrate the two.

As Harvard educational historian Lawrence Cremin put it, "A much broader view of education is demanded, one that sees schools and colleges as crucially important but not solely responsible."[9]

7. We have made schools our de facto nannies.

This is the dirty little secret we all share and for which we are virtually all to blame. Like all industrial societies, we have colluded to put kids away because we don't know where to put them if not behind the bulwarks of a school all day long. We have created a monster where parents, teachers, administrators, and the government are at odds because they all expect the school to take care of the physical, emotional, and intellectual needs of our children, and it can't be done without far more extensive involvement from society.

In a little more than a century, the school year has crept from 14 weeks to nine and a half months. International statistics show that nations with shorter school years perform better in competitive testing.

Contrary to popular belief, teaching is a good, reasonably well-paid, and secure job. Many teachers become discouraged with the mind-numbing routines and techniques of schooling and even come to recognize themselves as baby-sitters, yet they go through the motions because it's preferable to working in a corporate setting and less scary than the risks of entrepreneuring.

Learners know that the agenda of schooling is not paired to their needs. A certain percentage sees it in their interest to play the game, but many do not. Parents can generally conceive of no other option but to entrust their children's care and development to schools. It occurs to very few of us to conceive of alternatives. And government blames teachers, students, and the erosion of family for educational failure.

A second paradigm we need to shed is that of the school as nanny.

8. Learning has become equated with remembering.

Of course, we are all learning all of the time, but of what we learn in school, how much is remembered?

The renowned behaviorist B. F. Skinner, in his 1968 treatise on teaching (*The Technology of Teaching*), likened teaching humans to the training of pigeons. In the 1970s and '80s, it was frequently emphasized (influenced by the theorizing of Benjamin Bloom) that learning is a function of "time on task," another simplistic approach that underscored the drill and practice method. Without revisiting the application of learning theory in the classroom, suffice it to say that most of what we are charged with learning boils down to memorizing a bunch of stuff for a test.

Without boring you with statistics, just use your own memory and common sense to answer the question, How much is remembered? To be sure, it is a small fraction.

In designing a new architecture for learning, one of the basic questions underscoring the design of curricula ought to be "Is this going to be remembered in five years?" If not, why teach it? If something is deemed important to remember, how are we going to make the learning experience compelling enough to transfer it into long-term memory?

We need solid answers to these questions if school is going to become interesting, effective, and relevant.

Why do we ask a student to take a course that has no relevance whatsoever to a perceived need? If the need cannot be established, the course will be memorization of the most vexatious kind. Yes, of course, we use memory appropriately as part of the learning process. For instance, if we have a reason to be learning a language, memorizing vocabulary words will happen. And if we are going to actually use the language, we will tend to remember them.

Memory will always play a role in learning but not in the way it does now. As educators, we must learn to generate learning from appetite and not from control. As long as the process is so tightly controlled, it will mostly be distinguished by resistance (as in "Why am I learning this?") and forgetting (as in "OK, I passed the test—now I can forget it!").

The real problem with school doesn't hinge on what happens in the classroom but rather on the underlying theory of learning that generates what is happening. We make a mistake in expecting teachers and students to do better in the circumstances that are currently imposed on them.

It is as important for the brain to forget as it is for it to remember. The proportion of forgetting that now occurs is a function of the brain's common sense. "If I'm not going to use this, let's dump it!"

Consider an environment where learning was equated with growth or personal development and not a superior memory.

9. The United States is a dismal failure at vocational education.

In 2001, during the midst of a recession, 419,000 Americans with vocational/technical education landed jobs. Many such jobs went unfilled, and the situation is getting worse as many skilled technical workers are reaching retirement age. The average age of a skilled tradesperson is 48.

The types of jobs I'm talking about are those filled by construction workers, electrical workers, machinists, welders, medical technicians, and auto technicians. A commercial electrician makes up to $75,000 a year and a tool and die maker the same or more.

"Only 23% of work in the twenty-first century requires a four-year academic degree or higher; 43% of four-year college grads are underemployed, which means they have jobs that do not utilize degrees," according to Lucy Lazarony, writing for CBS *Market Watch.*

"Among college students who graduate with a professional credential (e.g., teaching engineering or accounting), only one in two will find related employment."[10] While the managerial/professional job classifications are generally at the top of the salary ladder, they represent only 20% of all jobs for which the competition is generally high.

Next in the salary pyramid are "craft, precision metal, and specialized repair" occupations in virtually every industry and every work environment—positions such as construction drafter, medical lab technician, manufacturing systems operator, computer repairperson, and paralegal—that pay well but require specific occupational skills available in secondary and postsecondary vocational-technical programs or apprenticeship programs.[11]

The type of employment described above is the fastest-growing segment of the labor market. The highest skilled and highest paid of these jobs require only a community college degree (two years) or a year of intensive education at a trade school.

Estimates indicate that only about a third of high school graduates have the aptitude and the academic preparation to succeed in college. In 1996, 27% of all college freshmen dropped out. Yet close to 90% of high school students indicate that they intend to go to college.

We have set up an expectation that will go unrewarded in the case of millions of young people—one that will create disillusionment and ill preparedness for the workforce. Much of this is the result of our attitudes about vocational education and our ignorance of the real exigencies of the labor market. These attitudes and this ignorance are alive and well in our secondary schools, which often consider the path that leads to vocational or technical education a lesser one.

Given that only about one-third of today's high school students actually benefit from a system that is geared toward preparing them for college, it would seem that we need a collective change of attitude and a better grasp of what's going on in the real world. Many other countries do not share our elitist view of college as the best destination for capable students. Many European and Asian countries have vocational education systems far more sophisticated than ours.

The most highly regarded approach to voc-tech training is that taken by Germany. Their system has been intensively studied and copied by many other countries. The German system is particularly well designed to prepare students for the real challenges of the workplace. The curricula are designed in accordance with actual vocational and corporate requirements.

The German system focuses on an apprenticeship where students make actual contracts to work for and be trained by an enterprise. Students then spend three to four days working at a company and one to two days at school. This process generally lasts three years and ends with an examination given by the associations or overseeing bodies of a particular industry.

Exams and examination committees in this system are made up of vocational teachers, the businesses students have worked for, and unions that represent the vocations. The curriculum is broken down into "learning fields" that correspond directly to a business activity. "A learning field is a complex set of knowledge acquirements and abilities necessary for performing a certain task."[12]

A learning field could be the production of a product component that would require a working drawing, determination of the correct materials, what tools will make it, and precise production specifications. It takes a great deal of work on the part of professional associations to continually update learning fields to correspond with technical innovations in the workplace.

In fact, new technical vocations are generated constantly. Information technology changes almost daily, and in an area as specific as metal processing, about 20 new compounds have recently evolved.

To keep up with this blinding pace, Germany's Federal Institute of Vocational and Technical Education and other research bodies are designing a system to "diagnose" qualification requirements and their changes ASAP. This involves analysis of jobs that remain vacant, new job descriptions, sending questionnaires to companies, and continuing analysis of existing voc-tech course offerings.

Only a commitment of this depth and magnitude can keep up with change in this world.

You may have noticed that we are importing the skills of more and more Indians, Russians, and East Asians to take these kinds of jobs because we simply aren't preparing young people in sufficient quantities to fill needed positions. It will get worse, and in a few years, the economic consequences will be felt as other countries develop superior technicians and vocational workers and, therefore, superior products.

The National Assessment of Vocational Education (NAVE) issued a five-volume report arguing that vocational (as well as general) education must improve substantially to prepare students for high-skill, high-wage jobs.[13]

Secondary voc-ed enrollments are dropping, and the percentage of disabled and economically disadvantaged people and immigrants enrolled in them has increased. We have a serious perception problem to deal with as well as a quality problem. Less than half of the voc-ed courses taken in our school system are actually used on the job.

For years, vocational educators and business leaders have been pointing out that our educational system is particularly unresponsive to the marketplace in vocational and technical occupations. As we move into the future, we need to think in terms of specific competencies (accompanied by certifications à la the German model) as key to a responsive educational system.

There are many certifications (e.g., desktop publishing, computer graphics, various information technology and medical technology skills) that could be learned in secondary school, providing certified students with substantial wage-earning skills.

Not everyone should go to college, and not everyone who goes to college should do so right out of high school. For a variety of reasons, economic, emotional, and developmental, many young people would benefit from developing a substantial earning capacity first as a foundation to build a career through further education in school or in the workplace.

This is a simple but difficult shift in point of view that many of us must make in order to embrace a blueprint for learning that is appropriate to the twenty-first century. In fact, 10 or 15 years down the road, prestige may begin to shift away from a college degree toward the kind and degree of certificates you hold, which would represent an integrated composite of marketable and bankable skills.

I hope the liberal arts degree never disappears, but we must be able to build in the world of formal learning a closer relationship with the world of work and its advances. In such a rapidly changing environment, blocks of learning (certificates) become a generally more realistic adaptation to the real world. In this world, a certificate, or three, from a community college here and a trade school there may have more monetary value than many baccalaureate degrees from prestigious universities.

10. The priorities of American education are "upside down and inside out."

"Upside down" refers to the order of priorities. In 1998, we spent an average of $5,371 educating a primary school student and $16,262 educating a university student.[14]

The World Bank has strongly advocated in its policy papers that countries will yield a higher social and economic return by reallocating government spending to reduce the cost of higher education and increase investment particularly in primary education.

If we think of schooling as a cognitive incubation process, it becomes very obvious where the emphasis of resources must be. Everything we know about how the brain develops tells us that we have only five or six years from the time kids begin schooling to build the biological foundation for self-directed "higher" learning. The first three to four years are most critical. Yet we expend our resources as if developing learners need more support as they age and progress through school.

This is where "inside out" comes into play.

Many, including myself, would argue that the dynamics we set in motion by not developing independent thinking and learning skills at an early age account for many of the problems that come with adolescence today. Remember, it was the American model of education that essentially created extended adolescence.

It is the "prime directive" of adolescence to begin taking charge of one's life. As this event occurs, we should have imparted the fundamental knowledge and age skills of independent learning, innovative thinking, problem solving, risk taking, and the ability to instigate and function well in collaborative situations.

If this were accomplished, secondary and higher learning would look very different. The pendulum of teaching would have swung over to learning. It is likely we would have different names for "teacher" and "professor." No more inside out.

As you imagine such an environment, picture yourself as a learning customer, with all institutions of learning having a primary responsibility to fulfill contracts you make with them. Imagine such institutions having the ethics of the Nordstrom department stores. "We are here to help and guide you, not to shove anything down your throat. If you are unhappy, if you haven't received the value you expected, we will make it right."

If the onus of learning has actually passed to the "learner," this picture is possible. You can't blame a facilitator for not learning, only for failing to fulfill obligations (of guiding) that you, the learner, have requested. It's a picture that requires much "suspension of disbelief" today. As we move into the future, the image should become easier to form.

It is the guiding principal in moving toward a new architecture.

Endnotes

1 Benjamin Rush, from "Plan for the Establishment of Public Schools," 1786
2 David F. Labaree, *How to Succeed in School without Really Learning*, Yale University Press, 1962, p. 114
3 See "15 Years after a *Nation at Risk*," *http://www.edreform.com/pubs/then&now.htm*
4 See Paul Krugman, "Death and Taxes," *New York Times*, June 14, 2000
5 Murat F. Iyigu and Ann L. Owen, "Risk, Entrepreneurship and Human Capital Accumulation" for the Board of Governors of the Federal Reserve System, 1997, p. 2
6 Averaged from ACT statistics, last available survey 1997
7 *Webster's New Collegiate Dictionary*, see "academic"
8 See Lauren Resnick, "Learning in School and Out," *Educational Researcher*, December 1987
9 Lawrence Cremin, *Popular Education and Its Discontents*, N.Y., 1990, p. 73
10 See Michael E. Wonacott, "Benefits of Vocational Education," ERIC Archives, 2000
11 Ibid.
12 Volker Ihde, "The Dual System of Vocational Education in Germany—Basic Assets of the System and Its Adaptation to the Challenges of the 21st Century," *http://www.ceaie.edu.cn/whatsnew/htm*
13 See "Vocational Education Here and Abroad," *http://www.ed.gov/bulletin/fall1994/voced.html*
14 Organization for Economic Co-Operation and Development, from the Centre for Educational Research and Development, "Education at a Glance," 1998 statistics

Part III:
The Future

Chapter 13

BACK TO THE FUTURE ALL OVER AGAIN

The future is here; it's just not evenly distributed yet.
—William Gibson

In times of change, learners inherit the earth,
while the learned find themselves beautifully
equipped for a world that no longer exists.
—Eric Hoffer

Becoming acquainted with the future requires, among other things, a leap of faith—in the case of learning, maybe the greatest. It's easy to visualize airborne automobiles, bio-domes, and "cruises" to Mars. You may have noticed in most portrayals of the future that people appear to be the same. Their clothes change, but their socialization, level of aggression, and overall wisdom seem to remain the same.

As Einstein put it, "*We can't solve today's problems with yesterday's thinking.*" So, we can picture things that haven't happened yet as long as they don't involve new paradigms of thought or evolved levels of humanity.

This journey into the future will invite you to think in new ways. It will encourage you to let go of cherished beliefs in order to conceive of new possibilities. This is the "muscle" that we most need to develop. It seems to most characterize the biggest brains as well as the most compassionate beings.

In fact, to begin portraying the future, we first have to catch up, to take an inventory of where we are, what we have become, what we are becoming, and what we can become. The answers to these questions form the basis for creating a new architecture. They also lead us to aim beyond the convenient and merely technical and toward specific human objectives.

Education has been pragmatic, learning in order to do. Doesn't who we are interact profoundly with what we do? If this is true, can we create learning design for being and becoming simultaneous to and integrated with doing? Can learning objectives actually include carefully defined changes in human consciousness?

To bring these questions to life requires some genuine understanding of how the world has changed; how our social, psychological, and spiritual development has or hasn't changed; and finally, some consensus on what and how we must learn to better exploit our cognitive capacities. To illustrate the point, let's provide an example or two.

Language is most essential to what made us human. Its first phase was speech.

About 5,000 years ago, in the area now called Iraq, writing was developed. Writing gave us recorded history. It brought what we refer to as "civilization."

Now we are entering a third human transformation. "With electronic yarn, we are knitting our disparate selves into a whole self."[1] "We can now transfer our eyes and our ears, instantly, to any point whatsoever. Our sensory reach has transcended a spatial barrier that has been in place from the beginning of time. Information that is available anywhere is now available everywhere."[2]

The world is now a global network requiring a different kind of social organization to support it. The human need to communicate is beginning to take precedence over physical infrastructure, including national boundaries. In the developing world, countries face critical decisions such as whether we should build freeways with current resources or invest in an advanced communications network.

The need for political factions and nations at odds to communicate has never been greater. Between the first and second Iraq wars, Saddam Hussein wanted the Iranians, whom he feared, to believe that he still had weapons of mass destruction. Yet he wanted very much to initiate a dialogue with the United States, presumably to let us know that he did not have them. Saddam was unable to open channels of communication. He did not understand the impact of 9/11 on the United States and ignored his own advisors' advice to issue a condolence. These are the high costs of our collective failures to communicate.

Skeptics might recoil at the notion that better communication is our best political and economic weapon, but the signs are hard to ignore. We have confronted the fact that we have the capacity to destroy ourselves and our habitat and are beginning to struggle with the implications. International governing organizations (i.e., the U.N., NATO, the World Trade Organization, the World Bank, the European Union) are proliferating.

Despite the seeming level of conflict in the world, international cooperation and trade are steadily increasing. International conferences are taking place in record numbers to address worldwide health, political, environmental, and economic problems. The issue of human rights for citizens of all nations is creating international laws and ostracizing nations that do not comply.

The growing awareness of differing cultures, ethnicities, and religious beliefs is creating a de facto global culture. We are entering into an age that will be largely characterized by an increasing "conceptual infrastructure of global civilization."[3]

Such changes are creating an obligatory "postmodern" global phenomenon where tradition, adaptation, and innovation must collide and, ultimately, interact. Tradition, contemporary (or popular) culture, and the synthesis of shared and diverse human experience are blending whether we like it or not. To participate in this process consciously is one of the great challenges of the new millennium and of education.

Alongside "globalism" and all it implies is another enormous evolutionary change. We are shifting from a century determined and shaped by physics and mechanistic principles to an era informed and reorganized according to biological principles. The twentieth century gave us railroads, automobiles, airplanes, space travel, nuclear bombs, telephones, television, and computers. The twenty-first century will provide us with genetic products that profoundly alter how we live and how we think about life.

As UC professor and futurist Gregory Benford puts it, "We stand on the threshold of the Biological Century … biology has turned aggressively useful." With increasing eagerness, we anticipate using genetic code to design microbes, rebuild body parts, build designer foods and drugs, and even augment the powers of our brains.

The mind reels: toothpaste with a designer bacterium that eats plaque; supermicrobes that live in your stomach or liver and eat bad bacteria that cause diseases; giant raspberry-flavored bananas; designer insects that eat mosquitoes, aphids, and all manner of destructive insects; an injection of T cells that repairs a damaged heart or kidney; seeds that can be programmed to grow into living inhabitable structures; designer organisms that release a measured amount of a drug according to the body's needs. We can't begin to conceive of the panoply of biological solutions to environmental, medical, industrial, agricultural, and energy production challenges.

At the microbial level, it is known that, through adaptation, microbes have long ago solved many of the problems scientists are still trying to understand. Microbes make up an estimated 60% of the earth's biomass. Less than 1% of microbial species have ever been closely described. Many can withstand extremes of temperature, radiation, and lack of light and thrive where no other forms of life can. The implications of understanding and transferring their adaptive capacities are enormous.

Discussion about the Information Age has heretofore tended to leave out the information inherent to genetic code and microbial sequences—biological information. The information to be mined from this endeavor is mind boggling. The limitations of biotechnology are clearly beyond our present ability to imagine. So are the threats.

Then there's the human brain, still with 10 billion times the capacity of our biggest "supercomputers." What happens when we can modify its biological "wiring" or change its chemistry to make us more focused, more alert, less inhibited, more joyful, imbued with photographic memory, or more compliant, more subdued, less emotional (e.g., violent)? What are the implications—good and bad?

How will the impact of "bionomics" affect society? When the rich can afford to purchase genetic immunities, cosmetic advantages, and better brains, what will happen to class separation? Will it become far more pronounced, or can we spread the benefits?

What is the dark side of biotechnology (biological weapons, economic slavery, designer microbes turning into unstoppable killers, ecological destabilization, genetic programming for frivolous or nefarious ends)? How do we balance opportunity and risk?

How do we even think about a world in which biological principles (i.e., self-organization, complex nonlinear responses, self-replication, and built-in adaptation) replace the deterministic and linear principles of mechanical laws? Surely, we face major and extended moral, legal, environmental, and religious debates. These issues present our brains with great and complex challenges. How do we incorporate these challenges into a new learning model?

Should we not be learning, in detail, about our ongoing status in the world? The United States is now the only true superpower. What are the responsibilities, the risks, and the opportunities that accompany this status? Should this not be an ongoing national discussion in which students vigorously participate?

Currently, there is an appalling lack of knowledge among our citizens as to the effects of U.S. policy on the rest of the world or the history that has led to many current circumstances such as the conflict in the Middle East. The founding fathers would almost certainly concur that we have wandered astray of the initial purpose for universal education—to create an informed populace that can comprehend the implications and consequences of our actions.

I have begun with the "what" of learning. What are we to focus on in the face of rapid technological and systems management evolution? To address the how and why is even more difficult because it requires that we approach learning design from inside the solution, attuned to the higher functions of our brains—a perspective largely outside of our experience. Surely, this is a design process that will require much discovery, calibrating our creative capacities to newly emerging domains of knowledge.

In approaching a new design, I will suggest a set of prime directives to guide the thinking and the design process. In the earlier stages of the book, I have deconstructed education to point out the thinking (or lack of it) behind our present course. Now we assemble the principles that give us a foundation for a new architecture of learning.

Architecture: def.

the art, profession, or science of designing and constructing (buildings) substitute *learning events, environments, learning tools, and experiences here.*

The term "architecture" conveys a comprehensive way of thinking about the physical, social, intellectual, and psychological aspects of things. Moorish architecture is a very different way of thinking than classical Greek. Architectures can become clearly obsolete and economically unfeasible as times change.

As has been already addressed in this book, the way we think about learning environments is simply obsolete. In order to rethink, to come up with a way of designing learning events and environments that embraces the world we inhabit today, we must create relevant theorems that guide our actions as did the Prussians in designing the system that became the last complete model for our current system of education.

The "prime directives" I identify in Chapter 14 are an initiative to launch a public conversation toward this end. The public didn't have any say in designing a school system that was recommended and funded by the richest American industrialists for their own reasons. Today, we are subject to that same system though it has been dressed up to appear more democratic. I propose that we who utilize and pay for this system find a way to define and endorse a new set of principles to guide it. I strongly suggest that those principles be focused on optimizing the process of learning itself.

In a very real sense, the future is here. Certain developments, issues, and conflicts are inevitable. Learning in the twenty-first century should be designed to anticipate and foresee just as it now records and remembers. This is a recent and crucial element of learning. On the brink of this millennium, it is reasonable to suggest that anticipation and vision must come more into the foreground of the learning process. Would it not be wise to benchmark this point in human evolution by holding education accountable for establishing and guiding us toward measures of evolutionary progress?

The most important thing to note about the future is that it steadily encroaches. Human ingenuity has far surpassed our ability to comprehend and integrate our capabilities—most of all to optimize their use on our behalf. Put simply, our wisdom has not caught up with our technology. Within this gap lies enormous untapped human potential. It is within our reach but not in our grasp.

Endnotes

1   See "Seeing the Forest—An Evolutionary View of Communication," *http://www.river.org/~jerry/forest.htm*

2   Ibid.

3   From "INGOs and the Organization of World Culture," John Boli and George M. Thomas, editors, Stanford University Press, 1999

Chapter 14

THE PRIME DIRECTIVES

*The scandal of education is that every time
you teach something, you deprive a child of
the pleasure and benefit of discovery.*
—SEYMOUR PAPERT

*We teachers can only help the work going on,
as servants wait upon a master.*
—MARIA MONTESSORI

The numbered subtitles that will follow here are intended to be the underpinnings, or "prime directives" of the new learning architecture. We begin with a radical statement made by Humberto Maturana on the nature of cognition.

As "rational" beings, we like to think of truth and reality as consensual. Closer examination, however, reveals that we all exist in and relate from subcultures of personality, family, ethnicity, language, and gender, each with their own reality and their own truths.

Making sense of the world stems from the interplay of multiple separate realities. What we think of as an individual is made up of memories, beliefs, values, instincts, impulses, appetites, and curiosities. All of these are components of our worldview. They are constantly affecting perception and, in turn, being altered by emotion. Emotion has more to do with what we learn and become than fact.

Set into motion the intersubjectivity of such "individuals" relating to one another and what happens to objectivity? What happens to the consensus reality in which we supposedly participate? What happens when one sets out to teach something of any complexity to another or to a diverse group?

1. There is no instructive interaction.

Chilean biologist Humberto Maturana made one of the most controversial statements of the twentieth century when he said, "There is no instructive interaction." What did he mean?

Without getting into complex biological ideas such as autopoiesis, epigenisis, and the ontology of cognition, the simplest explanation of Maturana's assertion is that learning happens only when we are teaching ourselves something that is relevant to us. That which is learned must be intimately connected to our priorities, our own beliefs and identities, our own path of inquiry. What becomes truly "known" to each of us is unique.

Furthermore, what we tend to accept as reality is riddled with ignorance. Not long ago, it was a reality that we could not transmit images and text messages instantaneously around the world. Today, it is reality that life is carbon based, that wars are necessary to solve conflicts, and that most of us won't live to be 100. "Reality" is not a static phenomenon or even a shared one. It is constantly emerging.

Teaching as we have generally conceived it supposes a primarily known universe in which knowledge is simply deposited from a teacher to a student. It creates an academic worldview in which the factual "objective" world is true and the "subjective" is unreliable. This does great injustice to the search for truth that is innate to all of us. It negates the trusting of our curiosity and our instincts, our subjective selves.

We are expected to believe that classrooms disseminate clockwork patterns of knowing and understanding in which we can all participate and in which what is learned is predictable. We are asked to accept that schools are repositories of a growing body of knowledge that we can universally understand and use.

We are schooled to believe that authority knows best. The result is that we live in an increasingly passive culture where we accept "truths" from a variety of sources without much question or concern for the consequences of our passivity.

The adage "*Are you believing what you see or seeing what you believe?*" is a key dilemma for today's schooled mind.

Teaching, as we have come to know it, does not readily acknowledge or accept a world of multiple realities and multiple understandings and truths. Such a view, under the current system, would invite chaos.

Yet, if we are honest, "teaching" a group of individuals is indeed chaotic. How can the outcomes be predictable? How can the lesson, as conceived by the teacher, have the same relevance to and impact on each learner?

Maturana's statement is the first prime directive of the new architecture because it recognizes what is most core about learning: that each person has unique needs, interests, learning style, and pace and, ultimately, a unique reality. When we make this the first axiom, we must not only organize around individual learners but also endeavor to understand and honor their views—what creates meaning and mission for them.

In a world where the largest professional occupation is teaching, this may be the toughest pill to swallow, yet we might call it the Golden Rule of learning.

The goal of the new architecture is not just to redesign learning but to repair a flawed worldview that science, the very discipline that created it, has long since debunked. The new worldview is one in which truth is not something we force-feed people but rather something we are constantly in search of and something that is altered by each perceiver. It is a model with biological rather than mechanistic underpinnings.

This biological worldview of learning begins with intrinsic motivation and self-organization, not externally controlled learning—hence Maturana's maxim. Implicit in this view is that learning is first and foremost about learning to learn—a shift from accepting packaged truths, mimicking, and memorizing to thinking for ourselves. It is a lifelong process.

2. Learning to learn is the primary objective of formal education.

The second prime directive underwrites a shift in emphasis from teaching to learning how to learn. This question will be raised: Are the two mutually exclusive? I am not arguing here for the elimination of teachers. I am arguing for a redirection of their focus and responsibilities. It would be a much wiser use of the word "teacher" if it was discriminately used by learners to describe someone from whom they could clearly say they have learned.

When the student is ready, the lesson appears.
—GENE OLIVER

If we stop thinking of teachers as stewards of knowledge, as responsible for the teaching of content, and start thinking of them as facilitators of learning, particularly learning how to learn, a major shift begins to occur—a shift in which the responsibility for learning, and the skills that go with it, fall into the appropriate hands.

In this schema, our primary resources in education go to developing the cognitive and intellectual skills of learners as they encounter questions and challenges that have captured their interest. The successful course of study is one where a learner has demonstrated new capabilities to understand big ideas, translate concept into practice, and comprehend implications not readily apparent. These criteria are not measured by the means we largely use today.

The third prime directive naturally follows from the first two. The first two are concepts or new ways to look at learning. The third is a precept, a call for action in the new universe our concepts create.

3. Learning is demand driven, not supply driven.

When children enter school, they are supercharged engines of curiosity. Their brains take in all that is in their path. It is seemingly random to the casual observer, but to them, it is always relative to their own journey. Curiosity is the engine of the journey, and self-directed inquiry is the compass. Only severe trauma or brain damage can impair this all-powerful momentum. Oh yes, and school can too.

To forego the design of our brains is perhaps the grandest human error. We make it too often and in many ways, but, most of all, we make it in deciding what each child should learn, deciding when, how much, how fast, and for what purpose.

> *The greatest sign of success to a teacher is to be able to say,*
> *"The children are now working as if I did not exist."*
> —Maria Montessori

Unbridled curiosity and spirited inquisitiveness—these are the true earmarks of optimal learning. We must not break this natural chain. A design process in keeping with the brain's own design will strongly signal to each learner that he or she is the steward of his or her own body of knowledge. Our strongest responsibility to learners is to help them seek out information that produces perspective, discernment, and trust in their own capabilities.

The instructionist view of learning is a form of social Darwinism. It assumes that the fittest (smartest) in the classroom will do well. This is tragic because the so-called fittest are not necessarily the smartest. The fittest in traditional schooling are often the pleasers, the performers, the average thinkers. Einstein was considered a near moron for a lengthy period of his schooling, as was Thomas Edison. They were not performers.

Creative thinkers, those who question things deeply, natural innovators, and leaders are often not suited to an approach that relies on teaching (pedagogy) as the prime route to learning. Too often, the "wrong" answer in a classroom is truth from a different perspective.

When we set out to organize around the learner, we summon the most powerful learning engine imaginable, the human brain. It has its own structure, its own "best practices." The search for meaning needs no mediation or motivation. The central questions Socrates asked, "Who am I? What is important to know? How do I know what I know?" are innate. As we learn to articulate and apply the meta-curriculum that engages the brain's innate capacities, getting the curriculum part right will be easy. It will have its own marching orders for each individual.

Learning on demand also means any time, any sequence, any pace, and any place. This notion tends to unravel traditional educators. "What about intellectual continuity?" Learners will follow the path of least resistance. They will go off on trivial pursuits to whet their peculiar appetites. "Where is the logical progression, the framework of organization?"

These are legitimate concerns, yet they are conditioned by our own schooling. Can we imagine how things would be different if school was widely perceived as **the** place for exploration and discovery, if it was seen as a staging place for forays of discovery and accomplishment in the real world—forays dictated by learners' emerging curiosity and commitments? What if play was an integral part of the learning process? These are the motivations for learning, and we have put them aside to make way for a linear process that gives us the illusion of control. The fact is that we never had control, and we never will.

Control we cannot have, but influence we do have. Learners naturally want to approach those who have knowledge that can help. When they know someone is there with the primary intent to help them along their paths, they will view this person, and others, as necessary to their success. Where learning is concerned, when we let go of control, we gain influence. To let go of control is to create an environment where learners, to the greatest possible extent, choose a broad-based inquiry into the world and ask for help when they need it.

Organizing around learners begs the question of how to keep an individual learning path broad and focused, rigorous and interesting, moving progressively toward higher objectives. Naturally, it will become necessary to council learners in a myriad of ways, to help them discover where proclivities, interests, aptitudes, and achievements might take them. Juggling multiple learning objectives will need a complex and interdependent parallel process using multiple advisors to identify next steps.

Advisor to a 13-year-old student: *Johnny, you are doing so well with numbers, and you seem to like solving puzzles. I've also noticed that you draw a lot of buildings. Do you have any idea what you might want to do with these skills out in the world?*

Student: *Well, I like to play video games that use math and puzzles, and I like to build things where I need to measure a lot. I made a fort out of Popsicle sticks at home.*

Advisor: *That's great. Do you know what geometry is? Do you know that carpenters have to use it to build houses? Would you like to be able to build a real fort, one that people will really use? In other words, would you like to start learning how to build more stuff?*

Student: *Yeah, that would be cool.*

Advisor: *Well, maybe we should start by introducing you to a few different kinds of things that you could learn to build. For example, a person who builds cars knows different things than a person who builds bridges. Even a person who builds big buildings like the one your dad works in knows different stuff than a guy who builds houses.*

Student*: I think I would like building houses like the new ones they are building by Kennedy Park.*

Advisor*: OK, that sounds great. Let's look at some things that will help you get good at that. I already mentioned geometry. I'll bet you never thought of this, but an art class can help you learn how to make a house look nice. You can even use your skill with numbers to make interesting art. Let me find an example of an artist who does that and show it to you. The person who designed those houses by Kennedy Park really knows how to make houses look nice. Don't you think?*

Student*: Yeah, I really like the way those houses look.*

Advisor*: Do you think you would like building houses more or designing them?*

Student: *I'm not sure, probably designing them.*

Advisor: *Well, let's see if we can help you figure that out. I've got a video on being an architect that will help you understand how a person who designs houses thinks and what that person does every day.*

Now, Johnny takes geometry and learns art with a purpose in mind. Along the way, he may likely discover that he is interested in other things. Maybe the art project he does inspires him to design things that are non-symmetrical. Maybe in geometry, he becomes interested in how to design a building that is round instead of rectangular.

Hundreds of conversations like this need to take place as a learner matures and acquires the skill to define his or her own direction or seek out from advisors the requisite skills to gain mastery over a discipline. Every course of inquiry should be considered an exploration into how what is learned can be used.

Curriculum itself becomes viewed as an ongoing conversation. Each learner is continually engaged in questions like, "What is important to you to understand? What do you see unfolding before you now, as a result of what you are learning? What questions do you have about a subject, and what questions arise from it about the world? What are you learning about yourself, and how do you see yourself in the world?" All of these questions turn back to learning about how to learn and learning about what to learn.

The facilitators who participate with learners in these questions are subject matter experts, psychologists, experts on developmental learning and cognitive style. They are also career specialists, able to break a practice down to its component skills, to shop talents in the marketplace, and to anticipate the needs of multiple industries and professions.

Grade levels and large classes are methods of organization that do not serve individual talents and interests, learning pace, or style. They may have some utility for early curriculum, the three R's, and the initial stages of learning skills training. But organizing around learners will cause a rapid destabilization of uniform learning process design.

I leave the particulars to experts, but I anticipate that somewhere around the third or fourth grade, a new architecture will progressively migrate toward unbundling learners. Grade levels will disappear as learners begin to codesign individualized learning plans. Traditional classes from this point on will commonly have learners of different ages, though often kept within certain age limits.

In such an organizational pattern, learners will accelerate in some areas, distancing others in their age group as they slow down in other areas to explore in more depth and retreat to places where better foundations can be built. These are the natural rhythms of learning. It is common for readers who start out seemingly stunted to be stars when their reading skills take off a year or more after other classmates'. It is critical that we accommodate these rhythms even in the early grades.

In principle as well as practice, we must recognize that organizing around the learner transfers a large responsibility and does not confer to the learner the privilege of becoming a petty tyrant. The loosening of controls need not promote a narcissistic orientation to knowledge.

4. Building knowledge is a social activity.

We strive to make sense of the world just as the world needs to make sense of us. We share the fundamental need to be in relation with one another. Our drive to understand and the language that enables us to do so permanently bind us together.

We all participate in a collective consciousness. It is our nature to seek a higher level of consciousness—to comprehend the human condition so that we may be guided forward. Communication is the sharing of a common context, a bond of knowing, and a bond of learning—about one another, from one another. Civility (and a civil society) does not evolve without discovering the standards of participation and reciprocity in a community, the tacit knowledge that informs convivial and cooperative behavior.

Yes, we are individuals in this. We make our own way. But this is possible only through the collective intelligence. Without participation in the capability of a group to use its complementary skills and interests to decide its course and act upon it, we literally cannot learn. The first group is family, the next community. The world is a community with common interests, though this may seem an oxymoron at times—and this above all, the human condition, is what drives us to learn.

There are specific skills and proceedings that enable participation in communities. We learn to appreciate and seek out what "has gone before" in an accumulated body of knowledge. We learn to recognize what others offer that completes our own perspectives. We learn what makes us more learned for having contributed to the knowledge and capabilities of others. Perhaps most important, we alter our consciousness from paying attention to the good of a group.

If we extend ourselves into the world, the possibility of stimulating, inspiring, and like-minded communities expands. Community is no longer only a function of place. If you are the only single Jewish motorcyclist in your little town, the possibility now exists to find or create a community of SJMs from all over the world.

Communities are clearly essential to the learning process, yet we have failed dismally to make use of their resources, to involve them more directly in education. The new architecture makes this an immediate priority. Intelligence is primarily the capacity to learn, discern, reason, adapt, imagine, and create. These are the core needs of social beings.

Communities form the crucible in which we learn to resolve conflicting desires and discover many of our innate talents. By working things out with our neighbors and peers, we become less egocentric and more capable of making our way in the world. Clearly, schools do a poor job of fostering these capacities and of using communities and the family to do so.

We often berate children as uncivilized. Could this be largely because we have isolated them from family and community in schools?

5. The nature of knowledge is building connections.

After Albert Einstein's death, neuroscientists were eager to examine his brain to find out whether it was bigger. They found that it wasn't bigger, but it had stronger and significantly more neuronal connections, the infrastructure that allows the brain to link one source of information with another.

The parsing of knowledge into disciplines has a purpose, and it has negative side effects. If we could look at all knowledge, it would look like an intricate borderless web: all values, all sectors, and all meanings linked to one another. Neural networks within the brain work the same way.

And, yet, what we have in the formal world of learning is the compartmentalization of knowledge into academic subjects. The pursuit of these subjects leads to mountains of compiled data, and, as writer/teacher James Burke put it, "People tend to become experts in highly specialized fields, learning more and more about less and less."

Specialized pursuits, while leading to technical advances, have produced avalanches of information that no human being can keep up with.

Understanding becomes narrow instead of broad. Thus, we breed increasingly more specialists. What is learned often becomes inert if its implications are not explored across disciplinary borders, if it is not applied from one's own view of things.

Cognitive science combines such disparate fields as philosophy, linguistics, neurology, anthropology, computer science, and biology. The complexity of understanding ecological science involves at least as many disciplines. Perhaps this is why so many today cannot grasp the implications of ecological instability. Deeper learning, today more than ever, involves the decompartmetalization of knowledge.

The kind of "understanding" we now disseminate in schools, devoid of context and real application, is not conducive to developing the higher-level cognitive skills that lead to the integration of knowledge and, ultimately, wisdom.

It is common for a student to get excited about one course or subject and then apply his or her interest and learning skills only within that discipline and only to school-related assignments. It is far less common to see a student become voraciously curious about a subject, explore sources of knowledge on his or her own, and then jump into other disciplines as a direct result. Yet this kind of behavior is far more indicative of brilliant and innovative minds.

Universities have increasingly created departments of interdisciplinary studies to try to correct the kind of minds we have created in primary and secondary schools. Of course, the right place to make this correction is where it happened in the first place. When deficiencies in areas of knowledge are identified, they are often the result of combining fields of study.

Were we to develop cross-disciplinary thinking early, we could expect a renaissance in the search for deeper understanding. To move in this direction begins with a much higher degree of focus (in learning design) on the implications of what is supposed to have been "learned."

As an example, suppose that we follow up with a discussion of the implications of the Magna Carta in a high school European history class:

We now have a phrase that is used in conversations about politics and what is needed to build a civilized nation. It is called "the rule of law." How did the Magna Carta bring this idea to England? What was the idea about law before the Magna Carta? How were landowners better off with the Magna Carta? Did the Magna Carta benefit non-landowners in any way? The Magna

Carta was made into many handwritten copies with the king's seal on them and then read publicly all over England. Why was this important? In what other ways was life different before this? How did this change the way people started to think?

Questions are more key to understanding than answers. They invite reasoning, more inquiry, the consideration of implications, and deliberation among peers.

When the English started coming over to America to start colonies for England, they brought charters (copied on paper with the king's seal) guaranteeing them and their children "all liberties and immunities of free and natural subjects." How were they able to bring these freedoms over to America? How was monarchy everywhere changed by the Magna Carta? Since the colonists in America did not wind up getting the freedoms they were guaranteed, what did they wind up doing about it? Do you think they had that right? What might give you the right to revolt now? How did the Magna Carta lead to the idea of democracy? Who were the next nations to revolt against a king? How do we get rights today that we don't have? What are some examples of this? Can you think of any important rights that are not being honored here in the United States today?

An event in history, important enough to be an exam question, accompanied by a few spare comments by a teacher, can easily become an extended discussion where implications, past, present, and future, are explored. Key to cultivating deeper understanding and curiosity is the posing of questions that link events, ideas, and disciplines with subjects that are important to individuals. The more we do this, the more we elevate a diminished capacity in our culture to connect the dots from history to philosophy, science, art, technology, and contemporary issues.

Extended conversations like the one above might diminish the breadth of curriculum in favor of depth. But, what is anchored in memory while exploring a subject in-depth will accrue to it unfolding strings of inquiry and knowledge due to its importance and universality.

Gregory Bateson, a multidisciplinary scientist and one of the great thinkers of the twentieth century, frequently spoke of the "pattern that connects." He went to great lengths to point out that at the core of learning is the recognition of patterns: physical patterns, historical patterns, patterns of behavior, and, most of all, patterns of meaning.

The advancement of knowledge is a great dialogue among civilizations, big ideas, scientific disciplines, and technical endeavors. It is a dialogue among philosophy, science, religion, art, and commerce. Each domain of thinking is its own society with its own values, assumptions, and practices. To comprehend the differences is to think in patterns while simultaneously learning to think outside of them.

The composer thinks in patterns as does the poet. To bring the skill of a poet to science, the talent of a composer to business, this is the stuff of applied genius.

Bateson observed a tool of thought that was absent at all levels of academic learning. It was ignorance of the presuppositions that guide a discipline of knowledge. In identifying patterns that connect, Bateson often pointed out that entering into knowledge is inextricably bound to accepting what is already presumed to be so. Without examining these tacit assumptions, the wherewithal to question and push boundaries becomes stunted.

For example, a tacit assumption of the study of medicine is that we wait for a person to exhibit symptoms of a disease before taking action. There are many implications of such an assumption. It is these kinds of understanding that need to be flushed out in order to create learners who ask powerful questions and pose innovative solutions.

Today, there is no discipline whose core purpose is to explore the effects of combining disciplines of knowledge, of searching out the frontiers of knowledge itself. In schools, we seldom question how science impacts religion, how physics impacts art, how literature impacts philosophy. As Bateson put it, "The combinations, harmonies, and discords between successive pieces and layers of information will present many problems of survival and determine many directions of change."[1]

Should you think this an impractical course of learning design, consider this. Have we evolved through our knowledge? It can certainly be argued that we don't even have the good sense (inherent in most animals) of knowing when to fight versus when to cooperate. We ignore the effects of our knowledge on others and others' knowledge on us. We cut down rain forests in the Amazon and destroy the habitats of indigenous people and even jeopardize the stability of our biosphere.

The notion that interacting systems of thought and practice create new possibilities and new values is still barely emergent. If the idea of globalization is to become something other than a manifesto for trade, we must build an ecology of knowledge. This means you train your intellect to look for the patterns that connect. Parochial understanding combined with the prioritization of short-term over long-term needs will insulate knowledge from progress.

For example, we Americans have an appalling lack of knowledge of the impact of our economic and political policies and social influence on the rest of the world. Sound policy and good global relations in the future will depend on correcting this. Recognizing the social value of what we learn is a key component to our growth as a nation and to educational policy. If knowledge is interconnected, then what we "know" affects what insurgents in Iraq know, to what the Chinese know about how to compete with us, to what Europeans know about the American character, etc.

6. For learning to "stick," it must be context driven and have utility in the present.

The most obvious example: when we teach mathematics, we leave both context and application out.

Structural engineers, carpenters, chemists, navigators, optical designers, surveyors, economists, statisticians, and rocket scientists all use mathematics for very specific purposes. They use different kinds of math and understand its application differently.

To understand math, one must get into the mind, the motivations, of the practitioner: the NASA scientist proposing a rocket design that can withstand atmospheric reentry and glide to a landing, the architect designing a domed football stadium, the carpenter putting a roof on a house. If a learner has no inclination whatsoever to go there, what is the use of learning geometry? Why learn to do quadratic equations?

The notion that all eighth graders must take algebra is simply ludicrous. I had no idea why I was learning algebra then, and I have never had occasion to use it since. It is true that we do not produce the amount of scientists, engineers, and technicians that we need. In third world countries, people learn these disciplines because they are told they must. They are told that prosperity awaits those who embrace science and technology.

Here at home, it is not that simple. If we are to interest learners in science, we must first and foremost make it interesting, real world, and practical. Then, we must divert learners with the right aptitudes into apprenticeships that lead to jobs in science and technology.

The obvious culprits, math and science, are not the only subjects that suffer for lack of context. Professionals who write include journalists, editors, playwrights, TV writers, business analysts and planners, speech writers, and technical writers. We must help learners enter these worlds, discover their sensibilities, and face their challenges.

Pilots learn to fly airplanes in "simulators" that are very real. They learn all the instrumentation, how to take off, and how to land without ever entering the airplane they are learning to fly. We must learn to build courses that are simulators of real-world occupations and real-world skills.

Imagine what it would be like if you were presented as a young student with a variety of self-paced, largely independent study courses such as Spend a Day as a Heart Surgeon; Rebuild a Bridge in Iraq That Was Destroyed During the War; Manage a Baseball Team in a Rebuilding Season; How Did David Emery Discover That Chicken Feathers (the waste of the poultry industry) Could Be Made into Auto Parts, Medical Devices, Dollar Bills, and Termite-Proof Building Materials?; Become the President of the United States for a Day; A Day in the Life of an Investigative Reporter; Build a Case to Defend Someone Accused of Murder; Run a Campaign for Governor of Your State; Start a Nongovernmental Organization and Host a Conference for World Peace; Work on a Cure for Cancer; Become the Head of the Federal Reserve Bank; Work on All Phases of an Automobile Assembly Line; or Turn around a Teen Fashion Department at Macy's.

Each of these courses begins by immersing you in the world of a profession. What are the daily responsibilities, what are the various skill sets, and what are the challenges, the frustrations, and the rewards? Then, you spend some time learning the skills to take over the job. Next, you are actually thrust into the job on a real-time, real-life-situations basis. When you fail, you discover why and are given the chance to make corrections. When you make a good decision or conduct a procedure effectively, you are acknowledged for it.

When you are finished with such a course, you receive a certificate of introduction to a real-world occupation. The certificate delineates the academic pursuits that would lead to higher learning and mastery. It points out other directions in which such pursuits might lead the learner. It becomes the possible beginning for a course of study.

Educators will argue that focusing on a single end result of learning, the choice of a career path, is putting cart before horse and excluding possibility. They will say that we must focus on a broad-based approach that concentrates on basic skills that will eventually stimulate and empower learners to make many choices that affect their lives, including the choice of a career.

This is a compelling argument if real-life scenarios were designed simply for the purpose of steering learners to specific occupations. The trick of designing such courses is to expose learners to how patterns of knowledge, specific skills, talents, and inclinations come together to make a professional occupation. This is much more than occupational training; it is preparing learners for the real complexities of work and making life choices.

For instance, before you can "Become the Head of the Federal Reserve Bank," you have to know what an economist is and does, the basic principles of economics, why you would be chosen for the post, the duties and responsibilities of the post, and why someone rises from being a talented economist to the top economist in the country. You are exposed to principles of management, interacting dynamics such as the stock market, employment, interest rates, and prices. Then there are issues of politics, ethics, and pleasing various constituents.

When you get inside the worldview of a carpenter or the head of the Federal Reserve Bank, you begin making all sorts of connections, between emotions and values, between ideas and actual practice, between things you want to know and things you want to do. This is the real stuff of learning.

Before you assume the role of a trial lawyer, you learn interesting facts about the law. For instance, 70% of all lawyers in the world are here in the United States. Learning about a profession might well lead you to inquire further about its place in society. "Why do we have so many lawyers?" would be the subject of a great independent study project.

Once you have entered into the real world (knowledge, interests, and practices) of a scientist, journalist, politician, doctor, or inventor, you are obliged to come back to your staging place for the real world and reflect upon the overall experience. What did you like and not like about it? What did it make you want to know more about? If the answer is nothing, why?

When you have been immersed in a different world, how can you apply what you have learned today, in your own life?

This might be easy to do if you have just tried on being a carpenter, but how do you apply "Being the President of the United States for a

Day"? This becomes one of the big challenges of learning. And once the practice of finding application becomes routine, it becomes a key condition of entering into any learning experience. "How might I improve as a person or get better at something important to me from this experience?" If we lived inside of such questions, our time and efforts would be greatly leveraged.

7. The world is the new classroom.

Mingling with the world and having real obligations outside of home and school should be part of an early education. Some learning experiences need to be designed to require learners to engage in public service, become an apprentice, or become part of a real-world community.

"After 12,000 hours of compulsory schooling, high school graduates have no skills to trade for income or even any skills with which to talk to each other."[2] Is this acceptable? I can think of nothing that would do more to provide adolescents with self-esteem and the impetus to become part of their communities than to acquire a marketable skill.

Having a skill is the foundation for venturing into the world and finding out how and why you want to better yourself. It is how we are weaned from parental control and dependency.

In our national zeal to preserve childhood, we have partly derailed the fundamental drive of adolescence, which is to become an adult. Of course, adolescents create their own cultures to define themselves in contrast to the adult world. This is a necessary step in the maturation process. We undermine the process by not providing adolescents with clear transitional opportunities to join the world they have been cloistered from by families and schools.

Such opportunities naturally present themselves in the form of community service, employment, and apprenticeship. It is these very occupations that build responsible families and communities. And we must not simply urge children to "be successful" as many of us have. As stewards of learning, we must challenge the young to discover what is important to them and be successful at that.

Even our earliest learning experiences can and should include projects that necessitate leaving a school setting and finding ways to understand real-world events, places, and activities. A curriculum component for six-, seven-, and eight- year-olds could be making them into investigative reporters. Individuals or groups come to the "assignment desk" and choose an assignment or petition the "news department" for an unlisted assignment by justifying its importance in their learning process. Just like in the real world, the best expository journalism is acknowledged and offered to the community—offered as an example of what kids have found the wherewithal to illuminate through their own resourcefulness.

"Current events" is a very good focal point from which to stage forays into history, sociology, science, politics, economics, the arts—all of those things we have broken down into discrete subjects. To move from a current event into an in- depth examination of a person's life, how genes carry the information that makes us what we are, why a sports team has been winning year after year, etc., calls on multiple cognitive skills. To make routine connections between events happening today and the deeper issues that events raise is a fundamental component of cognitive development.

When a learner of any age ventures into the world and accomplishes something on its terms or brings back insight born of his or her own initiative, it makes sense to reward this kind of activity above all else. The same priority is shared by all learners but is suppressed, even undermined, by current schooling.

Key capabilities such as courage, resourcefulness, communicative competence, collaborative skill, narrative ability, and organization are potential components to every challenge that the world offers. Such capabilities are honed in by real-world participation. Teaching with words is one dimensional. Functioning in the world involves a complex system of emotional intelligence, kinesthetic challenges, and intellectual capability. If these components of development are not engaged together, complex knowledge eludes us—the consequence of an excessive and narrow focus on intellectual development, of making the classroom a place apart from the world.

It is the natural inclination of immersion in learning to want to improve things. To improve things, we have to have a real-world knowledge of them, one that appreciates the challenges and dynamics that keep things from changing. This is a sensibility, once cultivated, that will drive inquiry—a kind of integrity that says, "If I am going to know about something, to participate in making things better, I am obliged to learn as much as I can, not just from those who teach but from those who do, not just from reading about a place but from going there to see it for myself."

We should be encouraging learners to want to make the world better and to tell us how they would do it. But, when a student cannot demonstrate knowledge of what is currently considered good practice, we must ask how he or she has reached these conclusions without understanding the logic of what is widely accepted now.

The Internet has made the world accessible. As soon as we begin learning Spanish, we can communicate with English learners in Mexico, or Spain, or Argentina. We can use the Spanish we are learning as the basis for exploring the Hispanic world. What countries speak Spanish? Where are they? Which one interests you the most? Why? Get yourself a pen pal in Costa Rica (if that's your choice), and find out as much as you can about him or her. Tell us what is different about living there. What interests you about your friend, and what interests your friend about you?

This kind of relationship accelerates the learning of a language, gives it context, leads to an interest in other cultures, provides contrast enabling better understanding of one's own culture, and more. It could also lead to an encounter with your pen pal here at home and/or in Costa Rica.

A group of adolescent students learning about government could have a designated component to their course that involves communicating with a group of students in Iraq and a group in Israel. Students in all places are asked to explore open-ended questions like "How is your government structured? What do you think of your government and your president? What are your opinions about the U.S.A.? How is life different in Iraq or Israel because of your government's positions and the policies of the United States?"

Such encounters help create a global context for inquiry. It is important to know what others around the world are thinking about, what their struggles are, and how they see us. We learn from their perspectives where ours might be lacking. We move in the direction of compassion for others. We begin to comprehend the boundaries of our own knowledge. As the world gets bigger and more complex, we develop humility and naturally want to learn more about it.

It is difficult to think of an interest too peculiar or too esoteric not to find others on the Internet who share it. Furthermore, there are whole communities of interest waiting to be joined or started. A community may be broken down into experts and novices, professionals and hobbyists, extremists and moderates, but with some form of access to all. Some communities exist through formal Web sites, others informally through chat rooms, blogs, and listserves.

A larger community on the Internet can often stimulate a learner to find three, six or ten others in his or her geographical area to physically meet. The networking possibilities are endless. A component of digital literacy will become the ability to instigate encounters with communities of interest and communities of practice.

Complex knowledge is first theoretically constructed. Big ideas are laid out in broad strokes by those in various stages of understanding. A learner is trying to explain something he or she is struggling to fit into a worldview. The ability to access others in various stages of the same process is key to a learner-centric model of education. If we work to make the world increasingly accessible to learners, the excuses for not having support simply disappear. Every teacher should be working to promote (and, when necessary, help design) a system that takes away the excuses for not finding help 24/7. "The world is your classroom. If you are not finding help, you need another session on **finding help when you need it.**"

The Seven Prime Directives of the New Learning Architecture

1. **There is no instructive interaction**—This marks the shift in emphasis (and design) from teaching to learning.

2. **Learning to learn is the primary objective of education**—Literacy and numeracy give us the foundation. Thinking and research and communication skills empower us to become the best teachers of ourselves.

3. **Learning is demand driven, not supply driven**—This stands the present hierarchy on its head and says the learner dictates what he or she learns, when it is learned, how it is learned, at what pace, and in what format. This will require a massive reorganization of resources around the learner, including guides and facilitators to identify barriers, set objectives, make sure objectives are broad and learned in sufficient depth, and measure progress, competencies, aptitudes, and proclivities.

4. **Building knowledge is a social activity**—This recognizes that the construction of knowledge requires a scaffolding provided by collaboration, reciprocity, deliberation, and a collective consciousness.

Much of what we call knowledge exists only as a socially mediated and recognized process. The primary challenges that present themselves to individual learners occur while doing something with others. What we come to know is always in danger of "objectivization" without the challenge from outside that says "How do you know that?" "Here is another way to look at it," or "What is most important about what you have said?"

5. **The nature of knowledge is building connections**—This calls for an approach to curriculum that allows inquiry to cross boundaries and pick up connections and new interests from segregated disciplines. This directive recognizes that the brain's own structure does not recognize knowledge as strictly organized into categories.

6. **For learning to "stick," it must be context driven and have utility in the present**—Before we learn something, we must have a reason why, a justification that becomes our own. If it cannot be used in the present, it will not be integrated into long-term memory. It will not drive further inquiry.

7. **The world is the new classroom**—School has come to be associated as the place for learning, but we all know that this is not so. Learning happens anywhere and everywhere, formally and informally, by design and by accident. We must all come to see and use the places of instruction and formal learning as staging places for forays into the world—our neighborhoods, other continents, other cultures, and new frontiers.

Endnotes

1   Gregory Bateson, from *Mind and Nature*, Chapter 2
2   John Gatto, *A Different Kind of Teacher*, Berkeley Hills Books, 2001, p. 201

Chapter 15

SO, WHAT DO WE TEACH?
WHAT DO WE LEARN?

Here we are with some new principles, albeit muddied with the detritus of our own schooling. Now what?

Let's meet the thorniest issue head on. In a learner-centric world, do we really need three million teachers? In a word, no. What, then, happens to them? The simple answer is some of them go, some of them stay, and others are retrained for new responsibilities.

Most of us are aware that many teachers are little more than nannies, paid to ensure that students pass tests that allow schools to receive federal and state support. This is not the teachers' fault. Public education long ago established that the needs of individual learners were subordinate to the needs of the state.

Most teachers really care about the needs of children. Many have much more to contribute than they are allowed. The simple truth, however, is that we cannot afford the luxury of 80,000 eighth-grade history teachers and 30,000 fourth-grade math teachers,[1] most of them less than stellar, teaching pretty much the same thing.

In a learner-centric education design, teaching becomes a profession ruled by economies of scale. If 80,000 history teachers cost us an average of $2.8 billion annually, what if we hire three top historians, a film producer, two or three top history instructors (even historians from Europe with contrasting historical views), a couple of the world's premier instructional designers, someone to design a history video game, and a few Internet resource experts to design and assemble the best eighth-grade history course ever made?

Suppose it costs us $30 million to design and produce this course and an additional $2 million every three years to update the course. Now we eliminate 50,000 of those teachers over time—some retire, and some become counselors or work in other school-related jobs. Many, regrettably, just have to go. The best 30,000, those we have accorded the status of master teachers, are kept on, and their salaries are doubled.

The course we create is now offered to all who take what we would now call eighth-grade history. It is even given to the master teachers to help with their instruction. We have just eliminated roughly $700 million from the cost of teaching one course, the biggest part of educational overhead except for administration. We will get to that later.

We have improved a single course, across the board, and reduced its cost dramatically. Can we do this with the majority of curricula offered at the K-12 level? I believe the answer is yes.

Is this an oversimplification to make a point? Certainly! The real equation will be more complex and subject to a national level of cooperation in education that doesn't currently exist. In the context of this book, it would be unrealistic to take on the problem of how you get states to buy into uniform standards and the sharing of resources. Still, economics of scale are extremely persuasive—particularly when the public is presented with such an alternative.

"But, I don't want to get rid of our teachers," you might say. An understandable sentiment until common sense prevails. How many teachers have you had that really lit a fire under you, got you excited about diagramming sentences, solving algebra equations, or learning about American history? Most of us can count them on one hand. The really good ones we remember vividly along with an ogre or two. The mediocre ones we have long forgotten.

Learning without a teacher in line of sight has been going on for millennia. Now, we have new tools to make courses very rich, individualized multimedia learning experiences. Designed correctly, these courses will hopefully make learners take to them with far greater zeal than they do a mediocre to bad teacher.

It would be grand if some teachers had waiting lists of students jockeying to get into their classes while others left because students elected to use alternative means. Some will argue that this would force teachers to become entertainers first. Perhaps so, but they will not survive on the ability to entertain alone. Many of the great teachers are capable of handling large classes well. If teachers were primarily judged by the clamor for access to them, we would be on the right track.

So, exposure to a live face-to-face teacher is diminished, but what remains is of the highest quality. Access to other great teachers can readily be increased through the use of visual media and computers. What we "teach" through conventional means becomes less important than the question of whether we are supplying the means for all students to learn.

"*What do we learn?*" is the more complicated question. To move from uniform, commodified learning to diversified learning is by far the biggest challenge to a learner-centric model. The shear enormity of providing an array of resources to accommodate an infinite variety of learning paths is, at first, overwhelming. To many traditional educators, it is viewed as impossible.

The problem is not one of content or information. Enormous repositories of information are available to be repurposed as learning events—learning modules. Tens of thousands of high-quality courses now exist that do not rely on a live teacher. How does a large variety of learning resources get organized into a user-friendly matrix? This is the big challenge of the next 20 years.

We have whole courses, some live, some on video, some delivered over the Internet. Then, we have bits, chunks, and comprehensive collections of supplementary information: visual, auditory, and written information. How do the learner and his or her advisors cobble together an intelligent combination of available resources to fulfill the requirements to receive credit? How do you know you have credible sources of information? Ninety-eight percent of a report on the decline of NASA's space program may be factually correct, yet the author may have an axe to grind and may slip in just a few brief comments indicating that NASA should not survive because the real use of space should be for military purposes. How do we identify strategically placed hidden agendas in otherwise acceptable educational material?

The honest answer: We can't.

In an unregulated system of information like the World Wide Web, where knowledge has no official stamp of approval, our first duty is to make learners into discriminating and increasingly expert consumers of information. When it comes in bits rather than sanctioned packages, it becomes obvious that we need to have the skills to analyze, classify, and organize it. The skills and attitudes of effective research and effective thinking become the price of entry into an open learning system.

These are the very skills Socrates prioritized almost 2,500 years ago. He exhorted all to be skeptical of official knowledge and the acceptance of anything as truth without thorough investigation. Bias and inaccurate information abound even in our present textbooks despite the efforts of committees to screen them.

Yes, it's an information jungle out there. How do we equip learners with the skills to survive in the jungle? Whether you refer to the present, 20 years ago, or 20 years hence, information has always had a bias. The first thing we need to learn after the three R's is to think for ourselves. Thinking for oneself in the digital age combines critical thinking skills with digital learning skills.

Educational writer and researcher Kathleen Cotton synthesized the research on critical thinking, saying it was "variously defined as":

- Reflective and reasonable thinking that is focused on deciding what to believe or do
- The disposition to provide evidence in support of one's conclusions and to request evidence from others before accepting their conclusions
- The process of determining the authenticity, accuracy, and worth of information or knowledge claims.[2]

For a more complete breakdown of critical-thinking skills, see the list developed for the North Central Regional Educational Laboratory (Appendix A).

In *A Primer on Digital Literacy*[3] Paul Gilster explains that "Critical thinking about content is the Internet competency upon which all others are founded. You cannot work comfortably within this medium until you have established methods for judging the reliability of Web pages, newsgroup postings and mailing lists." Gilster's book *Digital Literacy* "deals with strategies for evaluating the content of what you find online, verifying its authenticity, and placing it in the context of other information sources."[4] He provides a series of exercises to help learners develop these skills.

Critical-thinking skills and digital-learning skills are important enough to be core components of the curriculum. Some refer to them as a meta-curriculum, a set of exercises and practices attached to standard curriculum to make sure that a lesson has relevance to the learner and has been turned into applicable knowledge.

In a disintermediated world, students are turned loose to seek knowledge from anywhere and everywhere. Learning facilitators must learn to insert exercises into found information that help extract meaning for each learner. This, of course, requires intimate knowledge of a learner's interests, capabilities, and challenges.

Official versus Personal Knowledge

If you take on the cumbersome task of studying education as a discipline, two conversations (themes) you will encounter often are "democratic education" and "the hidden curriculum." The conversation about democratic education asks how we provide everyone with similar access and quality. Are we respectful of race and ethnicity? Are we creating good citizens in keeping with our constitutional beliefs and practices? Do we respect different points of view and religious differences? Are we responsive to the different talents, interests, and aptitudes of diverse learners?

The conversation about the hidden curriculum is about the implicit messages sent to us by the way schooling is organized and managed. What impact does the design of a textbook, the ringing of bells every 50 minutes, regimented classrooms, the lack of self-determined activity, and the application of uniform standards have on us?

Perhaps most significant is how the priorities and methods of education are affected by our approach to measurement. This is true at all levels of learning. Unfortunately, our methods of evaluation tend to reinforce a simplistic learning style that regurgitates the explicit meaning of learning materials. Studies have shown that academic achievers tend to be those who play by the narrower rules of teaching rather than the broader, more personalized rules of learning.[5]

The same dynamics persist into adult learning environments and account for a widespread learned dependence on teachers and trainers. The emphasis on "official" knowledge depersonalizes what we learn and makes it into a commodity that many of us cannot relate to our own needs. *When the student is ready, the lesson appears—when the STUDENT is ready!*

We often go to great lengths to try to make a curriculum relevant. Textbooks change to reflect modern images and trends. Corporate training invests a great deal in finding real-life situations to which employees should be able to relate. Whether we know it or not, most of us feel manipulated by an agenda that tells us what should be important and then explains why. Yet every K-12 textbook is essentially designed around such assumptions.

The conversations about democratic education and the hidden curriculum become largely moot when we:

- Put learners in charge of projects and assignments that are mutually agreed upon as important
- Allow learners to pursue a subject at their own pace, through means chosen by them from multiple available pathways (both official and unofficial)
- Empower them with the mental skills to evaluate their progress and, most important, the freedom to make their own connections—to decide what is important and why. *Then and only then might a facilitator suggest other points of view, missed significance, relevant topics, and alternative sources of input.*
- Recognize the social and intellectual connections that are a consequence of a learner's own efforts and use them to guide learners forward
- Reinforce in every way possible that the rewards for every learning event, every emerging capacity, and every developing interest are intrinsic. The way we evaluate learners must, first and foremost, reflect this value.

All real knowledge is both personal and valued in collective consciousness. It occurs to us through personal relevance and is arrived at through our associations. When the authority of meaning resides in teachers and prepared courses, it will inevitably become superficial and dictatorial, the result of a system that desires and rewards obedience and passivity. Our association with teachers and official texts is nonreciprocal and gives us no place to voluntarily engage or disengage.

"Easier said than done" will be the natural exhortation of the old school. Woodrow Wilson said, "It is easier to change the location of a cemetery than to change the school curriculum."[6] This indeed may be true, but no less than the erosion of our cognitive capacities is at stake.

Beginning with early schooling, how do we use our "old school"-trained minds to envision and encapsulate new possibilities? What do we teach, and what do we learn as the experience of the new school begins and becomes its own invisible curriculum? How do we transition, as quickly as possible, to a condition where a curriculum and the methods by which we learn it are a participatory experience?

The One-Room Schoolhouse

Now, in the early grades, we teach kids socialization skills and learning skills, but mostly we teach them how to read and write and have a basic understanding of numbers. Until these skills are mastered, it makes sense to focus on them as the foundation of all learning—with a few modifications.

For a powerful metaphor of early learning, let's return to an educational setting that was widespread in the early part of the last century and tweak it a bit. I am lucky enough to have experienced the one-room schoolhouse. It was a rural public school in California that was composed of local farmers' kids and kids from an adjacent military base. There were roughly 30 kids in my class, a fairly even mix of first, second, and third graders.

What I remember the most is that the help I sought out in the classroom was from older kids. I sought help frequently, older kids were glad to help me, and the teacher was very supportive of this process. I saw the teacher as a helper of last resort and my peers as better able to zero in on my needs.

Such environments were common in the past. Why not now? Naysayers might point out that we have too much diversity in today's classrooms to make this work or that in more urban areas with widespread sociological problems (i.e., broken families), kids need more individual attention.

These are some of the very reasons that the one-room schoolhouse would be more effective. What better way to facilitate social skills and use diversity as a learning experience than to have children learning from their peers *and recognizing early on that learning is an interdependent phenomenon that causes them to choose, value, and respect peers for helping them to learn?*

The one-room schoolhouse, I believe, would work best at early ages (six to nine), when children are steeped in *participation consciousness* and are most inclined to see helping their peers as an integral part of the learning experience.

There are several intrinsic dynamics to the one-room schoolhouse that are crucial to early childhood development and key to a learner-centric school design:

- Everyone can be a teacher and at any age. The certainty that, as a learner, you will also be called upon to teach invites a greater degree of mastery. It is the best weapon against complacency.
- Environments that encourage interaction and response, especially among peers, establish the "prime conditions for developing the more complex neural networks that appear to be the hardware of intelligence." When we have insights or master learning materials, the act of turning to a peer and sharing what we have learned builds the "association cortices" that embellish and anchor new ideas.[7]
- Learning from peers reinforces the awareness that one has the built-in capacity to learn—that learning is not tied to the "elders" and to formal teaching. This awareness may well have a greater effect on self-esteem and self-directed inquiry than we can now calculate.
- Schooling as we know it isolates children from their families and their communities and from each other. The notion of the one-room schoolhouse serves to establish a context of school as a place of associated living, a microcosm of the world where learning is primarily a conjoint communicated experience. It establishes the principle that school is a form of community and lays the groundwork for learning communities as a primary form of later learning.
- The notion that learning is neither linear nor homogenous is strongly reinforced.

The old one-room schoolhouse looked similar to today's classroom, but, of course, it lacked the media that provide access to the world today. The modern one-room schoolhouse must use technology and architectural design to convey that "the doors are open to the world here" and that "when you want to venture out into the world, you have multiple ways to do so." And finally, the means of engagement for young learners must involve a high degree of choice and constructive play.

A large room is organized into social spaces. Areas are designed to create comfort, warmth, and a sense of separation from the other spaces. One area is for building things and another for discussion with peers, and another has work stations where kids can download videos on computers, search for answers and information sources on the Internet, watch educational TV programming, play educational video games, communicate with others through chat rooms, discussion groups, Weblogs, e-mails, etc. There is separate area for quiet contemplation and rest. There is a separate lecture room where a teacher can present material, show a video, or stage certain activities.

A serious component of the new architecture or "new school" will be the design of physical spaces. One of the chief components of this new design will be the challenge of creating environments that learners own as theirs. Many early-education teachers go to great lengths to do this now, but it is difficult in an environment where kids sit in neat rows, bells ring to signal a regimented move somewhere else, and what is learned (and how) is controlled by others.

Learning as Play

Play is your brain's favorite way of learning.
—Diane Ackerman

"Play and imitation are natural learning strategies at which children are experts."[8] In fact, there is an array of inherent capability to be found in children at play—leadership skills, creativity, organization, initiative, conviviality, and more. It is often said that play is the "business" of children. Many children exhibit forms of emergent talent through their play. Play provides children with multiple forms of engagement, niches for their unique capabilities, and the ability to explore and experiment on their own terms.

Children need to engage in nondirective play of their own design and on their own terms. But I am also talking about play as a curriculum. There are role-plays in which children adopt vocational, parental, community, and fantasy roles—roles where they can explore being competent at something outside of their experience.

There are sophisticated computer games in which children learn by designing, fixing, building, and anticipating evolutionary steps. It is very supportive of cognitive development to have children learning to design their own games illustrating scientific, social, and economic principles. By so doing, they begin to develop the same cognitive capacities necessary to understand how learning takes place.

An interesting version of play as a curriculum is the "microworld," a term coined by Seymour Papert of MIT's Media Lab[9] to refer to a closed artificial environment that learners actually inhabit and explore to uncover or dig up knowledge. Being in a sandbox or a space station is a microworld. Engineering a bridge with an erector set and specific design constraints is a microworld. Role-playing a jury deliberation after a trial is a microworld, as is re-creating the conditions and experiments leading to a scientific discovery. It can be an abstract environment that creates a mathematical puzzle to solve.

Microworlds create immersed action in narrowly prescribed circumstances that mimic real-world problems. They can be created in a computer, in a classroom, at work, or at home. They allow for a self-paced natural progression from simple to complex problem solving. It is easy to create microworlds that involve small groups in a collaborative effort. Groups can then report their experiences and findings to a larger class.

Instructional designers, educational labs, and computer game designers are hard at work designing microworlds. Predesigned, modifiable microworlds will become a significant type of learning experience. They can be used for all ages. Design that propels learners from a simple case to increasingly complex variations that alter the microworld so that it expresses increasingly complex ideas is the ultimate challenge. (See Appendix C, "Mircoworlds Resource Page.")

Simulations are another means for creating powerful learning experiences. Simulations differ from microworlds in that they are near approximations of reality involving consequences for missteps. The most well known is, of course, the flight simulator. Flight simulators are such effective training devices that the first time professional pilots usually fly a new model aircraft is with a full complement of passengers—having learned the nuances and controls completely on a simulator.

To get the experience of a simulation, you need only purchase and play any one of a number of excellent commercially available video games: "SimCity," "Silent Hunter," "Baseball Mogul," "Microsoft Flight Simulator," "Myst," "Riven," "Doom," "Civilization," or "Plant Tycoon," to name a few. Simulators are realistic in the precision that you are able to alter the course of action and/or in the richness of detail and possibility that lends reality to an endeavor.

What one is left with from playing a "Sim" is the sense of complete immersion: "The computer feels like an organic extension of your consciousness … you may feel like an extension of the computer itself. The game can grow so absorbing, in fact, your subjective sense of time is distorted."[10]

Not only is a form of reality approximated but also so is the consciousness of the game creator. You emerge from a simulation having made a continuous series of crucial decisions made "so quickly and intuitively that you have internalized the logic of the program. … Losing yourself in a computer game means, in a sense, identifying with the simulation yourself."[11]

This more nearly approximates how natural learning by doing occurs. It is a visceral as well as an intellectual process, with continuous feedback between what you are doing and how the environment or the object you are acting upon reacts. You get the sense of what it feels like to design and manage a city, fly an airplane in combat, be the ruler of an entire civilization, build a baseball team, etc., through your decision-making process.

There is a downside to simulation in that it generally simulates a point of view about reality. Again, this is why it becomes necessary to provide learners, above all else, with thinking skills that generate perspective and discernment. The strength and weakness of "Sims" lie in the inevitable internalization of the programming logic that created them. If the process is conscious, meaning the learner has understood the logic and perspective of the programmer, we have an effective and empowering learning experience. If the learner becomes grandiose, thinking he or she knows how a plane is flown, a city is built, or a war is fought, we have mischief that leads to misunderstanding.

Self-contained-learning games and simulations would benefit from a component much like what is built into a typical DVD these days. The author or director discusses his or her approach to the project and to making the Sim. Or, even a step further, a critic offers alternative perspectives that help establish the point of view of the Sim.

On the face of it, one might assume that "SimCity," a game that allows you to buy land, build roads, create zoning restrictions, build sewer and power plants, and manage a city budget, is neutral because of the choices it allows. However, the game has been criticized by political ideologues on the left and the right (i.e., for favoring low taxes, for encouraging growth, or for discouraging nuclear over conventional power).

As long as such learning events are mediated with alternative perspectives, they will become increasingly favored as highly effective, low-cost (relative to the labor-intense model of teaching) forms of curriculum. If the attributes of various types of play are combined, they suggest a different kind of learning environment "where structure and motivation are optimized without subverting personal discovery, exploration, and ownership of knowledge."[12]

The argument for curriculum as play is extremely compelling, yet we face a widely held belief that play invites coddling, chaos, and time-wasting activity.

The child begins with a question that comes from curiosity about his or her immediate environment. What is the Milky Way? Why does it look like a cloud? If a cloud is made of water, how much does it weigh? Why doesn't it just fall out of the sky? Can people make clouds?

One thing leads to another, like poking around in a flea market. You find a unique end table, and then you want to look for a lamp to go on it. You find a really cool old lamp, and then you want to find out where and what period of time the lamp came from so you can find other things to go with it. Exploration drives curiosity and then discovery and further interaction with the immediate environment.

Curiosity is never satisfied, never diminished until we begin to funnel it down prescribed channels: telling learners what they need to know, not only that they all need to know the same things but also that they all must learn them the same way, at the same time, and at the same pace. We have turned learners over to middlemen who stop the nomadic "poking around in a flea market" process of learning and short circuit the interactive process, causing inquiry to diminish. Questions still come but mostly for different reasons. Curiosity has taken a back seat to conformity and performance.

To reverse this process, we must provide a wide variety of resources to learners in their immediate environment with various media. Let them **play** at mastering their worlds and discovering new ones. We have to make the outside world apparent and vivid by taking them out into it and by bringing it vividly into the classroom.

A great deal of attention is placed on play in early childhood curriculum (ages three to eight). Why stop there? We all know that adolescents love to play. So do people in their 20s and 50s if encouraged.

Computers are not the only vehicle for making games and making them fun. Learners of all ages need to play in physical space, with others in proximity and in their various communities. Computers do, however, present enormous potential as a platform for play-based curriculum. No medium except for sports has created the intensity, the adrenaline rush, the zeal for practice and mastery that computer games have.

Unlike sports, computer games can control all of the action, be played with people all over the world simultaneously, be both action oriented and reflective, graduate challenges according to skill, build in as-needed information, provide widely varied graphic settings and "atmospheres," make participants into game creators/modifiers, be constantly amended and upgraded, and provide infinite layers of content and variety.

Author, professor, and computer games expert James Gee perhaps summed up the potential of digital learning games best when he said, "Learning works best when the learners are so caught up in their goals that they don't realize what they are learning, or how much they are learning, or where they actively seek new learning inside and outside the game."[13]

A well-designed video game is a thinking lesson, a brain builder. Some developers are taking this observation seriously and are developing games that aim at improving specific cognitive functions. David Stevens, a Ph.D. graduate in education from Harvard, is the director of advanced research and design at Lexia Learning Systems in Lincoln, Massachusetts.

With a $2-million grant from the National Institute of Standards and Technology, a federal incubator for technology research and development, Stevens designed a suite of games he calls a "visual-spatial gym." "Lexia Cross Trainer," as the product is called, develops 22 cognitive skills including visualization, visual memory, mental rotation, visual tracking, spatial orientation, and multiperspective coordination. Some of the skills addressed by "Cross Trainer" are included in aptitude tests for kids but are not taught in school.

Some of the skills, in early clinical trials of the games, increased markedly. The 23 children who participated in the trial went from an age equivalent of 9.8 years to 12.9 years on the Stanford-Binet Pattern Analysis, a spatial orientation test that is standard in IQ measurements.

Much more research needs to be done. A great many more educational games need to be developed. Digital games are expensive to create. They are presently lacking in human interactions with consequences based on choices (questions and answers). They need more built-in tutorials. All of these challenges are now being addressed in the game design world. Game designers need to be paired on equal footing, with academic experts to lay out designs for learning around specific topics. In the world of play-based learning, their talents are equally important.

What computer games do remarkably well is combine levels of frustration with gratification in reaching staged mastery—this is an enormous contribution that will be exploited in many more ways. The next big thing for game design is to attack real-world complexity. Back to the micro-world for a moment, where we can immerse learners in the experience of being a newspaper editor for a day, making a set of ethical decisions in a medical setting, re-creating the complexity of life in a space station, with different cultures, languages, and competing priorities for being there. We can determine the best way to help a needy village in a developing country within the constraints of culture, religious beliefs, and available resources. We can be thrust into worlds that involve complex interactions between analysis, action, morality, technical know-how, economics, and human diversity.

Serious gamers spend hours learning how to alter games to make them more satisfying. They read manuals and learn more about facts that enable resolution to a problem. To transfer this level of thinking and enthusiasm to a domain of knowledge using similar strategies and techniques will be extremely useful in a learner-centric world. Seen as part of a whole curriculum, actively linked to discussions, books, and re-creations of learning in real-world situations, games become a powerful vehicle for blending action with reflection and learning from mistakes and repetition. Digital games add dynamics to a learning environment that have been absent in traditional classrooms. Like traveling and living in other cultures, they allow people to temporarily rearrange their psyches and their world of familiarity and by so doing re-create themselves.

> *In the past, education adapted the mind to a*
> *very restricted set of available media; in the*
> *(new architecture), it will adapt media to serve the*
> *needs and tastes of each individual mind.*
> —SEYMOUR PAPERT

For further investigation into the world of game-based learning, I recommend all of the following books:

What Video Games Have to Teach Us about Learning and Literacy, James Paul Gee, Palgrave Macmillan, 2003; *Digital Game Based Learning*, Marc Prensky, McGraw-Hill, 2001; *The Children's Machine—Rethinking School in the Age of the Computer*, Seymour Papert, Basic Books, 1992.

What we teach must follow some set of standards yet allow for individual interests, learning styles, aptitudes, and pace. Pace cannot be associated with intelligence until we fully understand the varieties of intelligence, the exigencies of each unique developmental path. We are worlds away from such understanding. Still, as stewards of a society of learning, we must attempt to leverage the learning process of each learner without overtaking it. We must ensure that learners do not become sophomoric, one-dimensional, or experts in minutiae. We must follow an evolving plan customized to each individual.

In a learner-centric architecture, this will involve three core practices:

- A cradle-to-grave learning management system—the decoded DNA of learning; each person's record of intellectual evolution and cognitive fingerprint; the trajectory of learning as defined by each learner in conjunction with advisors and professional observers; a shared system of accountability for learning, personal evolution, and productivity
- A highly sophisticated organizational structure and search mechanism for information and knowledge, one that has been designed with a global set of standards for the virtual world and establishes and maintains a form of organization in the physical world
- A new set of roles and standards for human intervention in the learning process, one that addresses the variety of conscious and unconscious human needs for intellectual, emotional, social, and vocational/career development.

I will begin with the learning management system as it is the central organizing platform from which the other practices are formed.

Endnotes

1 Granted, a fourth-grade "math" teacher teaches other subjects as well. However, if you separate the specific skills of teaching math or teaching science, many teachers fall short.

2 Kathleen Cotton, *Teaching Thinking Skills*, Northwest Regional Educational Laboratory, *http://www.nwrel.org*

3 See *http://ibiblio.org/cisco/noc/primer.htm*

4 From *A Primer on Digital Literacy* (see above)

5 One study "showed that those students who achieve the highest academically are actually those who prefer to work individually, who show adherence to existing rules and procedures, and who **do not** enjoy creating, formulating, and planning for problem solution." (F. Cano-Garcia and E. Hughes.) "Learning and thinking styles: an analysis of their interrelationship and influence on academic achievement." *Educational Psychology*, 2000, 20 (4) 413–427. Quoted from Andrew Seaton, *Reforming the Hidden Curriculum: The Key Abilities Model and Four Curricular Forms*, see *http://www.andrewseaton.com.au/reform.htm*

6 Ibid., p. 2

7 Quoted from "Education in the Decades Ahead," an essay by distinguished neuroscientist and teacher Marian Cleeves Diamond, from a series of "Perspectives on Educational Change," compiled and edited by Dee Dickinson for New Horizons for Learning. For more on the issue of how environments impact the brain, see Marian Diamond, *Enriching Heredity*, Free Press/Simon and Schuster, N.Y., 1988.

8 L. P. Rieber, "Seriously considering play: Designing interactive learning environments based on the blending of microworlds, simulations and games," *Educational Technology Research and Development*, 1996, 44 (2) 43–48

9 See Seymour Papert, *Mindstorms: Children, Computers and Powerful Ideas*, Basic Books, N.Y., 1980

10 Ted Friedman, a graduate student at Duke University, "Semiotics of SimCity." See *http://www.firstmonday.dk/isuues/issue4_4/friedman/*

11 Ibid.

12 L. P. Rieber, ibid.

13 Quote taken from "Some Notes on Educational Games—Feb. 18. 2004" at *http://www.watercoolerrgames.org*, see archives

Chapter 16

LEARNING IS A TWO-WAY STREET
Shared Accountability, Shared Evaluation

If we are to continue bearing the cost of educating all Americans, accountability will remain a crucial part of the social contract, as it should. But, it is too important an issue to politicize. We must acknowledge our failures and design accountability into the system using valid methods until we get it working at an acceptable level.

I don't need to reiterate my comments on traditional standards of measurement from Part II, Chapter 8. Suffice it to say, on the issue of accountability, we are on a course of failure. Anyone who sees the tragic results should be speaking out. You don't have to know the solution to bring attention to the problem. Though the outcry has been great, the course remains the same. Time to turn up the volume!

Conservatives, who have largely carried the banner of the "standards" movement for some 25 years, are right to insist on accountability in public education. That said, we all must dig deeper to arrive at authentic and effective standards for guiding and measuring learning progress.

Who would argue that we can do much better than using multiple-choice, norm-referenced, memorization-based tests to move learners through the system? These are not tests of real-world knowledge. It would be so easy to prove by simply giving the tests to the citizens of every school district. It has even been done on a small scale. Not only were the test results horrendous, but also the comments were overwhelmingly negative on the "standards" being used to measure so-called knowledge.

Our schools are now so preoccupied with preparation for testing that subjects such as "science and social studies have been severely trimmed in states that do not include those subjects on standardized tests."[1] Investigation into big ideas and "in-depth" learning are on the decline. The testing apparatus now controls curriculum and most of what happens in schools. Dropout rates have risen at an alarming rate, especially among people of color. We now have the highest dropout rate of any Western country. Twenty-five years ago, we had the lowest.

The standards we use to evaluate learning are the equivalent of evaluating this book strictly by looking at my spelling and punctuation. We need a deeper and more comprehensive method of evaluating the process of learning several times in a week rather than once a year or so with standardized tests.

Any valid method of accountability ought to be using gauges and standards designed to equip learners with awareness of their own learning skills and readily apparent indicators of the skills yet to be learned. That should be "standard" number one. The record of what has been learned is important but secondary.

Conservatives who care about accountability in schools should be the first to decry present circumstances. Perhaps we all want something to cry out for, not just against. Here is a vision for the new system of accountability.

In a learner-centric architecture, the work of learning is a managed process that knows how to respond to each individual's own path. When it doesn't know how, it has the capacity to expand its awareness of learner needs. It is an adaptive system, increasingly in tune with the development of each brain.

The Learning Management System

In the corporate world, there has been much talk in recent years about "learning organizations," "just-in-time learning," and creating delivery systems that provide learning on demand. Learning on demand is an important idea, but like traditional schooling, corporate employees are largely told what is important for them to learn and then are supplied with a specific course or method in which to do it.

The vehicle of choice now used to deliver learning on demand is called a learning management system (LMS). In the corporate world, it is primarily used as a platform to deliver courses and learning modules mostly online to individual employees. It provides reporting and tracking capabilities to make decisions about staff and further training needs.

The LMS is essential to a new architecture if conceived as the record and tool that makes the learner the primary agent in his or her learning process. It directs learners to:

- better ways to learn
- relevant learning content
- ongoing Internet discussions that pertain to their interests
- suggested next steps on the path to their learning objectives
- ongoing feedback from peers, mentors, community members, and learning facilitators to help evaluate progress and identify areas of concentration
- others who may wish to collaborate on learning objectives
- a comprehensive profile of their learning path (i.e., strengths, weaknesses, gaps in meeting core learning objectives, emerging aptitudes, and interests)
- a log of significant learning events and issues
- portfolios of their representative work

Such a device would be a cybernetic system with feedback loops that continuously mediate between the learner, the learning process, and specifically defined objectives. It would be the record that apprises all learners of their intellectual profile from cradle to grave.

As such, it would be highly confidential, accessible to only those who have received the learner's specific authorization. As an intellectual record, it would be very important that it is not accessible to anyone who might be motivated to use a person's beliefs and assessed levels of capability against him or her.

Certain data could be made available to outside agencies by permission. Data such as learning objectives, unique interests, learning styles, and distinguished accomplishments can be used (by private learning facilitators and creators of smart software products) to calibrate responses tailored to individual needs.

The basic LMS ought to be a universal software platform, resident on the Internet and designed so that the same basic instructions, tutorials, technical assistance, and updates would apply to all who use it and feed utilities or information into it. Its user interface and basic organization would be similar to a Windows desktop, allowing outside sources to input and receive information from it reliably. It would, of course, support existing open industry standards for Web deployments such as XML, URIs, and SOAP.[2]

It would also support existing learning standards such as SCORM and IMS.

It would have customizable features that allow users to give it a look and feel they are comfortable with and single-click access to capabilities that require greater degrees of sophistication to use. As learners progress developmentally, the LMS "desktop" would introduce more complex features.

Using an LMS as the central organizing platform for learning design, inquiry, testing, evaluation, planning, and organization is now no more than a concept. Yet it is a concept that I see as central to a new learning architecture. It very much impacts major educational costs and issues such as testing, curriculum design and management, administration, guidance, and learner focus.

As a concept, the proposed features of an LMS suggest its capabilities. Certainly, further research on the uses of an LMS is needed. Subject matter experts in various areas, such as curriculum, administration, and testing, will need to collaborate toward a design that meets a variety of real learning needs and optimizes human capabilities.

For starters, here is a suggested list of features for an LMS to be used in a K-12 setting:

- **A calenda**r of scheduled commitments, required attendances, and optional events that tie into each individual learning plan. Learners who have been absent for a time can pick up assignments they missed, though this need will occur with less frequency as learners move to a self-paced schedule.
- **Collaborative work software or "groupware"** that allows a group of learners, experts, and facilitators to be linked in while working on learning assignments and projects. There are existing models for this in higher education such as Lotus Notes.

- **E-mail access** to teachers and facilitators, including FAQs and online discussion threads pertaining to common issues a teacher/facilitator may be dealing with.
- **The Knowledge Browser**—The official link to all data that has been evaluated and categorized for learning purposes. It would be similar to search engines such as Google or Yahoo except that all Web pages and sites will be registered, evaluated, and "tagged" as to their educational purpose and value. A *Good Housekeeping*-type seal of approval with a rating system will be attached to any for-fee products and services accessed.
- **Academic Management System** (AMS)—Provides ongoing feedback to learners regarding meeting core requirements. The AMS functions as a kind of compass to guide learners in the direction of resources that explain unmet requirements and suggest means by which they can be met. Learners then consult with learning facilitators to come up with a plan to meet a requirement that is then incorporated into the LMS.

  An ongoing gap analysis puts completed increments of core requirements on a grid and then maps the terrain between what has been accomplished and what remains to be done. It analyzes the overall direction and concentration of a learner's work and then indicates possible gaps that may impair learning progress in meeting stated or required objectives.
- **Record of learning strategy**—This delineates how each learner seems to best go about mastering a particular subject. It details methods used to show competence in specific subjects and correlates those methods with overall learning style. Most important, it identifies patterns that show efficiency in learning and a tendency to excel in mastering a subject—patterns that are tied to specific methodology.

  For example, a person identified as particularly visual/verbal oriented may have exhibited a tendency to not follow verbal directions or process lectures well. He or she may have naturally migrated toward activities that have a high visual component and kept extremely detailed notes in order to remember what has been learned. This person likes to read and to do research on his or her own. He or she encounters difficulty with higher math unless it can be made logically visible through graphs, diagrams, and real-life examples he or she can visualize. Testing may have predicted or confirmed this. It is useful guidance to the learner and to all who may be providing lessons and facilitation.

- **Fee-based learning services** (that could be either public or private) such as **Find a Tutor** (on or offline) or, **Find a Learning Community**—which initiates a specialized search to find a suitable community of interest or practice for a student to seek association with like-minded people. The student is then welcomed by a personal e-mail from a community member.

  Best Solutions-Best Practices—Define a learning problem or goal and an extensive search is initiated to list highly rated on and offline solutions. Best methods to learn are identified relative to specific exercises and objectives.

- **Tests**—Provide pretesting information to help prepare for standardized tests. Students can download standardized tests according to preset instructions, download tests designated by teachers and facilitators, and use evaluative data to suggest optional "instruments" that may help learners identify learning styles, competencies, interests, and career inclinations. Facilitators and testing experts team up to design evaluative exercises for individual learners.

- **Learner Portfolio**—The principle demonstration of each learner's development and special talents is a portfolio of completed work. Each example in the portfolio is chosen to exemplify a learner's developmental progress and developing capabilities. The portfolio is the principle vehicle for teachers, mentors, and facilitators to review work, make comments, and explore new directions with individual learners.

- **Key Abilities Index**—Based on the identification of core skills that are needed to evolve to totally self-directed learning and preparation for the professional world. One key abilities model (*see http://www. andrewseaton.com.au/overview.htm for an overview*) identifies six key cultural and economic abilities: multiliteracy, problem solving, creativity, self-management, and knowledge of self, others, and the environment.

  The "index" provides an ongoing assessment of key developmental skills that a learner can progressively use. It would, of course, include access to how teachers, facilitators, peers, and tests are evaluating them.

- **Journals**—Whenever a long-term project or subject is undertaken, the keeping of a journal to identify milestones in the learner's odyssey (i.e., big questions that arise, how those questions get addressed, implications for how one's life is to be lived, how knowledge will be applied down the road, new areas of interest that arise, how they were identified and followed up on) can be among the most useful forms of accountability. Learners must understand that they are, above all, accountable to themselves. Using journaling skillfully will reinforce this awareness and keep learners on the path that is unfolding in front of them as a result of the questions they ask, the truths they discover, the connections they make to the world, and the new horizons they identify. Journaling ought to be a skill that develops commensurate with the ability to write.

- **Challenge mechanism** for tests, evaluations, and required curriculum—Needless to say, evaluations are human, and tests are imperfect. When a learner has a big issue with either teacher/facilitator comments or test results, he or she should have the opportunity to make a case for his or her point of view. If the case is weak, the LMS record would record a challenge with no change. If the case is compelling, the challenger should often have the option to repeat a test or receive a modified evaluation.

  When a student wishes to opt out of a required course, he or she files an alternative plan with a counselor, to be evaluated for its validity as part of a comprehensive educational plan. The plan is evaluated in committee, accepted or rejected, and recorded in the LMS.

  As it stands now, standards are seen primarily as an objective method of evaluation and an extrinsic motivator for improvement. Neither perspective is useful. If learners see a system designed to make themselves accountable for understanding and gauging their own progress, and one that lets them inject some of their own terms, they will be motivated to use it and open to its feedback.

- **Blended learning profile**—A composite picture of the best way for a learner to choose a course of action when beginning a new subject, course, or learning project. The notion of blended learning refers to what forms of learning are suitable for a course of study (online course, game-based learning, traditional class, community of practice, apprenticeship, independent study, etc.). Applied to an individual, a blended learning profile would analyze how each learner has responded to specific forms of learning activity. Does he or she like and respond well to audio lectures? Has he or she demonstrated a strong affinity for certain types of interactive learning games? Does he or she do well in an independent learning situation, or does he or she need a packaged course? Perhaps he or she does well independently with some subjects but needs more structure and direction in science and math.

This kind of information helps a learner design his or her own independent inquiry, and it can help a teacher/facilitator put together a "learning package" to match an educational objective.

All of the features I have described above need much further design and detail. The overall notion of an LMS is both sound and key to the notion of a new architecture. Why? Because a living record is essential to establishing feedback loops that distribute accountability evenly and appropriately between a learner and his or her advisors.

One of the underlying concepts of a learner-centric architecture is that learners need to explain things to themselves rather than having explanations handed to them. The present system of standards and accountability is, perhaps, the worst offender in that it doles out an explanation of learner progress with very little participation on the part of the learner.

Again, think of learners as the customers of education. With an LMS, they can evaluate and modify products in coordination with customer service experts (facilitators). This makes each learning process visible and puts learners in a position where they have the leverage to influence and maximize what a given area of knowledge has to offer. In such a context, learners stand a far better chance of becoming their own best critics as well as their own best teachers.

A Diary: Three Days with Mary (Age 10) and Her LMS

Monday morning

9 a.m.: On Saturday, I had some time, so I tested out of literacy level 5. It was the last requirement after my last book report and the video my team made comparing the cultures of three cities here in Michigan. I just finished the specifications for my core requirements in literacy level 6. I get to do most of it on independent study, and I'm really looking forward to the project where I get to learn what it's like to be an investigative

reporter. I don't think enough attention is being paid, by the president and others, to the issue of global warming, so I've chosen that as my topic. Mr. Conway, one of the teachers here, is going to be my editor, and he has already asked me to draft an outline of the proposed "conditions of satisfaction" that will make my story worth telling. I found a reporter at our local paper who has done stories on global warming, and she has agreed to be on my facilitation team. She, Mr. Conway, and two students are on the team, and we will communicate by e-mail and have a couple of meetings at the school after phase one and phase two. As soon as the specifications are approved, they go on my calendar with four deadlines to get my story ready. I've already printed out some articles I found on my Knowledge Browser. There is a really good one from *National Geographic* magazine. I have to name the source of every piece of information I provide.

11 a.m.: I met with Mr. Thomas, my academic advisor, about the fact that I haven't progressed in math as far as in other subjects. He knows I don't like math, but I agreed with him that because I like science, especially biology, I might get interested in some kinds of math. He told me about some kinds of math I have never heard of. I'm going to watch a video on chaos theory, and because he knows I am interested in genetics, I've put in a request for a video about genetic algorithms. It's about how they use math in genetic research. I really like looking at stuff under microscopes, so Mr. Thomas is trying to get me an internship in the lab at the hospital so I can use microscopes to find out real things. Mr. Thomas looked at my academic management system with me, and I think everything else is pretty well balanced.

"Balanced" just means I'm not ignoring something or unaware of something that will probably make me wish I'd paid attention to it later. They're not going to make me do math until I can see that I need it to do something I want to do.

2 p.m.: I just got out of my Jamestown colony microworld. We got some audio links from the Web to help us learn how they talked in 1609. We also went to virtual Jamestown and read letters that people there wrote. These were the first English people that came over to start an English colony. We are learning about what kind of food they ate and what kind of clothes they wore, and we are going to make clothes like they made them and talk like people from Elizabethan England and serve a dinner for the community. Our plan is to raise enough money so we can go to Jamestown and Williamsburg on a field trip.

We're bringing in some more people to our group to be the Algonquin Indians in Virginia then. They have to learn what is was like to deal with English people, and we have to learn what it was like to deal with them. We didn't get along very well because they killed more than 300 of us after we had been there only about 15 years. We have to learn why we didn't get along. I really want to understand because the Indians seem like they were cool to me. Why couldn't we understand each other and share the land?

Then, we are going to bring in some people to be Africans. The first Africans came to America in Jamestown. They weren't slaves though. They were indentured servants. We're going to find out what it was like to have indentured servants and get along with Africans, and we are going to find out what it was like to be an indentured servant.

I love doing microworlds. For me, they are a great way to learn about things that I might not be interested in by just reading a book or something. I said this in my blended learning profile so that my teachers and advisors will help me to find other microworlds for new things I am learning about.

3 p.m.: I saw a TV program on the Evangelical movement in America, and I thought it was very interesting because they see things very different than I do. At first, I thought they were just ignorant because they don't believe in science and they think that Adam and Eve was the real beginning of humans. When I told my mentor, Ann, she said that before I decide what they are like, I have to understand more about what they believe and why they don't think science is right about some things. I think they believe that Buddhists and Hindus, and all the other religious people, are doomed to go to hell unless they become "born again" Christians. I want to find out if this is true and what "born again" means. Ann thinks she can work with my academic advisor, Mr. Thomas, to get me two or three credits for this project. She is also trying to find me a way to get an e-mail pen pal about my age who lives in an area where there are lots of Evangelicals. I hope we can turn this into a project for credit. My dad says that there might be 100 million Evangelicals in the United States, so it seems important to understand why so many people believe in stuff that is so different from what I, and the people I know, believe.

Tuesday

11 a.m.: I slept late because I went to a movie with my parents last night. I am doing independent study all day and working at home. I'm

doing some stuff for my key abilities index to show that I can manage myself and my time. I'm keeping a log of everything I do and then putting together a plan for my next independent study day. I am keeping a planner and noticing how I can get more done by planning things. My learning facilitator, Miss Bradley, thinks I will be much happier with my own work when I can organize and plan it a little better. I can already see that she is right from my progress so far.

2 p.m.: I'm taking my Spanish course by CD-ROM on the computer. Different native Spanish-speaking people, like a waiter in a restaurant or a salesperson in record shop, talk to me, and I talk back to them. They even tell me when I said something wrong or didn't pronounce something right. I watch one movie a week in Spanish. I can stop the movie when I need to, and write down words I don't understand. I'm reading Spanish comic books too. Also, I have one pen pal in Costa Rica and another one in Argentina. We talk in Spanish about stuff that kids are doing. They send me pictures of places around where they live, and it makes me want to go there. I like it much better than taking Spanish in a regular class because I am talking to Spanish people, learning about different places that speak Spanish, and mostly, I can make it go as fast or as slow as I want. Sometimes I get bored and stop, and sometimes I get really into it and go longer than I had scheduled on my calendar.

4 p.m.: I'm learning how to make a résumé and do a job interview. It's part of my literacy requirement. Right now I'm studying about computer graphics designers because it's the next job I'm going to interview for. Each week I learn about a new type of job, and I have to watch a video and look up stuff on the Internet to prepare for my interview. Mr. Harley, our literacy coach, interviews me for all the jobs and tells me every time what I did well and what I can do better. Sometimes I watch other kids interviewing with Mr. Harley, and I can interview twice for a job if I really want it and did well on the first interview. I think I'm really interested in graphic designing, so I'm going to talk to Mr. Thomas about how I can get credit for a unit in computer graphics. If I get interested in a particular kind of job during the interview, Mr. Harley makes a note and then helps me find videos and simulations that will really help me to know what it is like to do that job.

Wednesday

8 a.m.: The specifications that I submitted for my literacy level 6 requirement were mostly accepted, but they want me to strengthen two

areas: "communicative competency" and "contrast and comparison." Mr. Thomas thinks I can work on both in my Evangelical Christians project if it is defined right. I will have lots of opportunities to compare and contrast Evangelicals with other Christians and people who think science has to be included in a religious education. Also, I'm sure it is going to test my ability to communicate well when I find myself disagreeing with my Evangelical pen pal. If we can't communicate well, I won't be able to learn much of anything. We are working on those new specifications (and a way to evaluate my progress) now.

10 a.m.: I love using my LMS because it gives me a way to see what I have learned, how well I am learning, and what I need to learn more about. I don't have to agree with it or with my advisors, but usually I do because I know they are spending a lot of time understanding me. The tests are good because they give me feedback, and I can challenge them if I, or even a counselor, think they are wrong. Everything is there in one place, and I can use it every day to help me learn. It's getting easier for me to combine requirements with things I want to do because I can usually combine them like I'm doing with the Evangelical project.

1 p.m.: I'm taking the rest of today off. I got a lot of things done lately, and I just want to fool around, do some things that aren't on my learning calendar. It's funny though. Every time I take some time off, I find a better way to do something that's hard for me or something else I'm interested in that I can try to turn into credit. The best way I can tell I'm doing well in school is when I can actually help create the courses and projects that earn me credit.

Complex Accountability

I'm convinced that the main key to the process of learning is discovery: discovery of truth, discovery of new domains of inquiry, deeper understanding of oneself, and discovery that expands the horizons of knowledge. Without a managed process that allows for self-directed inquiry, self evaluation and thus, discovery, we ignore the element of learner participation.

The same is true for setting and enforcing standards. They cannot be effective as a set of measures uniformly applied to each individual and for identical learning outcomes. Standards must be used to enable learners to make their thinking and learning processes visible. If a model for accountability cannot achieve this, it can achieve little else because it creates a milieu in which performance outweighs genuine learning—where knowledge is externalized and divorced from personal values and personal evolution.

Such standards do not tell us what has really been learned nor do they tell us what to expect from a person—with one exception. They tell us who the pleasers are, those who have surrendered to extrinsic motivators to make their way in life. Is this the type of society we want education to reinforce?

Accountability in the real world is messy. It involves a network of promises, requests, and shared explorations. A key mediator in the real world of accountability is the right to say no. "No, I can't deliver by this date. No, I don't want to take algebra. No, I'm not ready to accept this course plan yet; I need to know more." To make the world real for learners, they need the same rights. They need to be viewed as consumers of a highly customizable product.

The product, and just how customized it can be, will be discussed in Chapter 18—from domains of knowledge to subjects, to courses, to lessons, to modules, to learning objects, to discrete bits of information—how do we categorize, sort, and organize it all in a world the providers cannot control?

Endnotes

1 Alfie Kohn, *What Does It Mean to Be Well Educated? And More Essays on Standards, Grading, and Other Follies,* Beacon Press, 2004, p. 62

2 Very technical, but see *http://www.w3.org* for a breakdown of architectural standards for the World Wide Web if you want to learn more.

Chapter 17

CHAOS THEORY AND
THE BRAIN UNLEASHED

Compared to the pond of knowledge,
our ignorance remains atlantic.
—RONALD DUNCAN/MIRANDA WESTON SMITH

In 1960, a meteorologist named Edward Lorenz was using mathematical
equations to try to predict the weather. Lorenz eventually gave up
trying to predict the weather accurately, but by looking at graphs of his
calculations, he discovered a phenomenon that gave birth to chaos theory,
one of the three most important sciences to come out of the twentieth
century.

Chaos theory was perhaps most elegantly encapsulated in the following oft quoted passage from a book called **Does God Play Dice?**:

> *The flapping of a single butterfly's wing today produces a*
> *tiny change in the state of the atmosphere. Over a period of*
> *time, what the atmosphere actually does diverges from what*
> *it would have done. So, in a month's time, a tornado that*
> *would have devastated the Indonesian coast doesn't happen.*
> *Or, maybe one that wasn't going to happen does.*
> —IAN STEWART

215

Stewart's scenario has prompted scientists to often refer to this phenomenon as the "butterfly effect."

The first observation of this new science was that a tiny change in initial conditions could change the long-term behavior of seemingly random phenomena, or chaos. This led to later observations in physics, biology, and neuroscience that many of the mechanisms we study in isolation are coupled with much broader processes outside of our awareness. The principles discovered in observing complex, seemingly random phenomena are now being applied to economics, organizational theory, and many other disciplines.

What is being observed across all disciplines is that a large variety of physical and human systems exhibit seemingly chaotic behavior, but behind their apparent randomness is a higher degree of organization. Chaos isn't chaos after all but an implicate and higher order.

Nowhere is this more apparent than in biological systems. Take the heart, for example. What we think of as a rhythmic beat is, in fact, not at all like a metronome. Hearts routinely beat somewhat arrhythmically, skipping beats and speeding up and slowing down, even when the body is at rest. Says Dr. Yasha Kresh, professor of cardiothoracic surgery and biomedical researcher, "When that variability (of the heartbeat) converts itself into a regular monotonic rhythm, you can pretty much be certain that is the beginning of disaster."[1] Evidently, an irregular heartbeat is a sign of the heart's ability to regulate itself to changing conditions in and outside of the body.

In the brain, chaotic patterns are created when enormous collections of neurons link electrically in response to unknown stimuli. In the same way that dreams are helping us to complete mental processes begun during the day, neural activity in the brain is continuously accessing memory and known experiences to reference new ones. That is, it depends on chaos to create higher orders of discernment and knowledge.

Researchers from the Core Research for Evolutional Science (CREST) at the University of Tokyo have been studying a particular area of the cerebellum where nerve cells jump from moderate coupling to chaotic firing that "effectively recodes the high-frequency information into slower signals (integrated assimilation of inputs) by imparting information within the rhythm rather than just the frequency of nerve firing." CREST researchers refer to this phenomenon as "chaotic resonance" and assert that chaotic stimulation to the brain seems to aid learning.

Much of what has been learned about the brain seems to suggest that at its highest functioning level, it seeks that which is emergent from seemingly random inputs. Simply put, the brain seeks chaotic inputs to "engage in continual learning—categorizing a novel input into a novel category rather than trying to fit it into an existent category."[2] It seems to be willing to surrender its sovereignty, knowing that it stands to gain from mining the unknown.

Yet the very foundation of current learning design (or if you prefer, the lack of it) is to ignore our basic need to discover the world and make meaning for ourselves. This foundation also ignores the fundamental truth that most a priori "knowledge" is socially constructed, a product of what is already unconsciously accepted as truth without question. Together, these inadvertent blunders make for an antibrain infrastructure.

To flourish, the brain requires stimulation generated by moving from the known into the unknown and back again. To maximize its gain, it must have suitable feedback loops designed to have it review its own thinking processes and how it comes to know what it knows.

To begin building such a brain-compatible process, we must recognize that brains need to wean themselves from outside nurturing and control just as infants wean themselves from the breast. As learners are weaned from their dependence on frequent intervention and plentiful assistance, they take responsibility for their own learning so that their brains may be free to develop as they were meant.

Knowing this, we who facilitate learning are compelled to construct a thorough plan that gives learners the skill, the mental constructs, and the confidence to manage their own learning. In a reversal of tradition and closely held beliefs, this also means we decommodify, unpackage, and disintegrate educational resources.

Coming up with the "right" answers is appropriate only to the learner who has deemed a source worthy of having information he or she wants—answers he or she can use. This usually comes from an array of diverse searches and inputs. To the brain, "chaos provides the constant source of disequalibration, the awareness of complexity, and sensitivity to initial conditions"[3] that leads to higher organization and patterns of knowing.

The canvas of learning must present the sustained, open-ended uncertainty, the great cloud of unknowing that mirrors the brain's actual grasp, as well as the humility of truly learned people. Learning design must intentionally generate enough chaos to constantly renew each learner's sense of wonder and curiosity.

As young (preschool) children and professional adults, we are thrust into a maelstrom of discovery daily. We fend for ourselves in a society that generally supports our initiative. We must constantly adjust to and learn from disequalibrium. We must put these two worlds together and re-create the middle ground, the most intense period of formal learning, so that we progress with the delight and the wonder of children and the autonomy and responsibility of productive adults.

If we come into knowing and understanding from a view of the world (and of knowledge) as unpredictable, emergent, and largely obscured, we must learn to imbue everything we undertake with our own unique wisdom: a wisdom that respects those who have truly examined ideas and capabilities and most of all a wisdom that equates humility with respect for learning.

Schooling as we know it has a vested interest in controlling what is learned and how knowledge is doled out. It is a great deal to ask to relinquish this status quo, to convert to an open-ended learning process. As in the "butterfly effect," we must learn to look at each rock turned over by an individual learner as the flutter of a butterfly's wing—the possible initiation of great forces outside of our perspective and control.

The science of learning, given the dominion it deserves, will be the most significant science of the twenty-first century. It will set into motion forces that defy imagination, forces that will redefine what it is to be human.

Endnotes

1 From an interview with Dr. Kresh entitled "The Brain and Heart of Chaos," see *http://husol.hahneman.edu/chaosjk1.htm*

2 David Gross, *The Importance of Chaos Theory in the Development of Artificial Neural Systems*, see *http://wwww.geocities.com/ResearchTriangle/3324/neuro1.html*

3 From *Ignorance, Error and Chaos: Local Learning/Global Research*, translated from Japanese and published in English on the Web by John R. Jungck, Beloit College, see *http://biology.beloit.edu/jungck/ignorance.html*

Chapter 18

MANAGING AND ORGANIZING CHAOS

We live in a "connected" world of fiber optic cables, satellite signals, and twisted copper wires. More important, we are connected by language, aspirations, commerce, and culture. The primary connector in all of these human characteristics is information.

All information (useful, misleading, illuminating, pernicious, and necessary) is now available to us anytime and anywhere. From the perspective of a learning designer, there is an absolute glut of information.

Creating the efficiencies that deliver appropriate information to individual learners is clearly the biggest challenge of an "open (learner-centric) architecture." In the scope of this book, I cannot provide detail. Hopefully, I can provide a cogent overview.

Of course, the whole of the "info-sphere" is simply unorganizable and should be cordoned into that which is evaluated, sanctioned, indexed, organized, and optimized for such factors as:

- Ease of use
- Assessment—allowing for clear demonstration of progress within prescribed parameters
- Appropriateness for developmental and academic levels
- Facilitation indicators that say how a lesson or "chunk of information" might be supported by learning facilitators and used as a component to a packaged learning event

- Operability—instructions that enable learners to use technology components such as in a game or a test
- Probable learning outcomes—including links to more comprehensive or advanced follow-ups
- Point of view—directs learners' attention to such questions as "Whose view of society is represented here? Is there a political slant to this information? How would an environmentalist view this work? Whose way of looking at the world is promoted here? What is the agenda of this author?" etc.

Everything that is not optimized as described above is automatically part of the larger domain of "unconsigned." Is unconsigned information less valuable? Not at all! In fact, much of the value of investigation in this domain is giving it the utility and context offered in the "consigned" domain.

Of course, those who produce any kind of content in the unconsigned domain are dramatically limiting the market potential of their "content" for educational purposes. Defining the overall parameters of consigned content for educational purposes will reach across all ages, professions, nations, guilds, and associations as well as public and private institutions of education. Many will adopt generalized criteria and add criteria of their own.

To begin with, a glossary of terms might best describe some, but not all, of the component technologies of learning content. This offers the broad overview of what some may choose to rightly call managed chaos:

Hypertext is an educational device that almost everyone who owns a computer and a connection to the Internet has experienced. You click on an underlined word, and it automatically conveys you to another location: more words, sounds, animation, video clips, or games that further edify what you have been reading.

Hypertext builds a knowledge collage, linking together resources that have been chosen to expand on or validate the intended communication of simple text. It is the basic foundation of digital literacy and a much underutilized learning medium in schools—probably because reading words on a printed page is preferable to most teachers.

Hypertext and hyperlinking are the punctuation of authoring on the Internet. In traditional grammar, punctuation links words, sentences, and paragraphs. In cyberspace, linking creates nonlinear expression, a more cognitive-based form of communication. It can engage more of the senses than text by integrating sound and images.

I have already discussed the nonsequential and interactive nature of learning. Hypertext is, by nature, both. It is the basis for learning to write software, create Web sites, "blogging," and other essential means of digital communication. Moreover, by its nature, hypertext automatically engages those who use it in component skills of traditional literacy such as:

- Annotating text
- Cross-referencing
- Providing excerpts to elucidate a point
- Inserting bibliographic information/proof sourcing
- Inserting graphics to substantiate or clarify assertions

Connectivity in the brain certainly mirrors hypertext more nearly than traditional linear text. Much more research needs to be done relative to its effects on learning, but until it is routinely taught as a means of expression to young learners, the opportunity will be missed.

Learning Objects—By the shear force of volume, the Internet is viewed as a web of "knowledge." Before any discussion of using the architecture of the Internet to maximize learning can occur, I think it is necessary to distinguish between information and knowledge.

Knowledge is a process that exists only in a mind. When we express what we know, the message carried is not knowledge but information that becomes different knowledge in context of the relevance to each receiver.

Knowledge is not something that is "stored" inside the brain. It alters according to circumstance. My knowledge of how to ride a bicycle or write an essay is fluid. It is situational. The moment it becomes static, my mind is not engaged. I falter on the bicycle; I am no longer involved in writing the essay.

Information is exterior to the mind. It can be facts, observations, sensations, opinions, or interpretations. When information becomes integrated with the preexisting knowledge and experience framework of an individual, it can then become knowledge. Information is fuel. Knowledge is what our minds do with fuel. Information is stored in the brain.

Bottom line, when we send a learner in pursuit of knowledge, we must be aware that it does not reside somewhere where it can be captured. How information is presented, used, interpreted, valued, and applied is primarily influenced by our social connections. This applies at the delivery end of information as well as at the receiver end. We don't manage knowledge. We influence and add structure to an enormous chaos of information—much of it coming from sources we cannot control or foresee.

If we are to use the technology and vast resources of the Internet for learning, we start with this question: How does it get organized? Assuming that we can fuel brains with information, we ask the next question: How do we assemble bits of information and make them intelligible and relevant to inquiring minds?

Enter the notion of a **learning object**, or a unit of information that can have relevance to various learners. Don't we have to decide how big or small it can be? Obviously, we have to decide how it gets labeled and distributed to "consumers." It would make sense that we describe it, try to suggest how it becomes valuable in different contexts, and also make it easy for teachers and facilitators to apply it to specific learning goals.

All of these things are being debated, as are the common terms and technical standards by which they can be distributed (i.e., across developmental levels, schools, colleges, corporate settings, associations, governments, and international alliances). One group working on these issues is the IMS Global Learning Consortium. Visit the consortium at *http://www.imsglobal.org*. Much of the information you encounter will be highly technical, but the visit will acquaint you with the frontiers of creating an Internet learning architecture. I suggest clicking on "**Specifications**" to learn about the standards the group is creating and on "**Alt-I-lab**" to read some of the white papers that will introduce you to the level of thinking now being applied to this effort.

For purposes of discussion here, I will define a learning object as a resource that has some explicit and/implicit educational value and meets a narrow and well-defined set of learning objectives. A learning object can be nondigital such as the showcased "best efforts" of a group of inventors in Arizona or an exhibit at your local natural history museum.

For accessibility, it can make sense to reproduce an object or exhibit for the Internet. Let's take a museum exhibit, for example. Say there's an exhibit on diamonds somewhere at a natural history museum.

To turn the exhibit into a learning object, you must go through a sequence of steps:

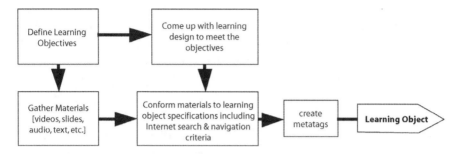

In defining learning objectives, you also need to define various audiences (i.e., interested in diamonds as jewelry, studying geology, gemology, mining, etc.). Once objectives and audiences are defined, then you can design and piece together the components of the object. Once the pieces conform to a learning taxonomy plus all other criteria and standards for producing a learning object, it is then tagged and placed in learning object repository. The act of placing it then triggers other events such as integration into other directories, linking to other objects, and additional tagging.

Learning objects can be as simple as a single picture or document, or they can be a complex assemblage of text and multimedia materials. They can exist in a public repository or a private one with restricted access. They can be free or have a cost attached to their use.

The future of this technology is potentially enormous, though there are many hurdles to realizing a system that really works as envisioned. This is an area where the federal government can play a role in such things as:

- Producing specifications for a uniform core curriculum that all states can agree on so that learning object repositories can service all state requirements for education equally.
- Funding the production of learning objects and producing uniform standards for private-sector providers.
- Funding independent research on learning object design and meta-tagging.
- Funding large-scale development projects, such as IMS, to build a national learning infrastructure.

- Initiating and funding "testbed" projects in large school districts to train personnel on the use of learning objects, the LMS, and other tools.
- Funding projects that accelerate the use of these technologies in small rural school districts where funding limits the use of human resources to make and support changes.
- Providing storage facilities (server farms) for learning object storage and retrieval.

When you combine learning objects and hypertext, you begin to have an information matrix that emulates brain functioning. There is no way of telling how much more active our dormant brains' powers can become by designing learning processes in this way until we implement the technology widely and do the research, but I suspect we are on the brink of unlocking new and higher levels of brainpower.

Teachers who now want to take a small step toward a more open-sourced approach to learning can begin to work with students to choose independent means and resources to meet current curriculum guidelines. It can be a very difficult step. "How can I manage such a chaotic process?" is a very common question.

Moving from control to support and facilitation will require new skills. Under the present circumstances of schooling—moving everyone through the same curriculum in the same way and at the same pace—it takes a visionary and a risk taker to take even the small steps toward managed chaos.

Learning objects form the nucleus of an enormous learning network that can deliver individually tailored "lessons" to millions simultaneously. As they become more plentiful, easier to locate, and easier to integrate into a larger course of inquiry, they will become more primary in the formal process of learning.

As this initiative becomes a reality for public education, its audience grows by tens of millions. The production of learning objects will most certainly spawn an enormous industry of cottage producers alongside big media conglomerates. Imagine billions of TV news archives alone converted into learning objects. The National Geographic Society might turn its primary focus on becoming a principal creator of learning objects.

Imagine the staffing needs for independent reviewing bodies and teachers producing learning objects under the employ of private companies.

Relationships among stewards of information, intermediaries, those who guard their monopolies over specific kinds of knowledge, and those who distribute forms of information are going to change radically in form and function. No one can see what will happen at this point though predictions and high-risk bets will be made.

Debates will rage about striking balances among the learning object world, the world of packaged learning products, and traditional face-to-face teaching. Much needs to be done to ensure that what is located in the managed chaos of a learning object economy is then given context and applied in the physical world. Encounters in cyberspace need to generate social encounters to keep the two worlds in a reciprocal embrace—challenging and empowering each other.

There is much to sort out around questions of intellectual property and who pays for learning objects—subjects for a later book.

Meta-data and meta-tagging—Meta-data, here, means information about learning objects that helps locate them and maximize their use. Meta-tags are the coding (attached to but not visible) in the learning objects themselves that provides a variety of descriptors for identifying, sorting, and distributing them. The card catalog in your library is meta-data about all of its books. Now imagine a card catalog that provides information about every indexed item in every book. Then take into account that each of these indexed items may be of interest to multiple audiences and might require separate cards. Now you begin to get the scope of providing meta-data for learning objects.

If this aspect of the technology is not done right, if it fails to provide a way to effectively manage, store, sort, identify, and retrieve the monstrous volume of discreet bits of learning media, it will not have a core role in learning as many now envision. The role of meta-data and its component information technology is very central to how things will play out. There are many questions yet to be answered.

Learning object repositories—These are the libraries themselves, the digital storage places for learning objects. Repositories will be located in multiple locations, some public domain, others privately held. There certainly needs to be a technology and set of standards for interoperability, like the World Wide Web (WWW) so that a networked "web" of discrete servers becomes one unified resource for all.

Specialized repositories will become the acknowledged source for specific kinds of information. Others may become known for their more sophisticated meta-data allowing for multiple objects to be packaged into more comprehensive or specialized learning resources. Certainly, as in the case of National Geographic, many large and high-quality archives of images, recordings, and data will be repurposed and repackaged as learning objects.

Learning agents and data mining—A learning agent is a software program that takes meta-tagged learning objects to a new level of complexity. It scans learning repositories and can respond to a set of commands entered by a learner or teacher and compose a set of learning objects into a course or course module.

Agents could program themselves to be adaptive to learning styles, recurring interests, and connections between areas of knowledge. Conceivably, they can point out when a set of learning objects furthers work already completed by a learner and subsequently alert the learner to new objects that better answer previous inquiries.

Conduct a Google or Yahoo search under the acronym JAM (Java Agents for Meta-Learning) and you will find many papers on one such technology. In the schema I am describing, it will take some time before agents are developed that "understand" the meta-tagging in learning object repositories in an adaptive way as described above.

Clearly, however, such technologies add another level of complexity that can begin to meet and serve the true complexity of the brain. Especially when we can combine the left-brained functions of direct paths to information with the right-brained functions that intuit larger patterns, we provide the brain with an exterior console that begins to tap its capabilities.

Extracurricular Learning and Earning Academic Credit

By now, it is apparent that the issues of how learning is packaged and credits are assigned need a total revision. Some further thoughts:

Earning merits—What I remember liking most about the Boy Scouts was all the options I had to learn practical things. And when I fulfilled the rigorous requirements for a subject area, I received a bright, colorful emblem, a merit badge to show what I had earned. I wasn't evaluated in the subject area or compared to others who studied the same area. I was acknowledged for fulfilling its requirements. I remember thinking, even at the time, that merit badges were far more satisfying and meaningful to me than grades at school.

Clusters of certain kinds of merit badges created subcultures within the scouts, such as those who exhibited a strong interest in science. They were a way to establish an identity, a unique status within the community. Certain merit badges were required to advance to Star and then Life and finally Eagle Scout. Some scouts were proud of the fact that they had not advanced to the higher ranks but had a lot more merit badges than some in the higher ranks—merit badges that weren't required but showed that individuals were accomplished and maybe more important but just interested in different areas of life.

It was a fascinating way to build a culture around education, not an enforced culture but one that offered diversity and a way for all participants to earn a place for themselves. Today, there are well over 100 merit badges, and new ones are constantly being created. Others die out as they fade in popularity. Some examples of current badges are Atomic Energy, Astronomy, Animal Science, Archaeology, Aviation, Citizenship (separate badges for community, nation, and world), Crime Prevention, Dentistry, Electronics, Environmental Science, Oceanography, Public Speaking, Soil and Water Conservation, Theatre, and Weather.

In the scouts, there was the sense that you were earning a place in the larger world and at the same time discovering your passions. This is where schools can learn from scouting. I remember earning an archaeology merit badge, in part, by going out on a "dig" with the local archaeological society. We dug in an American Indian burial mound, and I actually found an artifact that wound up in a university museum in Berkeley, California.

I was given an opportunity to accomplish something of note, and at the same time, I learned that I was interested in cultural anthropology. I subsequently read a number of illustrated books on Indian cultures on my own. In that case, as well as others, the merit badge became less important than the curiosity it awakened.

Can we create the equivalent of merit badges as a parallel system to the vertical path toward completing core credits? Can we do away with grades—and even grade levels? Perhaps one reaches a certification level for having completed certain credits but also has the option to branch into areas of interest without advancing toward certification in the core curriculum—horizontal as well as vertical advancement. In the Army, you have noncommissioned officers who develop highly specialized skills and are respected within the ranks though they do not become officers—horizontal as well as hierarchical advancement, cultures with different values within a larger culture.

In the scouts, there are community service requirements for each level of advancement. Staged community service, or service learning as it is referred to in the educational world, can be the opportunity to try out interests in the real world as an apprentice.

Also in the scouts, most are encouraged to develop useful skills such as auto mechanics, cooking, life saving, and home repairs. This creates opportunities to combine eventually marketable skills with service learning such as being part of the crew building a Habitat for Humanity[1] house or winterizing cars for the elderly.

To build on the scouting model of education, I propose a four-part plan that incorporates the following:

1. Core credits—Identify the basic curriculum designed to fulfill the requirements for what we now refer to as primary and secondary education. Create a set of parameters for achieving these credits on a contract or independent study basis. Specific methods and criteria would be established for designing a course of study from resources other than a preexisting syllabus and designated texts. Core credits would be made available in the traditional classroom, but those who wish to tackle them in other ways would be encouraged to do so and provided with all the resources of the new architecture to assist.

The distinction between traditional schools, charter schools, and homeschooling would blur as learners cross hitherto established boundary lines to take a class from a teacher; take a class online with the help of a learning facilitator; negotiate a learning contract composed of a variety of resources to receive units of credit; work at home, at a library, at a community center, or at another designated safe learning facility.

The competition in such a system will likely be robust. At the same time, it should be relatively untainted by commercial mischief. The competition would be among modes of learning, levels of independence, and facilities that were successful at providing them.

The element of comparison would be so integral to the process of choosing what and how to learn that private providers would simply have to submit their wares to the same process of scrutiny as publicly created products. Whenever a product had a price attached to it, the consumer would be obliged to seek comparable free products. Private providers could compete only by having a product that fills an unmet need or is clearly superior in some way that consumers have demanded.

Outsourcing elements of education to the private sector would be a strategic issue for the public system. Deciding where private companies could be more responsive to changes in a subject or advances in technology would be key factors. Who would want to compete with the resources of the National Geographic Society, a leading computer games company, or Microsoft in areas where their expertise is clearly superior?

A feasible way to view the notion of vouchers is to provide every student with a book of voucher credits to be used for the purchase of privately sold educational resources. Hence, a percentage of tax dollars would be earmarked for attractive alternatives or supplements to existing curricula. Such a model would need complex checks and balances to avoid redundancy and ensure that a demand receives a quality response. Despite its complexity, this approach could be far more responsive to a learner-centric architecture than simply shuffling a limited percentage of students to private schools.

There will certainly be debates over what the core credits should be, though the need for debate becomes mitigated by the creation of a horizontal or "merit" curriculum that goes far beyond our prior notion of extracurricular subjects. At the primary level (grades 1–6), it would make sense to focus on a much expanded literacy curriculum (as described in Part II, Chapter 6) and basic mathematics and science. Many of the projects within math and literacy would cross over into history, social studies, and the sciences though they would always contribute to advanced levels of literacy and numeracy. The other curriculum would be cognitive studies (learning skills, critical thinking, etc.). If these two areas are mastered by the end of primary studies, presumably a learner is ready to begin managing his or her own learning activity, designing course modules, earning credits for specialized inquiry, and increasing the amount of time pursuing studies on an independent basis and in nonschool settings.

2. Merit Curriculum—When you unhook teaching from learning, there is no limit to what can be offered in even the smallest of schools.

Take languages, for instance. Many parents complain that third- or fourth-year French and Spanish are not available at their schools. Others want more languages. Using online and software-based resources, there are many excellent language courses available, some free and many reasonably priced. If this is a concern of yours or in your school, know that you could offer as many as 26 languages at your school tomorrow via *http://www.orbislingua.com/resettastone.htm*. Also check out *http://www. bbc.co.uk/languages/* for some excellent-quality free instruction.

Like merit badges, the existence of a large offering of so-called non-core subjects creates a world of learning that offers something for everyone—a place where individuals can follow their interests and receive recognition and credit for doing so. Like the scouts, it would be effective to create a visual system of recognition so that a completed credit in avionics or zoology would be acknowledged by a colorful certificate that could be displayed at home or at school.

Instead of grades, I believe it makes much more sense to emphasize accomplishments. A course completed would have to have met satisfactory standards for basic knowledge of the material in that course. If the course is not completed satisfactorily, no certificate. It may have been too difficult, abandoned for lack of interest, put aside for the pursuit of a more essential course, etc. None of these reasons should stigmatize learners. Making mistakes is an essential part of discovery—the discovery of real interests, limitations, and priorities. For those who like rewards, completing a course with honors could be the substitute for an A.

At the secondary level, it makes increasing sense for a significant percentage of curricula to be self-selected, self-designed (with guidance), and paired to declared interests. The notion of trying on different fields of study, occupations, professional challenges, and real-world responsibilities should gradually become a primary intention so that the person nearing the end of a secondary education is already building a useable skill set.

As long as the search for knowledge, like in the Boy Scouts, is equally seen as making a place for oneself in the world and discovering one's passions, the movement toward both ought to be parallel. At the secondary level, students should have practical skills, and they should be aware that learning is a lifelong process, often leading to several related or unrelated occupations.

Hypothetically, let's say there were 500 official merit curricula courses available to a learner. Once a course of inquiry such as avionics is exhausted through available courses, then a student and his or her advisors must decide whether it is appropriate, in the present, to pursue a customized course of study in avionics. If the answer is yes, they would then investigate options for designing further credits in avionics.

When is it too early to begin a diversion into a specialized field of study? How much diversion is appropriate before core studies become diluted? How uniform do we really need education to be? These are all questions that have not been adequately answered, in part because we haven't explored alternatives to the homogenized system in place now.

We think of primary and secondary schools as the arena for a basic education. But what is basic? Should basic mean an identical curriculum for everyone? How many people who study algebra ever use it? If the answer is 20%, and I sincerely doubt that it is that high, should algebra qualify as basic education?

On the other hand, if a 13-year-old discovers a passion for cooking or a 15-year-old becomes obsessed with veterinary medicine, should we discourage them from following their passions?

"Passion of the moment, you mean," a knowing parent might say. Yes, it may be temporary, but does that mean we don't follow our passions? So what if we abandon a course of study that involved some courses in veterinary medicine and an apprenticeship to a veterinarian? Was the investment wasted? If embraced with genuine interest, I think not.

Adolescents, in particular, are deeply immersed in a subconscious search for identity. Should we not make this process more conscious? Kids now find identities through rather narrow outlets such as sports, associations with friends, how they dress, and hobbies. The unique genius of the Boy Scouts (I assume the same principles apply to the Girl Scouts) is that they recognize the importance of association and identity formation in growing up. They provide a much bigger laboratory, in the form of diverse pursuits, for children to discover their interests and to put their interests to work in a community setting.

Merit curriculum should have the potential to become core curriculum for the student who sticks to a specialized learning path and particularly when that path leads to a practical skill that can be used for community service or a job. In fact, I go so far as to suggest that we make an essential part of secondary education the cultivation of a marketable skill.

Those who have made a definite decision to put off their careers until after a higher education should not be excepted from this. Although the subject is too big to elaborate on here, I do think it is a crucial right of passage into adulthood to have something you are good at, proud of, and can actually make a living at during adolescence. There are many such skills that do not require large investments of time: being a lifeguard/swim instructor, childcare, community volunteer, carpentry, cooking, etc. Part of the new social contract for education will be to include the creation of new competencies to enable young people to become productive and responsible members of society while still in the formal schooling process. Many of those competencies could well be associated with learning.

3. The social structure of learning: Competencies, CoPs, guilds, and PIWs—At some point in the formal process of learning, the world of understanding that each individual is building must begin to become personal. Paradoxically, it doesn't become personal without being realized within a social structure. As people are the creators and carriers of knowledge, it is through association and practical application that knowledge becomes professed. To put it in the simplest of possible terms, "Use it or lose it."

You can read a book about learning to ride a bicycle, but it doesn't enable you to know how to ride. You can read books about management or law, but they don't familiarize you with being a manager or a lawyer. Join a bicycle club and through association with those who are serious about it, you find that bicycling becomes a practice. Become part of a community of lawyers, listen to their language, witness their attitudes about the challenges they face, join in some useful part of their work and you begin to experience what it is like to be a lawyer.

Being and doing, these are the essential elements of learning that schooling cannot actually prepare learners for without extending their reach into enterprises and communities concerned with the practice and improvement of human skills and ideals. The new architecture will reach beyond preparing to enter the world to building a new component dedicated to that very end.

The Boy Scouts managed to make the world of accomplishment and civic involvement immediate yet staged. You could try on being and doing without having to be fully fledged. It was real, but it was also intermediate. It was a staging place for doing and becoming.

To create such a framework within the world of education, communities and the professional world will have to ante up and play an official role—the role of bridging from interest to real-world practice. At present, there is no mediating institution between the cloistered life of formal learning and the passage into professional and community life. What could be more important for the young than to engineer such a bridge?

To do so would involve a mass movement. In the corporate world, there has been much talk and research about "learning organizations" and "communities of practice." I suggest that the corporate world can further serve its needs as well as those of public education by looking to those who make public educational policy for an institutionalized bridge from school to a place in the world.

Such a movement would combine good corporate citizenship and collaboration between government and the professional world on building human capital. Furthermore, it would partner schools, communities, government, and the professional world in developing productive citizens.

It is a tall order. And there are many ways it could be co-opted for political or corporate agendas. That said, such collaborations are now called for if public education is going to evolve into a relevant twenty-first-century institution.

The form of such a movement is critical in that we need to design a hybrid of education and professional and community life—a form that shepherds the process of entering society. If the design for this form is part of the new architecture, if it is embraced by corporate, professional, and geographic communities, we will have the makings of a new era in public life.

When we bring communities and schools into direct relationship and then do the same with the occupational/professional world, we redefine schools as centers of knowledge creation rather than the false and misleading impression that they are places for the transmission of knowledge. Developmentally, children begin to have the capacity to integrate intellectual development, identity, and work during midadolescence.

I propose a set of forms. I use the word "form" because the idea is at the conceptual stage and will need much refinement and filling in before it can become action research. The forms suggested here, in particular, are submitted for thought and discussion as a composite group of social structures for learning:

- **Communities of Practice (CoPs)**—These are communities of people who practice or have practiced a profession or occupation combined with those who have an interest in learning what their work and their culture are all about. The community members meet to advance the work of their profession. They do so by creating a continuous learning culture that builds knowledge and experience in the community. Retired professionals are highly respected for their prior contributions and for mentoring young people who wish to understand the culture of lawyers, farmers, firefighters, teachers, those who hold an elected office, culinary workers, entrepreneurs, etc.

CoPs have local chapters whenever possible, but in rural areas where there may be no research physicists or automotive designers, an interested learner can become part of an online community composed of members around the country and all over the globe. When the community meets for an annual conference, rural members will have the chance to physically meet prominent members and sit in on their professional discussions and presentations.

As a sanctioned participant in public education, a CoP would have to adhere to certain rules and practices. Mostly, the required structure would ensure that working professionals gave back to their professional communities by embracing learners who deepen exposure to their world. They would do this by welcoming observers into their professional dialogues and by creating events that provided novitiates with opportunities to formulate and ask questions that would introduce them to actual issues and practices.

An excellent incubator and meeting place for CoPs would be community colleges. Most communities of modest size or larger have a community college, and it is a natural place for bridging academic learning and real-world practice.

Professionals who participate in CoPs strictly composed of working professionals enjoy camaraderie, knowledge sharing, and networking for professional benefit. Introduce CoP participants who are "courting" a profession and you add valuable dynamics that come from returning to basic ideals and motivations, asking fundamental questions about where the profession is going, showcasing the best and acknowledging the worst of things, and exhorting the young to take on long-term reform and evolutionary issues. A profession stays young by giving the young a provisional place in it.

Those joining a CoP as students would be entering into a social contract whereby they are committing to a working understanding of a professional world. Participation would center around volunteer work that exposes them to daily professional routines, sitting in on professional discussions and presentations, and taking on a large-scale project that would provide immersion in some facet of the profession. Teachers and learning advisors would work with CoP professionals to define, shepherd, and review the project as needed.

CoP projects would be of defined duration. Upon completion, academic credit would be received, a major entry would be placed in learners' LMS portfolios, including self-evaluation, learning facilitator evaluation, and professional and peer evaluations. If the completed project results in a desire on the part of a learner to further participate in the CoP (i.e., becoming a paid intern, volunteering, or accepting a regular paid position), a mentor (usually a retired professional) would be assigned to help provide the support needed in having the work contribute to skill and identity building.

- **Guilds**—A guild differs from a community of practice in that it is a social and professional home for someone who has actually decided to develop competencies in a given occupation, craft, or profession. A significant percentage of those who join a guild will go on to embrace its profession. Some will continue on a path to higher education, but many will be diverted, after meeting secondary education requirements, to an educational path offered and sponsored by the guild.

Guilds can offer those who are ready to enter the world of work a place that meets social, educational, and economic needs. In a world where job security has become a thing of the past, the guild will provide a stable home to those who have cultivated specific skill sets. They would primarily be organized around:

1. Ensuring financial security
2. Professional training, certification, and placement
3. Becoming a locus of social interaction and identification

In addition to these functions, the guild would help establish and verify members' skill levels and work records and would serve as the ultimate reference.[2]

Guilds sanctioned by and integrated into the public education system would provide the extremely important function of diverting millions of young people into technical occupations that are compatible with their ambitions, capabilities, and economic needs.

Early apprenticeships would likely identify the best young people to carry on guild occupations. Guilds would be specifically responsible for training their members in all industry-specific skills and taking over the training function from schools and the corporate world. They would award certificates of competency involving multiple skills and levels of expertise. In the particular occupation in which a guild member is certificated, this credential would equate to employability and status.

In a time where job security is mostly a thing of the past, guilds provide a new social infrastructure that builds a closer connection among current aspirations, working life, and future development. They also provide a more efficient path to knowledge on demand.

"Guilds—which operate at the intersection of individual career aspirations, informal networks where work and learning actually get done, and the enterprise's quest for competitive advantage—are where much of the innovation around learning, and around work-life integration, can be expected to surface in the coming years."[3]

- **PIWs**—These are communities for **Putting Ideals to Work**. For the young, it is critical that ideals are identified and put to a real-world test. There is a tendency for young people to abandon ideals or become frustrated in finding ways to express their ideals as they become adults and begin to face the world of work. The consequence of this tendency is disappointment, shutting down key components of their identities, and retreating to cynicism.

PIWs are specifically constituted to explore the relationship between ideals and finding avenues to make them happen in the world. Like CoPs, they are thematic, concentrating on a specific area of life chosen as a calling for each member. Here are a few examples:

- Building a better democracy
- Creating renewable energy
- Improving education
- Ending war
- Breaking the boundaries of thought—unlocking human potential
- Optimizing health and fitness
- Making friends with other countries and cultures
- Communicating to others through the arts
- Ending poverty and hunger
- Conserving natural resources

Of course, the possibilities are endless. Each of the above areas suggests many opportunities to further ideals through activism. The principal work of a PIW is to define an ideal and put it in a community context (i.e., "How can we contribute to ending war here in Madison, Wisconsin?").

The work of participation in a PIW would be to confront several challenges. First, it would be to rally a set of outside resources (community members, organizations, thought leaders, and activists) with the same cause. Then, it would require defining a project, organizing around its goals, and implementing it. Finally, it would necessitate keeping the cause alive in some form for other students to carry forward.

Of course, the litmus test for a PIW would be "Did we make a difference?" Again, community opinion, peer review, and feedback from learning facilitators would together provide answers.

Several other important areas of evaluation would be recurrent in such a structure. "Did we organize ourselves well? Did we define and plan our project effectively? What did we learn that will make us more effective in the future? What is our relationship to the ideal now that the project is completed?"

Together, the above "forms" represent a missing ingredient in contemporary education. Building real-world competencies should not wait until one has passed through adolescence. By putting this process off and divorcing it from public education, we have, in effect, extended adolescence beyond its usefulness. To have a useful skill, to put ideals to work in the world, to create an identity beyond the normal adolescent preoccupations would become the right of passage we now lack.

The dynamics of many families propel adolescents into the world sooner than we might expect. I think it would be wiser to embrace this process than resist it. By doing so, it is likely we would find that many who enter the world of work at an early age would gain useful life experience, self-esteem, and the ambition to carry themselves to higher goals.

For this and other reasons, it might behoove us to rethink the notion of "graduation." At present, high school graduation is the de facto dividing line between youth and adulthood. Many who graduate from high school put off the transition to adulthood while continuing their education. Others regard themselves as failures for having missed the mark of qualifying for a university education or for being from poorer families that lack the resources to support them while in college. Still others do not achieve the certificate of graduation and are stigmatized as having failed to reach the lowest rung of the socioeconomic ladder.

Recognizing learning as a lifelong process and acknowledging that for many, it will be interrupted for a variety of reasons and in a variety of ways, we can view progress as more diversified. It is reasonable and wise to expect learners to have progressed to certain qualifications in literacy and numeracy in order to fully qualify for social inclusion—to participate in educational and occupational communities. However, I do not see the usefulness of creating an arbitrary demarcation point that is now signified by a high school diploma.

When the educational communities I have described above become an integral part of the learning process and when a significant component of learning is self-selected and self-managed, the accomplishments of a 17- or 18-year-old will be far more diverse and difficult to subject to comparative standards. Graduation becomes a matter of degrees rather than an event.

The failures of such a system would lie primarily in the learners who, at 18, are not self-directed and are unable to progress into paid work or advanced education. It is impossible to predict in a learner-centric architecture the numbers who may fit into such a category though I suspect they would be far outnumbered by those who have "graduated" in the sense that they have taken full responsibility for their learning and thus for its consequences. In our present system, the link between learning and its consequences is so fragile as to be nonexistent for the majority.

The Boy Scouts have failed to stay as relevant as in the past for reasons that are not important here. I left them at 14 because I couldn't bear wearing the uniforms to meetings. However, they do, I believe, provide a more integrated view of learning, identity, and community—one that is relevant for public education.

With contemporary schooling, we have isolated young people from their communities and families despite the best efforts of caring teachers. We have failed to harness the differentiation energy of adolescents to welcome them into society and provide them with a meaningful place. Through the design of schooling, we encourage them to become rebels without a cause. The new architecture will reflect a view that an education system's prime measure of success is having created enthusiastic independent learners and young citizens who embrace a productive role in society.

Endnotes

1 Habitat for Humanity builds low-cost housing for the poor. See *http://www.habitat.org*

2 See *http://ccs.mit.edu/21C* working paper no. 004 for a more thorough discussion of guilds. Written for the Sloan School of Management at MIT's "Initiative on Inventing the Organizations of the 21st Century" by Robert Laubacher and Thomas Malone

3 Robert Laubacher, "Guilds and the Future of Learning," from *LineZine*, 2001, see *http://www.linezine.com*, Summer 2001, "Integrating Learning, Working and Life"

Chapter 19

DEFINING ROLES IN A CULTURE OF LEARNING

In writing this book, I am mindful that there are three million teachers out there who will be impacted by learner-centric education. If you are one of them and are having trouble with where all of this is going, I suggest the following:

Go to *http://www.mceetya.edu.au*, the Australian Ministerial Council on Education, Employment, Training, and Youth Affairs. Click on "Publications," and find and click on the report called "Learning Architecture Framework—Learning in an Online World." This publication will give you an idea about how Australia is moving toward the implementation of a learner-centric architecture.

Other countries, such as China, Indonesia, Malaysia, Canada, and England, are moving in this direction as well. The World Bank and the European Union are suggesting similar initiatives to prepare schools for twenty-first-century needs.

Go to the Web once more and find Roger Schank's "hyperbook" called *Engines for Education* for a leading American educator's view of a learner-centric model. There is a worldwide movement, still invisible to most American educators, to turn the present model upside down and inside out.

Many may argue that a comprehensive makeover of education is rash and untested. The model we are using now has been tested ad nauseum, and the facts, I would assert, are indisputable. The present system is obsolete and highly dysfunctional. The nature of learning is largely contrary to the design of schooling.

That said, we certainly cannot make an instant leap to what I have been describing. A transitional strategy will be necessary to make the incremental steps in the right order and use existing resources to the best advantage. Teachers represent the key resource in doing so **if** they are able to embrace a learner-centric view. This, of course, is the big *if.*

Making the shift to a learner-centric system radically alters the educational contract and the roles of both teachers and learners. Teachers and their supporting cast become facilitators, and learners take on a higher degree of responsibility.

The adverse effects of too much teacher control have dimmed learner enthusiasm, motivation, and confidence. Many of today's students will have a strong tendency to resist a system that makes them more responsible.

Today, the implicit contract is that teachers will impart knowledge directly to learners through their knowledge and "teaching" abilities. The new contract begins with the idea that "there is no instructive interaction." Clarity and understanding are internal, unique, and largely undetectable processes for which you, the learner, are entirely responsible.

Learner-centered teachers will have to know more about themselves and how their own cognitive styles affect communication with each individual. They will have to know more about each learner's background, values, and beliefs because they understand that this information is the bedrock from which each learner seeks and processes information.

Learner-centered teachers will help students exercise new freedoms in seeking and validating knowledge. Student involvement will vary dramatically depending on the degree to which each one has become responsible for his or her own learning. At the simplest level, teachers will provide a menu of varied projects and assignments to complete a course, from which each learner must choose the right combination.

As the process increases in complexity, teachers will begin to assess a learner's portfolio of self-selected activities, independent resources, and extracurricular work to assign credit for academic achievement. In the process, teachers will work with a supporting cast of testers, mentors, coaches, and counselors to assist learners in better selecting and completing curriculum.

If a system like this, one that requires so much more of teachers and learners, was suddenly implemented in the middle of the K-12 curriculum, it would be greatly subverted by resistance. It will have to be introduced gradually beginning in the early ages. Though students are tired of the control and tedium of school and teachers are tired of students who resist deeper learning, it is best to prepare for the likelihood that the current habits of teaching and learning will die hard.

So let's work backward from the future. I will start with a brief description of revised and new roles for teachers and learning facilitators:

Primary Master Teacher (K-6)

The qualifications and attributes of a great teacher differ when you separate early learning and development. Just where the dividing line is drawn is subject for debate. I am arbitrarily choosing the sixth grade or age 12 as the point where teaching begins to take a different course.

In the primary grades, children are transitioning from total reliance on adults for guidance to the preadolescent state of beginning to seek independence. A teacher during the primary phase must be well attuned to a child's growth and motor development, cognitive functioning, social skills, and family relationships. All of these areas break down into further categories and developmental levels. The core skill of a primary teacher is to determine in which of many developmental areas a child is troubled or lagging and where an intervention will prove effective.

Interventions may be in working with parents, managing social interactions, dealing with patterns of aggression or "acting out" behavior, setting behavior limits, improving sensory-motor development, just being there during tough emotional times, and much more. The shear complexity of the brain's development during this phase of childhood calls for a multidisciplinary approach to learning facilitation.

Primary teachers are focused on the subjects of literacy, numeracy, and basic science. The manner and depth of coverage need a new design that enables teachers to focus on individual needs. Teachers, at this level, are with or available to students for the better part of the school day. I don't think this should change at the primary level until learners show definite signs of competence at self-paced, self-managed learning.

In addition to teaching the primary subjects and attending to emotional and social development, the K-6 teacher is teaching kids how to learn. The shift to this primary emphasis will become a major change in the new architecture just as it will become the chief prerequisite for teaching ability.

The learning skills inventory for a primary teacher will include independent thinking, identifying different points of view, formulating questions, intellectual perseverance, making analogies, refining arguments and clarifying issues, distinguishing between facts and supposition, citing and evaluating sources, comparing perspectives and interpretations, self-evaluating reasoning processes, questioning assertions and beliefs, identifying most relevant and logical arguments, and comparing/contrasting theories or ideals with actual practice.

These are among the skills necessary to produce a competent, independent learner. Those who teach children up to age 11 or 12 should be keenly aware that nature has a timetable for building the infrastructure of intelligence. Roughly at age 11, the brain releases a chemical that dissolves neural fields that have not been developed and used.[1] These functional networks within the brain are built primarily through the development of thinking and learning skills rather than the memorization of classroom data.

Stimulating brain development, then, is the key role of a primary teacher. The secondary teacher does not abandon this process but subordinates it to putting intellectual capacity to work following individual intellectual curiosity. The primary teacher builds the brain's capacity; the secondary teacher ensures that the capacities of individual brains are used to the fullest.

Master teachers, then, attend to basic skills cultivation: reading, writing, speaking, listening, math, and basic science. They develop thinking skills as mentioned above and are mindful of the development of individual responsibility, emotional health, self-esteem, social development and collaborative skills, independence, and self-management.

The skill-set of such a teacher is very comprehensive. To have exhibited mastery in all of these areas requires knowledge of psychology, brain development, sociology, and cognitive science as well as excellent organizational skills to keep records on each learner and initiate developmental interventions.

The essential skill of a master teacher, however, is intangible—something probably not learned, at least so far as our present teacher training system goes. It is the ability to bond with children, to engender trust, and to inspire them to do what they most want to do anyway: learn.

The passage from primary to secondary school is often difficult for children. Many things are happening. Children are becoming driven toward independence and are less driven to please parents and teachers. The secure intimacy of a single classroom gives way to multiple destinations and learning agents. Children do not bond with their classmates as readily or often as in the primary grades. The process of individuation will become primary.

To smooth the path to secondary education, primary teachers must focus on preparing children for the new culture of disparate influences and associations—less like the home, more like the world. The last stage of primary curriculum will focus on this transition and will create an intellectual understanding and an emotional preparedness to take over the reigns of their learning and move from the venue of the home and classroom out into the world.

Secondary Master Teacher (ages 11–18)

If there is to be a diploma in the process of education, I suggest that a more appropriate dividing line, or right of passage, be the matriculation from primary to secondary education. It is at this point that learners would "graduate" to self-managed learning—in effect, embarking on the path of using the skills they have learned to complete themselves. It ought to be an auspicious occasion.

Teachers at this level are subject matter experts, renowned among their students for being able to bring a subject alive. Here is a testimonial to such a teacher:

> "I had some excellent teachers, but the man who I most admired was Richard S. Peterson. Neither he nor I realized the importance of the role that he played in my life until years later. Mr. Peterson was a brilliant 'master teacher' with a commanding presence who taught college preparatory chemistry and physics at Jordan High School.
>
> "Mr. Peterson taught these subjects so completely, so thoroughly, and so enthusiastically that many of his students chose to study the sciences in college. Those who did literally sailed through the first two or three semesters of chemistry and physics with very little effort. Even more important, we learned how to be good citizens, we learned how to work, we had fun, and, most of

all, by following his example, we learned personal values that have
influenced our lives long after we have forgotten various chemical
properties and physics formulas."[2]

Many of us have been lucky enough to have known a teacher like
this. The experiences are generally few and far between, but we remember
the "master teachers." Not only did they love their subject, they also in-
fected us with their love for it.

Presently, a student matriculating from the seventh through the
twelfth grades may have 30 different teachers. Alternatively, if we exposed
students only to master teachers, they would be lucky to have five during
the same period. If only master teachers "taught" in the traditional sense,
what would we have lost? Yes, sadly, many would have to find new roles
in education or new jobs altogether. The net effect on learners, I submit,
would be highly positive.

Teachers would be highly respected. They could ask more of students
because they would deliver more. The excitement for a subject learned in
a master teacher's classroom would be carried over into further pursuit
(perhaps with the teacher as mentor) or into entirely new subjects taken
on without teachers.

Do we need teachers who do not meet the standard of "master"? The
answer is unclear because of demand. The marketplace in the new architecture will quickly tell us whether we need more teachers or fewer. I think
it is important, however, to recognize that (1) the status and influence of
teaching is greatly elevated by keeping mediocrity out of the system altogether and (2) master teachers may be hard to come by, especially at the
primary level. To attract the level of talent we desire, it will be necessary
to pay them at least double what they make now. All master teachers I
have known are fully capable of making twice their earnings in the private
sector. They usually know it, their students know it, and the community
around them knows it.

I think it is difficult to assess the impact of declaring that teachers
are the most valuable resource in our society—that we are getting rid of
all but the very best and paying them something close to what they are
worth. I believe that this alone, with no further reform, would dramatically affect education for the better.

So imagine a world with less than half the teachers we have now,
especially when you are always hearing about teacher shortages. What or

who do we put in their place? We need a supporting cast of experts in specific areas who work primarily on a one-to-one basis with learners. A cast of people who, as a group, empower learners to become their own teachers: coaches who exact the best performance, mentors who develop specific interests and talents, counselors who raise questions and make suggestions about barriers that individual learners confront.

Questions regarding what kinds of supporters, what requirements, and how many we need per hundred students certainly require more thought and research. As a starting place, though, imagine a supporting cast that looks something like this:

- **Mentor**—Anyone who volunteers to become a confidant and general advisor to a K-12 student. Community volunteers would be welcome with some training on how to be an effective mentor. The chief role of a mentor is to gain the confidence of a learner and be an effective listener to any issue he or she might face: emotional, social, intellectual, or otherwise. A mentor would generally be a volunteer but could also be a teacher or learning facilitator who wishes to work with a learner over time. Generally, the commitment sought is for at least three years or longer if possible. A student could elect to terminate the relationship if it was not working well for him or her. Lots of community recognition would be poured on those who become mentors and especially those who continue with a learner for three years and beyond. A mentor would meet with a learner at least once a month and establish routine questions that get at the challenges a learner faces.

- **Peer Associate**—A fellow student of roughly the same age and/or developmental level. Peer associates are assigned to learners based on similar profiles. Their role is to meet once a week for at least 30 minutes and discuss issues they face with teachers, other facilitators, and fellow students. Peer reviews will be part of the LMS. Peers evaluate progress they see based on evaluations formed at an earlier date. The relationship is informal and collegial but serious in that it affords each learner the opportunity to frame an issue properly so that it may be worked out at the peer level or brought to whom it needs to be addressed. All peer associates will undergo training in conflict resolution so that they can attempt to resolve an issue among fellow students before it is brought to adults.

- **Peer Associate Fellow**—A student who has exhibited talent at resolving issues and conflicts and can be consulted by a single peer or peer dyad to sort out issues that are not being resolved. The act of formalizing helping relationships among peers develops collaboration and deeper associations around learning and life issues. A peer associate fellow becomes an early leadership designation that leads to community acknowledgement and more advanced training in communication skills, conflict resolution, and peer counseling. In a learner-centric design, peer associations will be taken seriously as the first stage of intervention in assisting learners to problem solve.
- **Cognitive Coach**—Advises learners on strategies for completing difficult assignments and projects and identifies learning skills that need further development. Interventions may be undertaken when another learning professional has identified a problem through testing or evaluations. The main job of a cognitive coach is to help students develop self-awareness of their learning process.

Learners are also encouraged to seek help whenever learning progress feels impeded. An effective cognitive coach gains the confidence of learners and displays competence in helping them achieve goals they have identified or issues they have acknowledged as "needing attention from a learning specialist." In a learner-centric educational system, the cognitive coach is the key person to turn to for help in completing learning credits or the more general goal of getting smarter. "Smarter," in this system, is not seen as a static phenomenon but rather a constantly emerging and evolving process.

Currently, **smart** is not a universally cherished attribute. In a learner-centric system, smart is the fuel that propels you forward. You don't have to be accelerated to be smart, and smart is not indicated by grades. It is judged by how well you use the resources around you to get what you want. This is a value few would reject and one that would be exploited in so many different ways. There are many kinds of smart, but "learning smart" is an attribute embraced and sought by all.

The cognitive coach is your ally in getting smarter where you want to and smarter where you need to, though it may be a challenge you resist. Taking away the need to resist is the key talent of such a professional. The training necessary would involve cognitive science, planning and organization skills, testing, specialized learning techniques, and a knack for coaching learners through their most difficult learning challenges. Certification would be necessary to hold this position.

- **Curriculum Advisor**—Helps learners with learning strategies, curriculum choices, and selecting activities and assignments that best take learners to new skill levels within a given course of study. A curriculum advisor is part of the evaluation team that determines when a student has shown competency in a core learning requirement and can move on to the next level. He or she will also team up with a student and a career and aptitude counselor to discuss specialized pursuits and how to go about them.

  Curriculum advisors have to keep an overall perspective on the academic pursuits of each learner. Their ultimate responsibility is to make sure that learners are moving forward at an acceptable pace, keeping up with core requirements, and creating acceptable standards to earn credits in their specialized pursuits. They play an important evaluative role in consulting with a learner's supporting cast to help accurately determine academic progress.

- **Career and Aptitude Counselor**—Meets periodically with students at the secondary level to identify emerging aptitudes and possible career interests. Every time an aptitude or career interest is acknowledged by both the learner and the counselor, it triggers a new learning event. The learner is provided with an overview (often a film) that introduces the world of a career or professional discipline through introducing exemplars, some narrative and visual exposure to what they do, what they like about it, and the attendant challenges.

  Aptitude testing becomes part of the advisement process, especially when learners have declared a new interest and want to know their current strengths and weaknesses relative to the interest. A missed opportunity of current schooling is the initiation of a sincere effort to introduce learners to the world of a profession or occupation. A big part of secondary education should become familiarization with what it might feel like to pursue an interest in research science, veterinary medicine, acting, or engineering. Windows into worlds of talent and professional practice are opportunities to bring various areas of inquiry alive and into a perspective that gives further meaning and possibility to daily work.

Testing Specialist—Not only administers tests but also works with teachers, cognitive coaches, and curriculum advisors to design effective tests and evaluation processes. The primary skills of such a person are to reduce the stress of testing and use it as a frequent measure of comprehension and academic progress. The true value of testing is not to leave a marker of how well a student learned (past tense) but to give students feedback about how well they are learning (present tense) and how they will learn better (future tense). The testing specialist will intervene to revise or redesign curriculum assignments if they are likely to promote better learning.

The testing specialist will cast himself or herself as a collaborator with students in every way possible. He or she will design processes and tests that "encourage students to encounter themselves as learners."[3] One of the chief ways to ally with students is to help them challenge evaluations that seem punitive or unfair. When appropriate, alternative evaluations or retesting will be implemented to better demonstrate what has been learned.

The bottom line on testing: grades on academic material matter far less than demonstrated learning. Competence and mastery are levels of learning rather than grade point averages.

With a collaborative team of mentors, coaches, counselors, and advisors, learners will have a much higher degree of one-on-one interaction specifically focused on their own needs. Furthermore, learners will become prime agents in the process of learning itself, using the resources of school to support them in discovering what they want to achieve and achieving it as efficiently and effectively as possible. The motivation becomes intrinsic rather than external.

The faculty of a learner-centric institution works in concert whenever possible, with the learner as conductor, to create an environment rich in interaction and geared toward autonomy and responsibility. Fellow students (i.e., peers and fellows) become part of that faculty and form feedback loops to generate self-awareness. The end goal is to produce motivated, self-directed, and intellectually mature learners.

A supporting cast supports. "The more structured (it) make(s) the environment, the more structure students need. The more we decide for students, the more they expect us to decide. The more motivation we provide, the less they find within themselves. The more responsibility for learning we try to assume, the less they accept on their own. The more control we exert, the more restive their response. We end up with students who have little commitment to and almost no respect for learning and who cannot function without structure and imposed control."[4]

Some master teachers in the new architecture will appropriately want to reach as many learners as they can. Technology and entrepreneurialism, of course, will enable such ambition. Being unsure of what form this might take, let me simply advance the notion of a teacher publisher. It would make sense for a teacher or group of teachers to band together with media and software professionals to build a franchise around specific subjects, fields of knowledge, or perhaps a niche component of education. They would form a company or perhaps be subsidized by the federal government to produce learning products.

History as Context

For an example of a niche teaching enterprise, take the issue of establishing context (discussed earlier) as the first unit of a new course of study. Every subject has a history, a story of how the subject was born, how it evolved into various human occupations, why it is important, and how knowledge of the subject is useful to various people and related occupations.

Even the most basic subjects such as reading and writing need to be understood historically to unlock their vitality and allure. Imagine an interactive DVD series produced by Stephen Spielberg on reading that re-creates what life was like before books and portrays the life of a typical tribe where life's experiences were recorded only in the minds of the elders and transmitted to others via storytelling. Then, there might be the story of a scribe in an abbey in the sixth century who produces an illuminated manuscript with commentary about how "knowledge" was kept alive by writing on the skins of sheep and was available to the very few.

Next, there might be a segment about Gutenberg, the explosion of the printed word, and the "great awakening," followed by contemporary celebrity readers talking about how their lives were enriched by books. Finally, there might be a segment with a researcher talking about how books develop imagination versus television and movies, followed by a series of writers talking about their craft: a novelist, a nonfiction book writer, an investigative reporter, and someone who writes film scripts. One of the interactive portions of the series would be becoming an editor for a writer who is trying to make a series of points to readers. The editor helps clarify the writer's narrative.

A private entity such as the Annenberg Foundation might take on the production of knowledge histories (or knowledge contexts) and produce a series of lessons to accompany the introduction to any subject from anthropology to zoology. A series of teachers would be hired to work with master storytellers to produce a knowledge history for literally hundreds of subjects.

The production of knowledge products, from learning objects to entire series of courses on specific subjects, will become an enormous industry requiring collaboration among learning experts, teachers, actors, multimedia specialists, game developers, film producers, researchers, and media giants. Again, this is an area where federal money can subsidize education by producing learning materials that exceed the quality and effectiveness of average teachers and curriculum.

In high-demand areas, publishers of successful educational products would remain together to capitalize on their success by producing follow-up materials. Teachers who can make subject areas come alive will often be the catalysts and leaders of such enterprises.

It is difficult to predict how teaching will evolve, except to say that it will follow the evolution of learning, having shifted from the role of master to handmaiden. It is certain that the textbook, as we know it, will give way to nonlinear forms of inquiry and to the use of mixed media. The combination of learner and learning tool (i.e., LMS, video game simulator, or collaborative software) literally extends cognitive capabilities, forming new dimensions of the noosphere.

What we now call teaching will become a collaborative process with various players who play their particular role in the learning process. The locus of knowledge will take its true place in the learner, empowered through his or her unique odyssey by many inside and outside the formal institution of school.

Endnotes

1   See Joseph Chilton Pearce, *Evolution's End*, Harper, San Francisco, 1992, pp. 100–101

2   Radio station KSL in Utah honors a teacher weekly, posting a testimonial at the "Teacher Feature" section of their Web site. They have been doing this for 11 years.

3   Maryellen Weimer, *Learner-Centered Teaching: Five Key Changes to Practice*, Jossey-Bass, N.Y., 2002, p. 11

4   Ibid., p. 98

Chapter 20

RADICAL CENTRALIZATION AND THE NEW FEDERAL ROLE

One of the great tragedies of schooling today is the endless bickering over exactly what should be taught. Why can we not satisfy everyone in a pluralistic society with plural ends and means? A large high school can be broken up into several schools within a school: one school is for science and engineering, another for the arts, and a third for the humanities. Each school nurtures a different culture and has different requirements to matriculate into higher learning.

Those who think religion should play a central role in education can start a charter school. Those who want the family to stay more closely bonded may want to choose homeschooling while availing themselves of certain institutional services and sports programs.

If any school cannot stay in the black or meet basic standards for moving kids into higher learning or school-to-work programs, it receives a probationary warning leading to censure. Parents begin to move their children to better-managed schools. Market forces determine a school's fate. Various approaches to education are available within a community. Moving from one institution to another is made as seamless as possible.

The radical decentralization at the local level, described in this book, creates accountability issues at state and federal levels. How do we accredit a multitude of institutions offering various programs and curricula? How do we transfer students from school to school without losing credits? How do we ensure that public funds are being used effectively to educate?

Right now, the resolution to these questions comes largely from state boards of education, local school boards, the federal government, and teachers unions. These bodies are often at odds with one another, their decisions are politically motivated, and they are in constant turmoil over who runs things. The question "Who really does run things?" is a hard one to answer.

If you add to this matrix of control testing organizations, textbook publishers, special interest groups, local administrators, crusading politicians, and corporate CEOs, the end result is that there's a lot of control-oriented behavior and no locus of control, and a highly dysfunctional system is perpetuated largely because control is so dispersed. Where do you go to institute change? Who resolves the endless turf wars of those attempting to wrest control from others who don't really have it?

Stepping back from this chaos, it would seem apparent that the act of taking away the need to assert controls (at least in certain areas) would leave those concerned about education to focus on different sets of issues. For example, as so much of the education wars are about content, why not do away with the source of the conflict by:

- Creating a federal nonpolitical agency to create standards for competence in all core academic subjects. The same entity will establish standards for the creation of acceptable learning materials and the assemblage of materials into custom courses for academic credit. This entity will be primarily composed of cognitive scientists (learning specialists) and subject matter specialists and will be strictly barred from entering into any controversies involving political disputes over curriculum. Their role will be confined to adequate coverage of subject areas and acceptable learning design of courses, course modules, learning objects, and any other design components therein. The charter of this entity would explicitly state that it cannot be influenced by political parties, lobbying, or any other outside influence.
- Instituting a second agency to establish methods and standards for assessing the achievement of learned competencies. This agency would work with professional organizations to continually ensure that academic standards reflect professional and industrial requirements. It

would be permitted to interact with watchdog groups that are specifically concerned with professional knowledge and standards as they apply to competent practice. For instance, the agency might meet with the American Geological Institute to go over significant new findings on the nature of oil formation.

The second agency, could then take new information to the first, or competencies, agency so that it could add to the body of knowledge and competency standards in geology. Only the second agency would bring new academic findings or professional concerns to agency #1.

The assessments agency, agency #2, would develop multiple means of assessing competencies so that no one method would become **the** standard. By avoiding the complete standardization of testing, responsibility for the evaluation of learners is placed in the hands of those who actually work with learners and have a far better sense of their real knowledge and talents. National tests could be developed to measure learning on a regional or school-by-school basis, but these tests would no longer be used to prevent individuals from passing a course or establishing a competency. That responsibility would remain local, with federal guidelines to provide for consistency across states.

Eliminating Bureaucratic Waste

Bureaucracy is the largest cost as well as the largest source of redundancy, conflict, and waste in public education. Private schools generally outperform public schools at less than half of the operating cost. Most of that cost savings is in leaner bureaucracies.

In the nation's second largest school district, New York City, there were some 6,000 administrators in the public schools and 25 in the Catholic schools. Yes, the Catholic schools had a quarter of the students that the public schools did.[1]

Fordham University Professor Bruce Cooper and graduate student Robert Sarrel published a study indicating that less that one-third of the money spent on New York City high school students actually reached the classroom.

A task force of Chicago business leaders published a study in 1989 pointing out to the Chicago Board of Education that the ratio of administrators to students in the Chicago Public School system was one to 143, while in Chicago's Catholic schools, it was one to 6,250.[2]

Wherever you have "inner" cities and large disadvantaged populations, bureaucrats seem to swell in proportion to employees who actually work with students. School bureaucracies, in particular, seem to have no real incentives to operate efficiently or respond to public needs.

I see no need for all of this bureaucracy and propose a radical downsizing of all state and federal educational bureaucracies by 75–90%. Those who remain of this group would exclusively devote themselves to collecting and analyzing data on school performance and quarterly reports submitted by school districts showing performance data and use of funds. Analysis of this data would, in turn, be made available to local citizen groups and school districts for purposes of reengineering and accountability.

As for cities and districts, I propose that they adhere to the same guidelines for bureaucracy reduction or answer to the public if they choose to exceed guideline expenditures. At the school level, I propose a requirement that all personnel (except facilities maintenance staff and a business manager) must spend at least 75% of their time working directly with students.

Principals and assistant principals can be teachers or facilitators performing those duties on rotation. Most administrative functions would be performed by teachers, facilitators, and volunteers. School leadership ought to be viewed as a joint effort between community members and teacher/facilitators.

I do not believe there is a need for school boards in a new architecture. To be sure, parents need to be involved with schools, particularly in facilitative or helping roles. School boards, however, seem to be a remnant from a time when it was thought that citizens needed to have an official role in school governance.

It was never clear what their exact role was except to provide community input into an institution that could be otherwise insensitive to community needs. The net effect of school boards has largely been to create political battles with administrators.

PTAs, or parent-teacher associations, have been shrinking dramatically since around 1960. Without going into the rival (and also shrinking) PTO movement, it is fair to say that civic involvement in schools, particularly involvement directly with kids, is now a fraction of what it was a few decades ago. If the energy being devoted to political debates in your local school board was redirected to rebuild direct volunteer involvement working with kids and teachers in schools, parent involvement could conceivably be resurrected.

All of the research points to the fact that parental involvement in education makes for better learners and better schools. I would propose that the new architecture include a volunteer Education Corps. It would be an amalgam of volunteers, low-paid staffers who seek an alternative service to the military, and retirees who must give one afternoon of service per week in exchange for their Social Security checks.

The core staff of an Education Corps would be devoted to teaching volunteers and staffers to carry out needed assignments within school districts. They would conduct recruitment campaigns to involve parents in volunteer roles and young people who wanted to earn further education. Staffers and volunteers would make specific time commitments to allow for human resource planning and development.

An Education Corps could well supply many of the current needs of our schools and add services such as arts and music that have disappeared over the years. It would reinvigorate the important element of civil involvement that has been in precipitous decline in the United States since the 1960s.[3] It could bring trained volunteers into poor and underserved communities to balance the resource gap that exists as a result of less tax revenue and single-parent homes that keep parents from being available.

A large, well-organized volunteer organization could provide a combination of local community involvement and outside resources on an as-needed basis. If its first priority was to correct the imbalance of human resources provided to poorer school districts, much could be done to create an awareness of the connections between socioeconomic issues and the ability to learn.

To provide resources in the trenches instead of in the administrative ranks would mark a major shift in how educational equity is now addressed. Furthermore, the resurrection of nonpolitical civic involvement in schools would provide the local support and oversight to allow for centralized services that can reduce costs and improve actual learning.

With an adequate volunteer base, every school district could provide the means to integrate schooling with family life. By installing parents, wherever possible, to participate in the daily routines side by side with students, parents begin to become partners in their children's education. In turn, parents could take kids out of school to help with work projects and civic involvement, leading to academic credit when possible. The policies of such programs could serve to strengthen families and build community.

The central agencies I spoke of earlier (standards for competence and academic credit and, then, for the assessment thereof) are critical to the design of a new architecture. Without them, communities would continue to be mired in political battles over what to teach, how to teach it, and how to properly evaluate student progress. If we can largely take these issues away, communities are left with the proposition of supporting individual learners within a structure that allows for their unique development.

When standards and routines are not homogenous, the effort to support a school becomes focused on individuals instead of uniform policies. Volunteerism is encouraged because parents want to be able to help an overall effort geared to individual need. Johnny's mother doesn't have to worry that Johnny is being stamped out in a particular mold or being made to conform to practices that don't support him. She wants to volunteer because she wants a level of service that can respond adequately to individual need.

The factory model of schooling has encouraged endless wars over product quality, how to run the factory, and how to compete with other "factories." When the impetus for these wars is removed, we have the option to design new challenges to occupy the attentions of learning facilitators and parents. If these challenges focus on the individual learner instead of the institution, we encourage a level of responsibility that has been culled out of the system with commodified schooling.

To achieve this end, we must ensure that the product we produce is for a market of one. It becomes an endlessly customizable product with lots of customer support around it to make sure it is used by each consumer to his or her own best advantage. Ironically, to produce an education (the product) for a market of one, there must be a uniform standard that can accommodate changes to make it richly modifiable. It is the difference between engineering for **a uniform product** and engineering for **uniform satisfaction** with the product.

Without centralization, we invite dynamics that have plagued the computer industry. Instead of creating a compatible cross-platform system for delivering multiple solutions, it creates competing products with multiple standards and operational functionality. The result is a kind of pandemonium where most of the development time is spent coping with changes in operating systems and incompatibilities between products and platforms. The result is extreme customer frustration and a level of accessibility that keeps all but the very sophisticated from ready access.

To reach this idealized state of centralization, much has to happen. Most important, we must agree to make it so. It will require cooperation between the federal government, the states, commercial interests, and the millions who facilitate learning. The first step in realizing a new architecture will be a congress of the players to organize around depoliticized centralization and a plan of action.

When you look at it this way, it suggests that politicians will get it. They will accept that they are fighting for a national rather than a state or local solution. Assume that they will never get it without your involvement. It is counterintuitive. After all, all politics are local.

Endnotes

1   From *Politics, Markets and America's Schools*, a 1990 study of 500 public and private schools for the Hoover Institution conducted by John Chubb and Terry Moe

2   From *Education Choice, a Catalyst for Reform*, released by the City Club of Chicago in August 1989

3   See Robert D. Putnam, *Bowling Alone*, Simon & Schuster, N.Y., 2000, for an extensive study of the decline of civic involvement and community in the United States

Chapter 21

HIGHER LEARNING: THE GREAT PARADOX

Suppose you had been admitted to Stanford University—at the hefty price tag of around $40,000 annually—and your parents approached you with this offer:

> "We know you are a capable learner. Every college, it doesn't matter which one, is going to make you jump through endless hoops to get a sheepskin. Much of what you learn will be irrelevant. We think you are capable of getting a better education by using your own instincts and judgment independently. Of course, the social life in college and the pure intellectual adventure of exploring various subjects with intelligent peers and professors can be great, but we believe you can achieve this in other ways. Because of our faith in you, we propose to give you the $240,000 it would have cost us for a master's degree. It will be set up as a trust fund for you to spend specifically on activities and pursuits that fulfill your desire to become learned and to become successful and prosperous in a profession."

A ticket to Stanford or $240K? Which way do you go? For many, the only hitch in making the decision would be questions like, "What becomes of me? Can I climb the corporate ladder without the Stanford pedigree? Can I even get a decent job without a college degree?"

As a young person, you could live comfortably for seven or eight years while using that money to pursue your dreams. You could find a captain of industry, a professional heavyweight, and say, "Teach me what you know. Help me to become the best, and I will work for you and learn everything you tell me to for free for the next four years."

With the help of some advisors and the ability to convince others of your sincerity, you could buy a much better education on the open market than you could get on any university campus and structure in three months a year of seeing the world as part of your education.

Going to college, for many, is a right of passage, a dividing line between the right and the wrong side of the tracks. It is also a socially conferred freedom zone—a buffer between parental oversight and indentured servitude, a place to experiment, to find out who you really are and what you want to be. These are legitimate reasons to say yes to higher education.

Most of us are not admitted to prestige universities, and I have never heard of anyone being offered the money instead of the degree. About one-third of college students drop out in their first year, and less than half (about 45%) finish college.[1] Roughly 15 million students are enrolled in colleges and universities at this writing. Most of these students have a very practical motive for attending college. About seven million are already in the workforce and are looking to upgrade their skills.

About 40% of those attending college are in two-year public institutions and are paying an average of $1,387 a year. This is a far cry from Stanford or Harvard. The more you break it down, the more you find that higher education is now primarily geared to human capital development.

But higher education has other purposes as well. It pushes the envelope of knowledge. It conducts research and develops new products, new fields of endeavor, and new technologies. It provides a broader understanding of the world for those who want to enter it with some intellectual ballast.

There is no question that higher education contributes much to society. And while K-12 education is an international embarrassment[2] in the United States, an American university education is has been widely sought after throughout the world. Since 1993 however, foreign enrollments to American universities and graduate schools have been dropping. The N.Y. Times (Dec. 21, 2004) reported that Chinese and Indian grad school graduates dropped by over 50% in 2003 while enrollments in European and Chinese graduate schools increased

The dark side to American higher education is becoming increasingly apparent. Simply put, a colleges are increasingly ineffectual at meeting the needs of the marketplace. The structure itself is every bit as outmoded as that of "lower" education.

Students enter colleges unprepared to take advantage of the many resources on campus and, upon leaving, find themselves unprepared to cope with the world of work. The practical effect of expanding access to education, under the current design, has led to lowered expectations, uniform outputs, and shallow performance tracks.

Employers complain that college graduates cannot read, write, calculate, or reason well. Most students go through the maze of college curricula and requirements with little to no advisement. Add to this the fact that completion rates are dropping while tuitions are soaring.

Earlier in this book, I pointed out that we finance college students in public education at triple the cost of primary schoolers. I, for one, would rather invest the money in early learning and in sending skilled, intentional learners into higher education.

Add it all up and it becomes apparent that higher education needs a new architecture as well, one that complements and builds on the changes to primary and secondary learning. Clearly, learning has been reframed as a lifetime occupation. Although higher education is very aware of the changing demographics and needs of learners, it has not responded at the level of fundamental redefinition and design.

Colleges and universities know that breakthroughs in research and knowledge mostly occur beyond the borders of a single discipline. They also know that the largest potential for revenue and growth comes from what is now called the "continuing education" sector. Unlike "lower" education, college policy makers are generally aware that the transfer of knowledge is no longer the primary goal of education. Yet, the lecture remains the primary modus operandi in the college classroom.

What, then, needs to happen to implement an architecture that makes higher education the sine qua non for higher learning? Many of the changes suggested for secondary education would apply. Here are some comments directly aimed at the Academy:

Making the transition to higher learning would be very difficult if colleges and universities maintained their present admission and transfer policies under the new architecture. How do you admit a student who has a custom education, no diploma, and no uniform grading? We could fall back on tests, but how do you apply tests when, instead of a college-prep track, there are dozens of varying preparation tracks already instigated before college?

What was already a fairly complex process becomes far more so. Any college or university serious about admitting quality students would need to rely heavily on the interview. The LMS, particularly portfolios, would provide much of the information used to evaluate applicants on their own terms. I would think an extensive essay covering one's history and reasons for pursuing higher learning and for choosing a particular institution would also be key to the process.

Clearly, the process of admittance would be far more labor intensive, but the result would be students who are admitted as a result of close scrutiny instead of scores on standardized tests and grades. The process of admission would build familiarity both ways and would provide invaluable information to both parties.

Faculty members would take on the primary role of educational consultants. Lectures would not disappear altogether, but faculty members would be available to every student for individual consultations on learning goals, putting ideas to work, standards of rigor, and specific learning projects. Divining each student's unique learning path becomes the principle role of a faculty member.

The choice of an institution would be made secondarily on the institution's reputation and primarily on the strength of departments and, most particularly, individual faculty. This being said, one institution may not employ all of the faculty in a student's course of study. Institutional flexibility allowing for intercollegiate enrollments would be commonplace in a world where faculty and departmental relationships are primary.

Again, this makes for a complicated world in which curriculum is the collaboration between faculty and students, with deans and colleges themselves providing oversight for quality assurance only. Faculty from varying institutions would have to develop procedures for shaping a course of study. Any challenge to quality would have to be substantiated with evidence to show that students were being underserved by a faculty member's standards for assigning credit.

When a faculty member ceases to be the "font of knowledge," he or she may be inclined to take on more crucial roles such as preparing students for leadership in the disciplines they are pursuing and working with other faculty to develop cross-disciplinary patterns and connections in an individual course of study. Ostensibly, the faculty member at a college or university has exhibited talent at facilitating the path from information to knowledge to wisdom.

Each step on this path requires very different levels of understanding. The faculty member who has been a successful steward will often develop a relationship that extends beyond the present course of study over a number of years. Learners might frequently return to faculty members to negotiate advanced learning contracts and build on the relationships that have formed around deep learning. Learning communities evolve out of faculty relationships. Faculties become more involved in the exploits of their students in the world.

The strongest impetus for seeking outside help in education would be where learners seek a faculty member because they have come to see his or her work, ideas, and values as a pathway to new understanding. This is the natural progression into higher learning.

Credit ceases to become the sole responsibility of an institution. The organization of work accomplished into credits is, perhaps, the greatest inefficiency of higher education. It is presently for the convenience of the credit-granting institution and, more often than not, is of little use to the learner and the professional world he or she will later enter.

In the early years of my professional life, when MBAs were beginning to get more popular, I remember when I and my co-workers would dread the hiring of an MBA into management because it pretty much ensured we would get a highly conceptual manager with little experience of the real world and a by-the-book problem-solving mentality.

At the core of this problem is the tendency for colleges and universities to confer degrees that do not correspond well to real-world occupations. Before the breakup of AT&T, a large-scale study of its managers determined that the best-performing managers tended to have liberal arts rather than business degrees.

This confirmed the Mark Twain maxim, "It ain't what you don't know that'll hurt you; it's what you're sure is true." The worst managers I encountered shared the tendency to be sure of what was true. While most armchair critics (myself included) tended to define this problem as one of ego, I am now convinced that irrelevant and incomplete education was as much at fault.

Every job comes with its own marching orders. Every ambition has conditions for satisfaction. Every individual has unique talents to bring to bear on both. When individuals are agents in identifying their own criteria for progress, particularly if they have learned how to learn, you have a cybernetic system in which feedback is constant and tends to be more accurate. Higher education and corporations are both guilty of ignoring this maxim.

The process of assigning credit might develop as follows:

- Deemphasize degrees and concentrate on competencies
- Make competencies relevant to industry standards, include industry participation, and update competencies to reflect better practices and new developments
- Award certificates for completion of competencies. A certificate designates competence in a specific occupational endeavor. A field of endeavor (teaching, cellular biology, nursing, law, avionics, economics, or philosophy) may have hundreds of competencies. It may be more attractive to hire a reporter who has certificates of competency in psychology, research methods, English literature, and journalism than one who simply has a slew of certificates in journalism. Certificates become far more indicative of specific capabilities and professional talent than a degree. Degrees are no longer the currency of professional advancement.
- Many who have been in the workforce for a number of years have competencies that far supercede academic credentials. Though this is true, it is often impossible for a person returning to formal education to receive recognition in the form of credit for existing competencies.

If this enormous flaw in higher education were corrected, tens of thousands would flock back to academic institutions to combine credit for life and work experience with new courses to achieve certificates of competency and degrees. A large new industry would develop, and an important socioeconomic need would be met.

To provide this service would require the same form of complexity higher education now eschews in favor of cookie-cutter credits and diplomas. Large departments of credit evaluators would have to form to meet the demand, or the effort could be centralized with a Higher Education Credit Board to assign credit on behalf of all institutions.

- It would be wise for individual institutions of higher education to get out of the credit business altogether. Again, a centralized credit-granting board could combine with industry appointees and professional associations to grant credit for certificates based on a combination of faculty recommendations, LMS reviews, and testing.

Where credit comes from—As things are now, we tend to regard the university as a monolith, a brand, a source of prestige. Everyone who has been to college knows you can have a great professor at your local community college and a lousy one at Stanford, or vice versa. Our way of seeing universities has remained a powerful myth that serves no useful purpose to the student.

As certificates become the unit of accomplishment and the symbol of prestige or merit, the actual faculty and departments that are directly responsible for them should receive the notoriety and engage in the efforts of making their accomplishments known. To browse through a university catalog, one would pay far more attention to departments, faculty, and their offerings than the broader reputation of the university.

Colleges and universities might also be segmented into schools organized around the core reasons for attendance. While a single enrollee may share more than one of these reasons, more often than not, they are separate:

- Schools devoted to scholarly activity and advancing the frontiers of knowledge
- Research schools devoted to specific technical advancements and to partnering with industry on entrepreneurial ventures
- Training schools that specifically serve the needs of industry and work directly with professional associations and corporations to provide for human resource development
- Traditional liberal-education schools devoted to providing students with a broad education in the liberal arts

Yes, these designations are similar to how schools are now organized. But if they were more clearly focused around specific areas of endeavor and excellence, it would be easier to build a reputation, promote achievements, raise funds, and enter into partnerships with private concerns.

Under this scenario, what used to be the college transcript would become an amalgam of credits, certificates, and extensive evaluations from individual departments, schools, and faculty. The notion of a single diploma from a single college or university becomes the exception.

Higher education becomes an open-ended process reflecting a higher degree of selectivity on the part of students and the lifelong process that learning has become. Of course, this trend would call for a yet-to-be-conceived model for higher education, one that the powers that be, particularly in light of their claims to success, would be hard- pressed to even consider.

Guidance—For most of us, stepping onto a college campus is bewildering. When we leave, two or four years later, we have become familiar with the buildings and a few teachers, but have we taken advantage of what the institution has to offer?

If guidance were truly a component of higher learning, it would encompass a process of deep reflection upon the emergent ideas, trends, and organizing principles that are shaping each person's learning process. The process would involve faculty, outside mentors, and the learner in distilling the weekly inputs of intensive inquiry and discovery into decisions that chart a course into the future.

Part of the guidance process is ensuring the students are taking full advantage of the available resources on a physical (or virtual) campus. For example, a good college library has directories of teachers and their areas of specialty, research projects currently under way, dissertations, research monographs, and faculty publications. It may also have written and videotaped lectures and specialized indexes of hard-to-find resources pertinent to specific areas of study.

If a need is not adequately addressed through on-campus resources, a learner's guidance team ought to be tasked with finding the right course, faculty member, or other resource elsewhere. By the time a student gets to college, he or she should be very skilled at locating learning resources. The guidance team is there to ensure that all available means are known to the learner, that no stone goes unturned. The very presence of such a resource creates an atmosphere in which methodical inquiry is the basis for discovery—for refining and moving toward learning objectives.

I have not addressed many of the issues in transforming higher education: accrediting bodies, the problem of rising costs and diminishing revenue growth, governance, and the use of information technology, to name a few. The marketplace exerts a larger influence on this world, but it will prove to be more resistant to change because each college or university, public or private, has its own character and its own constituent base and views itself, to a large extent, as independent.

The dynamics of influence are far different here than they are in the K-12 world. Taking them on requires another book. Suffice it to say that, even now, you can be more creative in pursuing higher education than you probably know. Push the envelope. If you are a full-time student in a local or virtual college, learn to negotiate the terms of a course for credit. Begin with the assumption that your professor wants to help you tailor a course to your needs. You may be surprised at what you can accomplish!

Endnotes

1   From ACT compiled national collegiate dropout and graduation rates, 2003.

2   Conduct a Web search for the Program for International Student Assessment (PISA) to see how U.S. students' academic performance compares to the rest of the world.

Conclusion

Ask yourself these questions: What kind of a society do I want to live in?

Do I want knowledge to be the province of an elite group who makes decisions for me?

-OR-

Do I want to live in a society where knowledge is widely valued and independently sought after, where the real diversity is diversity of thought, perspective and opinion?

Do I want to see the social value of our knowledge put to use so that we can work toward a collective intelligence?

Are you a spectator in your social and political world or a participant in building the one you want? If what you want seems out of reach, have you given up? Is there a cynical place inside of you now clothed in thoughts like "I'm a realist" or "God will eventually make it right"? To an extent, I believe this describes most of us. It is the Faustian bargain we make to be acceptable—to be civilized.

To have a vision for the society we want is important to education. Without it, we are not inclined to recognize the interdependence of knowledge. Knowledge becomes divorced from ethics. Without a vision, we become complacent. Knowledge becomes a commodity—a matter of expedience.

Most of us leave formal education and enter the world with poorly developed cognitive skills and an incomplete sense of what learning and knowledge offer us. We are then expected to become productive, often at the expense of our curiosity and our dreams.

It is clear that education has failed to improve the common mind. Formal education serves the collective by making us the same, by explaining the world to us, and by asking easy questions rather than hard ones. What is left out of it tells us more about ourselves than what we are "taught."

Without a vision that binds us together as a society, we do not seek to see a wider picture. We fail to grasp the coevolutionary possibilities of education and knowledge at the level of family, society, and the world.

We lack vision, I say, because our brains have been turned off. It has been bred out of us. Oh yes, we did it to ourselves but with a lot of help from schooling. What each of us learns, and what each of us does not learn, has an incremental and demonstrable effect on the world.

If you complete four years of college, you have spent roughly 19,000 hours over a 17-year period becoming acclimated and/or obedient to the disciplines, the unconscious messages, the psychology, and the judgments of schools. No other institution can claim such influence.

To what extent we are the product of schooling may be hard to calculate. And it will be hard to overcome without awareness and resolve. The best way to keep both alive is to become an activist.

The kind of society you want begins with what and how you learn. Until now, most of us have consigned this responsibility to educators and elected representatives. We pay them with taxes, votes, tuition checks, and faith in their judgments. Meanwhile, the return on investment has been steadily sliding as the means and the ends of education become increasingly obsolete.

If I deliver no other point in this book, it is that educators and public officials will never get it right until you take the reigns of your own learning process and do the same for your friends, colleagues, children, and society. Because so much of our crucial learning time is spent in schools, it behooves us to begin there.

First, be an educator in your sphere of influence. Understand the real issues and make them known. Learn to make the case for better learning skills and organizing schools around learners and how learning occurs. Find ways to emphasize brain-based learning in early-stage development because it will pay big dividends later.

Suggest alternatives. Find ways to communicate how miserably unacceptable the status quo is. Make the case, first to yourself, and then to others, of just how crucial the transformation of education is.

Use your own vision of the society you want to argue for a society of learning. We must build consensus on the society we want and learn to create it in schools.

The science of learning may yet become the most important of this century. I want to find and communicate with those who agree that it offers human possibilities beyond our reckoning. Its first challenge is to produce a new generation of enthusiastic and highly capable learners. Let us begin.

An Invitation

If you see the future of learning as a priority, I want to know who you are. I will be able to communicate with you if you go to *http://www.lessonsfortomorrow.com* and sign the guestbook. Let me know how you are involved with education or learning. Tell me what changes you regard as important and what you want to do about them. If there are enough entries, we may have a movement.

As a follow-up to this book, I am thinking of identifying some of the key architects of learner-centered education, defining their contributions, and interviewing them. What do you want to know more about? Let me know what you are thinking. —Edward L. Davis

Appendix A
Thinking Skills

The North Central Regional Educational Laboratory's Learning Research and Development Center (1991) lists the following higher-order thinking skills:

- "Size up and define a problem that isn't neatly packaged.
- Determine which facts and formulas stored in memory might be helpful for solving a problem.
- Recognize when more information is needed and where and how to look for it.
- Deal with uncertainty by 'brainstorming' possible ideas or solutions when the way to proceed isn't apparent.
- Carry out complex analyses or tasks that require planning, management, monitoring, and adjustment.
- Exercise judgment in situations where there aren't clear-cut 'right' and 'wrong' answers but more and less useful ways of doing things.
- Step outside the routine to deal with an unexpected breakdown or opportunity." (pp. 3–4)

Appendix B

Critical Thinking Skills

Paul, Binker, Jensen, and Kreklau (1990) have developed a list of 35 dimensions of critical thought:

"A. **Affective Strategies**

    S-1   thinking independently

    S-2   developing insight into egocentricity or sociocentricity

    S-3   exercising fair-mindedness

    S-4   exploring thoughts underlying feelings and feelings underlying thoughts

    S-5   developing intellectual humility and suspending judgment

    S-6   developing intellectual courage

    S-7   developing intellectual good faith or integrity

    S-8   developing intellectual perseverance

    S-9   developing confidence in reason

B. **Cognitive Strategies—Macro-Abilities**

    S-10   refining generalizations and avoiding oversimplifications

    S-11   comparing analogous situations: transferring insights to new contexts

    S-12   developing one's perspective: creating or exploring beliefs, arguments, or theories

S-13   clarifying issues, conclusions, or beliefs

S-14   clarifying and analyzing the meanings of words or phrases

S-15   developing criteria for evaluation: clarifying values and standards

S-16   evaluating the credibility of sources of information

S-17   questioning deeply: raising and pursuing root or significant questions

S-18   analyzing or evaluating arguments, interpretations, beliefs, or theories

S-19   generating or assessing solutions

S-20   analyzing or evaluating actions or policies

S-21   reading critically: clarifying or critiquing texts

S-22   listening critically: the art of silent dialogue

S-23   making interdisciplinary connections

S-24   practicing Socratic discussion: clarifying and questioning beliefs, theories, or perspectives

S-25   reasoning dialogically: comparing perspectives, interpretations, or theories

S-26   reasoning dialectically: evaluating perspectives, interpretations, or theories

C.   **Cognitive Strategies—Micro-Skills**

S-27   comparing and contrasting ideals with actual practice

S-28   thinking precisely about thinking: using critical vocabulary

S-29   noting significant similarities and differences

S-30   examining or evaluating assumptions

S-31   distinguishing relevant from irrelevant facts

S-32   making plausible inferences, predictions, or interpretations

S-33   evaluating evidence and alleged facts

S-34   recognizing contradictions

S-35   exploring implications and consequences" (p. 56)

*From North Central Regional Laboratories. See *www.ncrel.org*

Appendix C
Microworlds Resource Page

Here are a few Web sites to introduce you to the computer-generated microworlds:

1. *http://www.mulawa.net/mulawa/turtle/intro.html*—A good introductory site that allows a free download of microworld software (for 15 days). Teaches kids basic programming skills and comes with 20 basic lessons.
2. *http://www.microworlds.com*—A company with microworlds software. You can try various product demos.
3. *http://www.umcs.maine.edu/~larry/microworlds/microworld.html*—A brief overview of microworlds with links to several under development.
4. *http://mia.openworldlearning.org/*—A collection of microworld projects, lessons, and other resource materials for developing LOGO programming skills.
5. *http://www.rand.org/education/mcarthur/home.html*—A Rand Corporation project that features several microworlds developed under a National Science Foundation grant.
6. *http://www.mtlakes.org/ww/tech/webtools.htm*—Microworlds for elementary teachers.
7. *http://mailerfsu.edu/~flake/microworlds.html*—A good set of links to useful microworld sites.
8. *http://www.greatplaces.org/games/top.html*—A place to download several microworld games.

Please note: Web sites disappear and undergo frequent changes. If any of these links do not work, conduct your own search under *microworlds*.

Appendix D
Prominent Views on Education

Jacob Brownowski
It is important that students bring a certain ragamuffin barefoot irreverence to their studies; they are not here to worship what is known but to question it.

John W. Gardner
I am entirely certain that 20 years from now we will look back at education as it is practiced in most schools today and wonder that we could have tolerated anything so primitive.

Lillian Smith
Education is a private matter between the person and the world of knowledge and experience and has little to do with school or college.

Thomas Armstrong
The newer and broader picture suggests that the child emerges into literacy by actively speaking, reading, and writing in the context of real life, not through filling out phonics worksheets or memorizing words.

Daniel Goleman
Who does not recall school at least in part as endless dreary hours of boredom punctuated by moments of high anxiety?

Isaac Asimov
Self-education is, I firmly believe, the only kind of education there is.

Mark Twain

I have never let my schooling interfere with my education.

Albert Einstein

It is a miracle that curiosity survives formal education.

Agatha Christie

I suppose it is because nearly all children go to school nowadays, and have things arranged for them, that they seem so forlornly unable to produce their own ideas.

Howard Gardner

The single most important contribution education can make to a child's development is to help him towards a field where his talents best suit him, where he will be satisfied and competent. We've completely lost sight of that. Instead we subject everyone to an education where, if you succeed, you will be best suited to be a college professor. ... And we evaluate everyone along the way according to whether they meet that narrow standard of success. We should spend less time ranking children and more time helping them identify their natural competencies and gifts and cultivate those.

There are hundreds and hundreds of ways to succeed and many, many different abilities that will help you get there.

We should use kids' positive states to draw them into learning in the domains where they can develop competencies. ...You learn at your best when you have something you care about and can get pleasure from being engaged in.

Dorothy L. Sayers

What use is it to pile task on task and prolong the days of labour, if at the close the chief object is left unattained? It is not the fault of the teacher— they work only too hard already. The combined folly of a civilization that has forgotten its own roots is forcing them to shore up the tottering weight of an educational structure that is built upon sand. They are doing for their pupils the work which the pupils themselves ought to do. For the sole true end of education is simply this: to teach men how to learn for themselves; and whatever instruction fails to do this is effort spent in vain.

John Taylor Gatto

By bells and many other similar techniques, they (schools) teach that nothing is worth finishing. The gross error of this is progressive: if nothing is worth finishing, then by extension nothing is worth starting either. Few children are so thick-skulled they miss the point.

Teaching means different things in different places, but seven lessons are universally taught from Harlem to Hollywood Hills. They constitute a national curriculum you pay for in more ways than you can imagine, so you might as well know what it is.

(1) Confusion, (2) Class Position, (3) Indifference, (4) Emotional Dependency, (5) Intellectual Dependency, (6) Provisional Self-Esteem, (7) One Can't Hide. It is the great triumph of compulsory, government monopoly mass-schooling that among even the best of my fellow teachers, and among even the best of my students' parents, only a small number can imagine a different way to do things.

Carl Rogers

It seems to me that anything that can be taught to another is relatively inconsequential and has little or no significant influence on behavior. I realise increasingly that I am only interested in learnings which significantly influence behavior. I have come to feel that the only learning which significantly influences behavior is self-discovered, self-appropriated learning. Such self-discovered learning, truth that has been personally appropriated and assimilated in experience, cannot be directly communicated to another. As a consequence of the above, I realize that I have lost interest in being a teacher.

Ludwig von Mises

Education rears disciples, imitators, and routinists, not pioneers of new ideas and creative geniuses. The schools are not nurseries of progress and improvement but conservatories of tradition and unvarying modes of thought.

William Glasser

There are only two places in the world where time takes precedence over the job to be done: school and prison.

John W. Gardner

Much education today is monumentally ineffective. All too often we are giving young people cut flowers when we should be teaching them to grow their own plants.

Emma Goldman

Since every effort in our educational life seems to be directed toward making of the child a being foreign to itself, it must of necessity produce individuals foreign to one another and in everlasting antagonism with each other.

Oscar Wilde

Education is an admirable thing, but it is well to remember, from time to time, that nothing that is worth knowing can be taught.

Edith Hamilton

It has always seemed strange to me in our endless discussions about education so little stress is laid on the pleasure of becoming an educated person, the enormous interest it adds to life.

Will Durant

Education is a progressive discovery of our own ignorance.

Roger Schank

The school system has two flaws. … The first flaw is that the curriculum is wrong. They teach subjects that don't matter. The second flaw is how these subjects are taught. In the school system, learning is basically done by students sitting and the teacher is talking. Well, "You sit, and I talk" is not the way people learn.

Roger Schank

School isn't really about learning; it's about short-term memorization of meaningless information that never comes up later in life. The school model was never intended to help people acquire practical skills. It is intended to satisfy observers that knowledge is being acquired (for short periods of time).

Recommended Reading

During the three and a half years I spent writing this book, I read all or parts of well over 100 books. Rather than post a bibliography, I thought it would be more useful to list some of the books that I found most interesting and informative.

Abbott, John, and Ryan, Terry, 2001, *The Unfinished Revolution: Learning, Human Behavior, Community and Political Paradox,* Alexandria, VA: Association for Supervision and Curriculum Development.

Bateson, Gregory, 1972, *Steps to an Ecology of Mind,* New York: Ballantine Books.

Brown, John Seely, and Duguid, Paul, 2000, *The Social Life of Information,* Boston: Harvard Business School Press.

Bruner, Jerome, 1996, *The Culture of Education,* Cambridge, MA: Harvard University Press.

Davis, Stan, and Botkin, Jim, 1994, *The Monster Under the Bed,* New York: Simon & Schuster.

Gardner, Howard, 1991, *The Unschooled Mind,* New York: Basic Books.

Gatto, John, 2001, *A Different Kind of Teacher,* Berkeley, CA: Berkeley Hills Books.

Gatto, John, 1992, *Dumbing us Down: The Hidden Curriculum of Compulsory Schooling,* Gabriola Island, B.C: New Society Publishers.

Kohn, Alfie, 1999, *The Schools Our Children Deserve,* New York: Houghton Mifflin Company.

Langer, Ellen, 1997, *The Power of Mindful Learning*, New York: Addison-Wesley Publishing Company.

Papert, Seymour, 1993, *The Children's Machine: Rethinking School in the Age of the Computer*, New York: Basic Books.

Pierce, Joseph Chilton, 1992, *Evolution's End: Claiming the Potential of Our Intelligence*, San Francsico: Harper.

Perkins, D.N., 1986, *Knowledge as Design*, Hillsdale, New Jersey: Lawrence Erlbaum Associates.

Schank, Roger, *Engines for Education*, a "hyperbook," go to *http://www.engines4ed.org/hyperbook*. This one's free and quite an experience!

Smith, Frank, 1998, *The Book of Learning and Forgetting*, New York: Teachers College Press.

Index